Mathematics Higher Level
Topic 9 – Option:
Calculus
for the IB Diploma

Paul Fannon, Vesna Kadelburg, Ben Woolley and Stephen Ward

CAMBRIDGE
UNIVERSITY PRESS

University Printing House, Cambridge CB2 8BS, United Kingdom

Cambridge University Press is part of the University of Cambridge.

It furthers the University's mission by disseminating knowledge in the pursuit of education, learning and research at the highest international levels of excellence.

www.cambridge.org
Information on this title: www.cambridge.org/9781107632899

© Cambridge University Press 2013

This publication is in copyright. Subject to statutory exception and to the provisions of relevant collective licensing agreements, no reproduction of any part may take place without the written permission of Cambridge University Press.

First published 2013
Reprinted 2014

Printed in India by Replika Press Pvt. Ltd

A catalogue record for this publication is available from the British Library

ISBN 978-1-107-63289-9 Paperback

Cover image: Thinkstock

Cambridge University Press has no responsibility for the persistence or accuracy of URLs for external or third-party internet websites referred to in this publication, and does not guarantee that any content on such websites is, or will remain, accurate or appropriate. Information regarding prices, travel timetables and other factual information given in this work is correct at the time of first printing but Cambridge University Press does not guarantee the accuracy of such information thereafter.

NOTICE TO TEACHERS
Worksheets and copies of them remain in the copyright of Cambridge University Press and such copies may not be distributed or used in any way outside the purchasing institution.

Contents

How to use this book

Structure of the book

This book covers all the material for Topic 9 (Calculus Option) of the Higher Level Mathematics syllabus for the International Baccalaureate course. It assumes familiarity with the core material (syllabus topics 1 to 6), particularly Calculus (syllabus topic 6) and Sequences and Series (syllabus topic 1.1). We have tried to include in the main text only the material that will be examinable. There are many interesting applications and ideas that go beyond the syllabus and we have tried to highlight some of these in the 'From another perspective' and 'Research explorer' boxes.

The five main chapters are probably best covered in the order presented, although chapter 5 (except for the last section) only requires knowledge of the core calculus material. Chapter 6 contains a summary of all the topics and further examination practice, with many of the questions mixing several topics – a favourite trick in IB examinations.

Each chapter starts with a list of learning objectives to give you an idea about what the chapter contains. There is an introductory problem at the start of the topic that illustrates what you should be able to do after you have completed the topic. You should not expect to be able to solve the problem at the start, but you may want to think about possible strategies and what sort of new facts and methods would help you. The solution to the introductory problem is provided at the end of chapter 6.

Key point boxes

The most important ideas and formulae are emphasised in the 'KEY POINT' boxes. When the formulae are given in the Formula booklet, there will be an icon: ▌; if this icon is not present, then the formulae are **not** in the Formula booklet and you may need to learn them or at least know how to derive them.

Worked examples

Each worked example is split into two columns. On the right is what you should write down. Sometimes the example might include more detail then you strictly need, but it is designed to give you an idea of what is required to score full method marks in examinations. However, mathematics is about much more than examinations and remembering methods. So, on the left of the worked examples are notes that describe the thought processes and suggest which route you should use to tackle the question. We hope that these will help you with any exercise questions that differ from the worked examples. It is very deliberate that some of the questions require you to do more than repeat the methods in the worked examples. Mathematics is about thinking!

Signposts

There are several boxes that appear throughout the book.

Theory of knowledge issues

Every lesson is a Theory of knowledge lesson, but sometimes the links may not be obvious. Mathematics is frequently used as an example of certainty and truth, but this is often not the case. In these boxes we will try to highlight some of the weaknesses and ambiguities in mathematics as well as showing how mathematics links to other areas of knowledge.

From another perspective

The International Baccalaureate® encourages looking at things in different ways. As well as highlighting some international differences between mathematicians these boxes also look at other perspectives on the mathematics we are covering: historical, pragmatic and cultural.

Research explorer

As part of your course, you will be asked to write a report on a mathematical topic of your choice. It is sometimes difficult to know which topics are suitable as a basis for such reports, and so we have tried to show where a topic can act as a jumping-off point for further work. This can also give you ideas for an Extended essay. There is a lot of great mathematics out there!

Exam hint

Although we would encourage you to think of mathematics as more than just learning in order to pass an examination, there are some common errors it is useful for you to be aware of. If there is a common pitfall we will try to highlight it in these boxes.

Fast forward / rewind

Mathematics is all about making links. You might be interested to see how something you have just learned will be used elsewhere in the course, or you may need to go back and remind yourself of a previous topic. These boxes indicate connections with other sections of the book to help you find your way around.

How to use the questions

The colour-coding

The questions are colour-coded to distinguish between the levels.

Black questions are drill questions. They help you practise the methods described in the book, but they are usually not structured like the questions in the examination. This does not mean they are easy, some of them are quite tough.

Each differently numbered drill question tests a different skill. Lettered subparts of a question are of increasing difficulty. Within each lettered part there may be multiple roman-numeral parts ((i), (ii),...) , all of which are of a similar difficulty. Unless you want to do lots of practice we would recommend that you only do one roman-numeral part and then check your answer. If you have made a mistake then you may want to think about what went wrong before you try any more. Otherwise move on to the next lettered part.

Green questions are examination-style questions which should be accessible to students on the path to getting a grade 3 or 4.

Blue questions are harder examination-style questions. If you are aiming for a grade 5 or 6 you should be able to make significant progress through most of these.

Red questions are at the very top end of difficulty in the examinations. If you can do these then you are likely to be on course for a grade 7.

Gold questions are a type that are *not* set in the examination, but are designed to provoke thinking and discussion in order to help you to a better understanding of a particular concept.

At the end of each chapter you will see longer questions typical of the second section of International Baccalaureate® examinations. These follow the same colour-coding scheme.

Of course, these are just **guidelines**. If you are aiming for a grade 6, do not be surprised if you find a green question you cannot do. People are never equally good at all areas of the syllabus. Equally, if you can do all the red questions that does not guarantee you will get a grade 7; after all, in the examination you have to deal with time pressure and examination stress!

These questions are graded relative to our experience of the final examination, so when you first start the course you will find all the questions relatively hard, but by the end of the course they should seem more straightforward. Do not get intimidated!

We hope you find the Calculus Option an interesting and enriching course. You might also find it quite challenging, but do not get intimidated, frequently topics only make sense after lots of revision and practice. Persevere and you will succeed.

The author team.

Introduction

In this Option you will learn:

- how to find a limit of a sequence (the value that the terms of the sequence approach)
- about various methods for finding limits of functions, including L'Hôpital's Rule
- formal definitions of continuity and differentiability of functions, and some useful properties of differentiable functions
- how we can extend definite integration to allow one of the limits to tend to infinity
- how to decide whether infinite series have a limit
- how to use series to approximate various functions (Maclaurin and Taylor series)
- how to solve certain types of differential equations, both exactly and approximately.

Introductory problem

Consider a wedding cake with four layers:

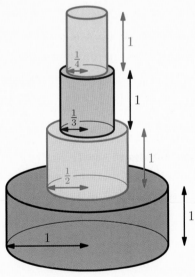

Each layer has a thickness of 1. The first layer has a radius of 1, the second a radius of $\frac{1}{2}$, the third a radius of $\frac{1}{3}$ and the fourth a radius of $\frac{1}{4}$.

Find the volume of the cake and the surface area (excluding the bottom of the first layer) that needs covering with icing.

Now imagine there are infinitely many layers to the cake. What can you say about the volume of the cake and the surface area that needs icing now?

The calculus option builds on many different areas of the course, using the theory of functions, sequences and series, differentiation and integration. Some of the ideas you will study here have interested many of the greatest minds in mathematics: Euler, Newton, Leibniz, Cauchy, Riemann and others; and have far reaching applications both within mathematics and other subjects such as physics and engineering.

The option is split into five chapters:

1 Limits of sequences and functions looks first at the behaviour of sequences as we take more and more terms. How can we determine which sequences head towards (converge to) a finite value when we take infinitely many terms, and which just become infinitely large? We then examine the values of functions as we get closer and closer to a particular value in their domain. The focus is particularly on quotients where both the numerator and denominator are tending to 0 or where they are both tending to ∞. Building on the idea of a limit of a function, we then look at where functions are continuous and where they can be differentiated, before considering two important theorems for differentiable functions.

2 Improper integrals looks at what happens when we take the upper limit on an integral to be ∞. Will this always give an infinite value for the integral (and hence an infinite area under the curve), or are there some circumstances in which that value (or area) is finite? And again how do we know which is the case for a given integral? This chapter starts with a look at the Fundamental Theorem of Calculus.

3 Infinite series builds on both the previous chapters and examines the sums of infinitely many terms. We have already seen with some geometric series that it is possible to add together infinitely many terms and yet get a finite value for the sum to infinity; here we look at a wide range of different series and develop ways to test if the series converges (has a finite value) or not. We also link improper integrals and infinite sums and look at ways of placing bounds on the value of an infinite sum.

4 Maclaurin and Taylor series establishes a way of representing many familiar functions as infinite series in increasing integer powers of x. We examine polynomial approximations for functions, and their accuracy, and use the series representation of functions for integration and to calculate limits, again particularly those where both numerator and denominator are tending to 0 or ∞.

5 Differential equations looks at setting up and solving differential equations, which are used to describe the behaviour of many processes in nature and engineering. We look at three methods for solving different types of these equations and then consider some methods to find approximate solutions to differential equations that are difficult (if not impossible) to solve in the standard way.

1 Limits of sequences and functions

In this chapter you will learn:

- to use algebraic rules to calculate limits of some sequences

- to find the limit of a sequence by squeezing it between two sequences that both converge to the same limit

- to apply similar principles to find limits of functions

- to use l'Hôpital's Rule to find limits of the form $\frac{'0'}{0}$ and $\frac{'\infty'}{\infty}$

- to determine where functions are continuous and where they are differentiable

- to apply Rolle's Theorem and the Mean Value Theorem to differentiable functions.

You should have met sequences in the core course, and will be familiar with using a general term u_n to define them. Our main focus now is to see what happens as we take more and more terms of a sequence: does there seem to be some finite value (a limit) which the sequence approaches, and if so does the sequence do so by increasing, decreasing, or perhaps by oscillating either side of the value?

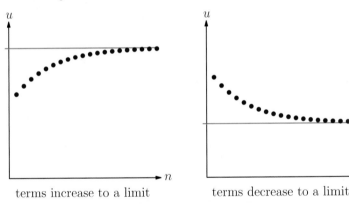

terms increase to a limit   terms decrease to a limit

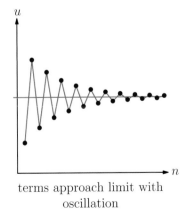

terms approach limit with oscillation

Alternatively, does the sequence not have a (finite) limit, due to just getting larger in magnitude or perhaps oscillating with the same magnitude either side of some value?

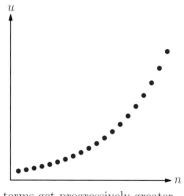

terms get progressively greater

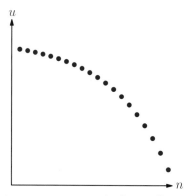

terms get progressively smaller

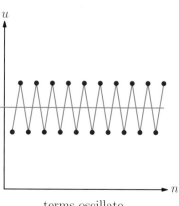

terms oscillate

Sometimes it is immediately obvious which of these is taking place.

For example, the sequence with general term $u_n = 2^{n-1}$
1, 2, 4, 8, 16, …
is clearly just getting larger term by term and will never approach a limit.

The sequence defined inductively by $u_1 = 3$, $u_{n+1} = \dfrac{1}{4 - u_n}$

$$3,\ 1,\ \frac{1}{3},\ \frac{3}{11},\ \frac{11}{41},\ \frac{41}{153} \ldots$$

seems to be decreasing, but it is not clear whether it will have a limit or if it does, what this limit might be.

In this chapter we start by looking at ways to answer these questions about sequences and then widen our focus to look at the limits of functions. We then use the idea of limits of functions to consider where a function is continuous and where it can be differentiated and finally apply these ideas to develop two well known and useful theorems.

1A The limit of a sequence

If the terms of a sequence u_k head towards a value L, we say that the sequence **converges** to a limit L, as $n \to \infty$ ('n tends to ∞') and we write:

$$\lim_{n\to\infty} u_n = L$$

This does not necessarily mean that any term of the sequence actually reaches the value L, but that, by taking more and more terms, the sequence becomes arbitrarily close to L.

For example, the sequence $\{u_n\} = \dfrac{1}{n}$

$$1, \frac{1}{2}, \frac{1}{3}, \frac{1}{4}, \frac{1}{5}, \frac{1}{6}, \frac{1}{7} \ldots$$

appears to be converging to 0, that is:

$$\lim_{n\to\infty} \frac{1}{n} = 0$$

although no term actually is 0.

Graphically we have (see alongside):

If the sequence does not converge then it is said to **diverge**.

Often, the behaviour of a sequence is not so apparent and we may want to find a possible limit without evaluating lots of terms or drawing a graph.

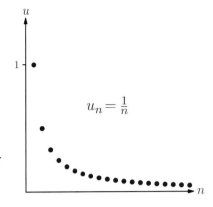

For a sequence such as $\{u_n\} = \dfrac{6n+72}{2n+97}$, we might consider trying to take the limits of both the numerator and denominator separately and then dividing one by the other. The problem here is that both numerator and denominator diverge and $\dfrac{`\infty'}{\infty}$ is not defined.

We can, however, take this approach if the limit of both sequences is finite, as then the limits do behave much as you might expect (or at least hope!).

KEY POINT 1.1

Algebra of limits

If the sequence $\{a_n\}$ converges to a limit a and the sequence $\{b_n\}$ to a limit b, then:

$$\lim_{n\to\infty}\left(pa_n + qb_n\right) = p\lim_{n\to\infty}a_n + q\lim_{n\to\infty}b_n = pa + qb \qquad (p, q \in \mathbb{R})$$

$$\lim_{n\to\infty}\left(a_n b_n\right) = \left(\lim_{n\to\infty}a_n\right)\left(\lim_{n\to\infty}b_n\right) = ab$$

$$\lim_{n\to\infty}\left(\frac{a_n}{b_n}\right) = \frac{\lim\limits_{n\to\infty}a_n}{\lim\limits_{n\to\infty}b_n} = \frac{a}{b} \quad (b \neq 0)$$

The algebra of limits only applies when the limits exist (they are finite) but we will often make use of the following two supplements to the final point.

KEY POINT 1.2

If the sequence $\{a_n\}$ diverges, then for any constant $c \in \mathbb{R}$ $(c \neq 0)$:

$$\lim_{n\to\infty}\left(\frac{c}{a_n}\right) = 0$$

$$\lim_{n\to\infty}\left(\frac{a_n}{c}\right) = \infty$$

While this might not seem helpful for $\{u_n\} = \dfrac{6n+72}{2n+97}$ where both numerator and denominator diverge, the following example illustrates a common way of dealing with this problem, allowing us to apply the algebra of limits result.

Worked example 1.1

Find the following:

(a) $\displaystyle\lim_{n\to\infty}\frac{6n+72}{2n+97}$

(b) $\displaystyle\lim_{n\to\infty}\frac{n^2+5}{2n^2-3n+8}$

Neither $6n+72$ nor $2n+97$ converges so we must rearrange the expression to give a numerator and denominator that both converge, by dividing through by n

(a)

$$\frac{6n+72}{2n+97}=\frac{6+\dfrac{72}{n}}{2+\dfrac{97}{n}}$$

Now apply the algebra of limits results

$$\therefore \lim_{n\to\infty}\frac{6n+72}{2n+97}=\lim_{n\to\infty}\frac{6+\dfrac{72}{n}}{2+\dfrac{97}{n}}$$

$$=\frac{\lim_{n\to\infty}\left(6+\dfrac{72}{n}\right)}{\lim_{n\to\infty}\left(2+\dfrac{97}{n}\right)}$$

$\displaystyle\lim_{n\to\infty}\frac{72}{n}=0$ and $\displaystyle\lim_{n\to\infty}\frac{97}{n}=0$

by Key point 1.2

$$=\frac{6+0}{2+0}$$

$$=3$$

Neither n^2+5 nor $2n^2-3n+8$ converges so rearrange the expression to give a numerator and denominator that both converge, by dividing through by n^2

(b)

$$\frac{n^2+5}{2n^2-3n+8}=\frac{1+\dfrac{5}{n^2}}{2-\dfrac{3}{n}+\dfrac{8}{n^2}}$$

Now apply the algebra of limits results

$$\therefore \lim_{n\to\infty}\frac{n^2+5}{2n^2-3n+8}=\lim_{n\to\infty}\frac{1+\dfrac{5}{n^2}}{2-\dfrac{3}{n}+\dfrac{8}{n^2}}$$

$\displaystyle\lim_{n\to\infty}\frac{5}{n^2}=0,\ \lim_{n\to\infty}\frac{3}{n}=0$ and $\displaystyle\lim_{n\to\infty}\frac{8}{n^2}=0,$

all by Key point 1.2

$$=\frac{\lim_{n\to\infty}\left(1+\dfrac{5}{n^2}\right)}{\lim_{n\to\infty}\left(2-\dfrac{3}{n}+\dfrac{8}{n^2}\right)}$$

$$=\frac{1+0}{2-0+0}$$

$$=\frac{1}{2}$$

EXAM HINT

To apply the algebra of limits result to a fraction, first divide through by the highest power of n.

It is tempting to think that the limit of the difference of two sequences that diverge to infinity is 0, i.e. that '$\infty-\infty=0$', but we must not apply the algebra of limits to non-convergent sequences. (In fact '$\infty-\infty$' might be 0, but it might be some other finite value or it might even be ∞!) In these cases it is necessary to manipulate the expression into a convenient form for applying the algebra of limits and/or Key point 1.2.

Worked example 1.2

Find $\lim\limits_{n\to\infty}\left(\sqrt{n^2+n}-n\right)$.

Neither $\sqrt{n^2+n}$ nor n converges so we can't apply the algebra of limits to the difference. Neither do we have the familiar situation of a quotient where we could divide through as in Worked example 1.1

So create a quotient by multiplying top and bottom by the same expression. The presence of $\sqrt{a}-b$ here suggests multiplying by $\sqrt{a}+b$

$$\sqrt{n^2+n}-n=\left(\sqrt{n^2+n}-n\right)\left(\frac{\sqrt{n^2+n}+n}{\sqrt{n^2+n}+n}\right)$$

$$=\frac{\left(\sqrt{n^2+n}\right)^2-n^2}{\sqrt{n^2+n}+n}$$

$$=\frac{\left(n^2+n\right)-n^2}{\sqrt{n^2+n}+n}$$

$$=\frac{n}{\sqrt{n^2+n}+n}$$

Divide through by n (this will mean dividing through inside the square root by n^2)

$$=\frac{1}{\sqrt{\dfrac{n^2}{n^2}+\dfrac{n}{n^2}}+1}$$

$$=\frac{1}{\sqrt{1+\dfrac{1}{n}}+1}$$

Now apply the algebra of limits

$$\therefore\ \lim\limits_{n\to\infty}\left(\sqrt{n^2+n}-n\right)=\frac{1}{\sqrt{1+0}+1}=\frac{1}{2}$$

Exercise 1A

1. Find the following limits:

 (a) (i) $\lim\limits_{n\to\infty}\dfrac{3n-7}{2n+1}$

   (ii) $\lim\limits_{n\to\infty}\dfrac{4n+11}{3-2n}$

 (b) (i) $\lim\limits_{n\to\infty}\dfrac{n^2+3n-1}{3n^2+5n-7}$

   (ii) $\lim\limits_{n\to\infty}\dfrac{4n^4+3n^3-10}{n^4+5}$

 (c) (i) $\lim\limits_{n\to\infty}\dfrac{5-3n}{2n^2+4n+9}$

   (ii) $\lim\limits_{n\to\infty}\dfrac{n^2-6}{n^3+5n-3}$

 (d) (i) $\lim\limits_{n\to\infty}\left(\dfrac{5-3n}{7-4n}\right)^2$

(ii) $\lim\limits_{n\to\infty}\sqrt{\dfrac{9n^2+2}{4n^2+n+1}}$

2. (a) Show that $\lim\limits_{n\to\infty}\dfrac{3n-2}{5n+7}=\dfrac{3}{5}$

(b) Hence find $\lim\limits_{n\to\infty}\left(\dfrac{3n-2}{5n+7}\right)^3$ *[3 marks]*

3. (a) Show that $\dfrac{n(n+4)}{n+2}-\dfrac{n^3}{n^2+3}=\dfrac{2n^3+3n^2+12n}{n^3+2n^2+3n+6}$

(b) Hence find $\lim\limits_{n\to\infty}\left(\dfrac{n(n+4)}{n+2}-\dfrac{n^3}{n^2+3}\right)$ *[6 marks]*

4. For the sequence $\{u_n\}$, whose general term is given by

$$u_n=\sqrt{n+1}-\sqrt{n-1}$$

find $\lim\limits_{n\to\infty}u_n$ *[6 marks]*

5. Use the algebra of limits to find $\lim\limits_{n\to\infty}\dfrac{\sqrt{n}}{\sqrt{n-3}+2}$ *[7 marks]*

6. Use the algebra of limits to prove that

$$\lim\limits_{n\to\infty}\dfrac{\sqrt{n+1}+\sqrt{n-1}}{\sqrt{n}}=2$$ *[4 marks]*

1B The Squeeze Theorem

In addition to the methods already described for finding limits of sequences, there is another result which we need to have at our disposal.

KEY POINT 1.3

> **Squeeze Theorem**
>
> If we have sequences $\{a_n\},\{b_n\}$ and $\{c_n\}$ such that
>
> $a_n\le b_n\le c_n$ for all $n\in\mathbb{Z}^+$
>
> and
>
> $$\lim\limits_{n\to\infty}a_n=\lim\limits_{n\to\infty}c_n=L<\infty$$
>
> then $\lim\limits_{n\to\infty}b_n=L.$

The Squeeze Theorem says that if we can find two sequences that converge to the same limit and squeeze another sequence between them, then that sequence must also converge to the same limit.

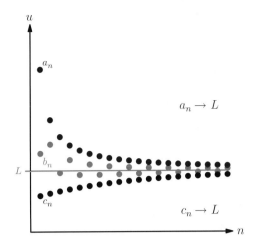

To use this result we often need known inequalities for standard functions.

Worked example 1.3

Use the Squeeze Theorem to find $\lim_{n\to\infty} \dfrac{\sin n}{n}$.

The obvious place to start is by bounding $\sin n$

$-1 \le \sin n \le 1$ for all $n \in \mathbb{Z}^+$

$\Rightarrow \dfrac{-1}{n} \le \dfrac{\sin n}{n} \le \dfrac{1}{n}$ for all $n \in \mathbb{Z}^+$

As both $\left\{\dfrac{-1}{n}\right\}$ and $\left\{\dfrac{1}{n}\right\}$ converge to 0 we can apply the Squeeze Theorem

Since

$$\lim_{n\to\infty}\left(-\dfrac{1}{n}\right) = \lim_{n\to\infty}\dfrac{1}{n} = 0$$

by the Squeeze Theorem

$$\lim_{n\to\infty}\dfrac{\sin n}{n} = 0$$

When you use the Squeeze Theorem it can be difficult to choose one, or both, of the sequences a_n and c_n. The following illustrates a common way of doing this.

Worked example 1.4

Show that $\lim_{n\to\infty} \dfrac{n!}{n^n} = 0$.

We can see that $\dfrac{n!}{n^n} > 0$ so we are looking for a sequence that is always at least as large as $\dfrac{n!}{n^n}$ but which tends to 0 as $n \to \infty$ so that we can squeeze $\dfrac{n!}{n^n}$

$\dfrac{n!}{n^n} > 0$ for all $n \in \mathbb{Z}^+$

$\longrightarrow$

continued . . .

To find such a sequence start by writing out the general term of our sequence long-hand

Next,

$$\frac{n!}{n^n} = \frac{n}{n}\frac{(n-1)}{n}\frac{(n-2)}{n}\frac{(n-3)}{n}\cdots\frac{3}{n}\frac{2}{n}\frac{1}{n}$$

Each numerator is less than n so use that to introduce the inequality.
We leave the final term unaltered so that not everything cancels out

$$< \frac{n}{n}\frac{n}{n}\frac{n}{n}\frac{n}{n}\cdots\frac{n}{n}\frac{n}{n}\frac{1}{n} = \frac{1}{n}$$

$$0 < \frac{n!}{n^n} < \frac{1}{n} \quad \text{for all } n \in \mathbb{Z}^+$$

Apply the Squeeze Theorem

Since $\lim\limits_{n\to\infty}\dfrac{1}{n} = 0$

we can conclude that $\lim\limits_{n\to\infty}\dfrac{n!}{n^n} = 0$

by the Squeeze Theorem

Exercise 1B

1. Use the Squeeze Theorem to find the following:

    (a) $\lim\limits_{n\to\infty}\dfrac{\cos n}{2n}$

    (b) $\lim\limits_{n\to\infty}\dfrac{4n^2 - \sin 3n}{n^2 + 8}$

    (c) $\lim\limits_{n\to\infty}\dfrac{n^n}{(2n)!}$

    (d) $\lim\limits_{n\to\infty}\dfrac{\arctan(n^2)}{\sqrt{n}}$

2. (a) Show that $\dfrac{6^n}{n!} \le \dfrac{6^5}{5!} \times \dfrac{6}{n}$ for $n \ge 6$.

    (b) Hence use the Squeeze Theorem to show that $\lim\limits_{n\to\infty}\dfrac{6^n}{n!} = 0$.

    [6 marks]

3. (a) Show that $(1+x)^n > \dfrac{n(n-1)}{2}x^2$ for all $x > 0, n \in \mathbb{Z}^+$.

    (b) By taking $x = \sqrt{\dfrac{2}{n-1}}$ show that $\left(\sqrt[n]{n} - 1\right)^2 < \dfrac{2}{n-1}$ $n \ne 1$.

    (c) Hence find $\lim\limits_{n\to\infty}\sqrt[n]{n}$.

    [8 marks]

4. (a) Find $\lim\limits_{n\to\infty}\dfrac{n}{\sqrt{n^2 + n}}$

    (b) Hence use the Squeeze Theorem to find $\lim\limits_{n\to\infty}\sum\limits_{k=1}^{n}\dfrac{1}{\sqrt{n^2 + k}}$

    [7 marks]

5. (a) By considering $(1 + x)^n$ for a suitable value of x, show that

    $$2^n > \frac{n(n-1)(n-2)}{3!} \quad \text{for all } n \in \mathbb{Z}^+.$$

    (b) Hence find $\lim\limits_{n\to\infty}\dfrac{n^2}{2^n}$.

    [8 marks]

EXAM HINT

It is a common trick to use part of the binomial expansion to introduce an inequality such as in question 3. Look back at the core course for a reminder of the binomial expansion.

6. (a) Find the value a at which the tangent to $y = \ln x$ passing through the origin touches the curve.

(b) Hence form an inequality involving x and $\ln x$ for $x > 0$.

(c) Find $\lim\limits_{n \to \infty} \dfrac{3n^3 + \ln n^3}{n^3}$.

7. (a) Show that $\dfrac{1}{n} < \ln n$ for all $n > 1$.

(b) Show that $\ln(1+n) < n$ for all $n \geq 1$.

(c) Hence show that $\dfrac{n}{1+n} < \ln\left(1 + \dfrac{1}{n}\right)^n < 1$ for all $n \geq 1$.

(d) (i) Find $\lim\limits_{n \to \infty}\left(1 + \dfrac{1}{n}\right)^n$

(ii) What assumptions have you made? *[15 marks]*

 The limit established in Question 7, part (d)(i) is one of the most important in maths. It is often introduced informally in the context of percentage increase, but has many wide-ranging applications. We will meet it again in chapter 3 of this option.

1C The limit of a function

The idea of the limit of a function $f(x)$ at a point a, $\lim\limits_{x \to a} f(x)$, is like that of the limit of a sequence: it is either the value that the function attains at a or approaches as $x \to a$. The difference is that the domain will not just be positive integers and that the limit can be taken as x tends to any value, not just as $x \to \infty$.

For example:

$$\lim_{x \to 3} x^2 = 3^2 = 9$$

$$\lim_{x \to \frac{\pi}{2}} \tan^2 x = \infty$$

$$\lim_{x \to \infty} e^{-x} = 0$$

While we cannot input $x = \dfrac{\pi}{2}$ into $\tan^2 x$ to get the limit in the second example above (as it is not in the domain) or $x = \infty$ into e^{-x} to get the limits of ∞ and 0 respectively, we can see that the functions tend to these limits by referring to their graphs.

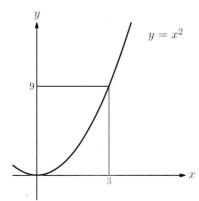

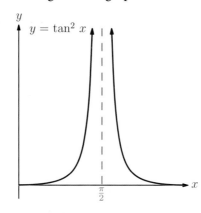

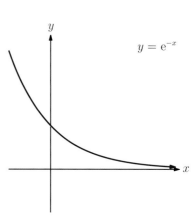

Using a combination of two of these limits, we could also say

$$\lim_{x \to \frac{\pi}{2}} e^{-\tan^2 x} = e^{-\lim\limits_{x \to \frac{\pi}{2}} \tan^2 x} = 0$$

This process of taking the limit 'inside' a function is valid for all the functions we will meet, but in general is not valid.

We can use the idea of the limit of a sequence to form a definition for the limit of a function. If we take a convergent sequence $x_1, x_2, x_3, \ldots$ and evaluate the function at successive terms of the sequence, we get a new sequence:

$$f(x_1), f(x_2), f(x_3), \ldots$$

If this sequence converges too, we say that the function converges.

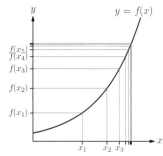

KEY POINT 1.4

If for any sequence $\{x_n\}$ such that $x_n \to x_0$ we have that $f(x_n) \to L$, then L is said to be the limit of the function.

Note that it need not necessarily be the case that $f(x_0) = L$:

for example, consider the function $f(x) = \begin{cases} 2x & x \neq 1 \\ 3 & x = 1 \end{cases}$

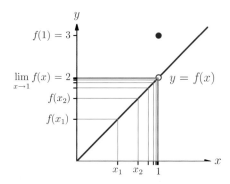

Taking any sequence that converges to $x = 1$, we will clearly get the function converging to $f(x) = 2$, that is $\lim\limits_{x \to 1} f(x) = 2$, even though $f(1) = 3$.

Finding a sequence that converges to a limit and then seeing how the function behaves as we evaluate it at successive terms of the sequence, raises an important question about how the sequence tends to the limit. For example, consider the function $f(x) = \tan x$ and choose any sequence that tends to $x = \dfrac{\pi}{2}$ in the following way, that is from the left or from below.

EXAM HINT

This definition is often most useful for showing that a limit does not exist at a point. To do so you need to find two sequences x_n and y_n that tend to x_0, but for which $f(x_n)$ and $f(y_n)$ do not tend to the same limit.

Worked example 1.6 demonstrates how this definition of limit can be used to show that the limit of a function does not exist at a point x_0.

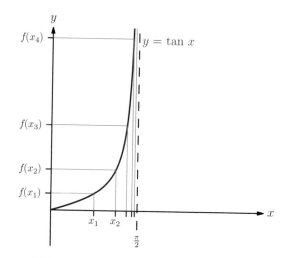

Here we would have $\tan(x) \to \infty$.

However, what if we had chosen a sequence that tended to $x = \dfrac{\pi}{2}$ in the following way, that is from the right or from above?

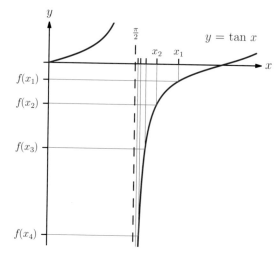

Now, we would have $\tan(x) \to -\infty$; a different limit.

Clearly we cannot have two different limits for a function at the same point and so in this case we say that the limit does not exist at this value of x.

KEY POINT 1.5

If we find the limit of a function at point x_0 by having a sequence that approaches from below, we write:

$$\lim_{x \to x_0^-} f(x)$$

If we do so by having a sequence that approaches from above we write:

$$\lim_{x \to x_0^+} f(x)$$

We need both the limit from above and the limit from below to exist *and* coincide for the limit to exist at that point. If they do then:

$$\lim_{x \to x_0} f(x) = \lim_{x \to x_0^+} f(x) = \lim_{x \to x_0^-} f(x)$$

The limits from above and below may not be equal at asymptotes (as in the case of $\tan x$ at $x = \dfrac{\pi}{2}$), and there might also be an obvious difference in the limits at a point where the definition of the function changes.

Worked example 1.5

For $f(x) = \begin{cases} -3x+7 & x \leq 2 \\ x^2 - 1 & x > 2 \end{cases}$ determine $\lim\limits_{x \to 2} f(x)$ (if it exists).

It is often a good idea to start by sketching the function. Here we see that the limit clearly doesn't exist

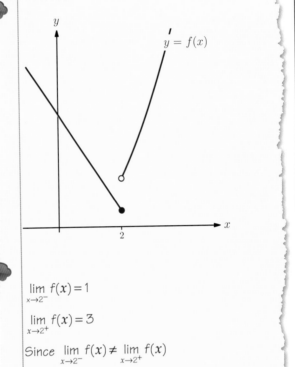

We just need to find the limits from above and below and show they're different to justify this

$\lim\limits_{x \to 2^-} f(x) = 1$

$\lim\limits_{x \to 2^+} f(x) = 3$

Since $\lim\limits_{x \to 2^-} f(x) \neq \lim\limits_{x \to 2^+} f(x)$

$\lim\limits_{x \to 2} f(x)$ does not exist.

Note that a function, such as that in Worked example 1.5, consisting of two or more pieces defined by different formulae, is said to be 'piecewise'.

EXAM HINT

It is often a good idea to sketch piecewise functions to understand their behaviour at different points in the domain.

With other functions, a limit may also not exist at a point if the function oscillates very rapidly as it approaches that point. This is rather like the case mentioned at the beginning of the chapter for sequences that oscillate without ever tending to a limit.

For example, $f(x) = \cos\left(\dfrac{1}{x}\right)$ behaves in the following way:

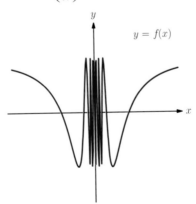

Worked example 1.6

Show that $\lim\limits_{x \to 0} \cos\left(\dfrac{1}{x}\right)$ does not exist.

> If we can find two sequences, x_n and y_n, that tend to 0 but for which $f(x_n)$ and $f(y_n)$ tend to two different limits, then the limit of $f(x)$ does not exist

Let $f(x) = \cos\dfrac{1}{x}$

> The sequence $a_n = 2\pi, 4\pi, 6\pi, \ldots$ has $\cos(a_n) = 1$ and the sequence $b_n = \dfrac{\pi}{2}, \dfrac{3\pi}{2}, \dfrac{5\pi}{2}, \ldots$ has $\cos(b_n) = 0$ for all n
>
> So take $x_n = \dfrac{1}{a_n}$ and $y_n = \dfrac{1}{b_n}$

Let $\quad x_n = \dfrac{1}{2\pi n} \to 0$

and $\quad y_n = \dfrac{2}{(2n-1)\pi} \to 0$

Then

$$f(x_n) = \cos\left(\dfrac{1}{\dfrac{1}{2\pi n}}\right)$$
$$= \cos(2\pi n)$$
$$= 1 \quad \text{for all } n$$
$$\therefore \lim\limits_{x_n \to 0} f(x_n) = 1$$

But $f(y_n) = \cos\left(\dfrac{1}{\dfrac{2}{(2n-1)\pi}}\right)$
$$= \cos\left(\left(\dfrac{2n-1}{2}\right)\pi\right)$$
$$= 0 \quad \text{for all } n$$
$$\therefore \lim\limits_{y_n \to 0} f(y_n) = 0$$

As $\lim f(x_n) \neq \lim f(y_n)$, the limit does not exist.

Just as for sequences, the Squeeze Theorem holds for functions.

Worked example 1.7

Show that $\lim\limits_{x \to 0} x\cos\left(\dfrac{1}{x}\right) = 0$.

> The difficulty here is the $\dfrac{1}{0}$ inside the cos function, so we cannot evaluate the limit directly

$$\left| x\cos\left(\dfrac{1}{x}\right) \right| = |x|\left| \cos\left(\dfrac{1}{x}\right) \right| \leq |x|$$

> However, since $|\cos x| \leq 1$, we can bound the function $x\cos\left(\dfrac{1}{x}\right)$ and potentially use the Squeeze Theorem

i.e. $-|x| \leq x\cos\left(\dfrac{1}{x}\right) \leq |x|$

continued . . .

We can now let $x \to 0$ since clearly both $\pm |x| \to 0$

Therefore, by the Squeeze Theorem, since
$$\lim_{x \to 0} \left(-|x| \right) = 0$$
and
$$\lim_{x \to 0} |x| = 0$$
we must have
$$\lim_{x \to 0} x \cos\left(\frac{1}{x}\right) = 0$$

The algebra of limits also holds for functions.

Worked example 1.8

Evaluate:

(a) $\displaystyle\lim_{x \to 3}\left\{x^3 - 5x - 8\right\}$

(b) $\displaystyle\lim_{x \to -2}\left\{\frac{(x+2)^2}{\sqrt{x^2 + 4x + 13} - 3}\right\}$

We can apply algebra of limits straight away

(a) $\displaystyle\lim_{x \to 3}\left\{x^3 - 5x - 8\right\} = \lim_{x \to 3} x^3 - 5\lim_{x \to 3} x - \lim_{x \to 3} 8$

$= 3^3 - (5 \times 3) - 8$

$= 4$

Since $\displaystyle\lim_{x \to -2}(x+2)^2 = 0$ and $\displaystyle\lim_{x \to -2}\sqrt{x^2 + 4x + 13} - 3 = 0$ we can't apply algebra of limits immediately as $\dfrac{'0'}{0}$ is undefined. However, we can simplify the quotient by using the trick from Worked example 1.2 and multiply top and bottom by $\sqrt{x^2 + 4x + 13} + 3$. This is an even better option when we notice that completing the square of the quadratic under the root will give us $(x+2)^2$ which is also in the numerator

(b) $\dfrac{(x+2)^2}{\sqrt{x^2 + 4x + 13} - 3} = \dfrac{(x+2)^2}{\sqrt{(x+2)^2 + 9} - 3}$

$= \dfrac{(x+2)^2}{\sqrt{(x+2)^2 + 9} - 3} \times \dfrac{\sqrt{(x+2)^2 + 9} + 3}{\sqrt{(x+2)^2 + 9} + 3}$

$= \dfrac{(x+2)^2\left(\sqrt{(x+2)^2 + 9} + 3\right)}{\left\{(x+2)^2 + 9\right\} - 9}$

$= \dfrac{(x+2)^2\left(\sqrt{(x+2)^2 + 9} + 3\right)}{(x+2)^2}$

$= \sqrt{(x+2)^2 + 9} + 3$

Now apply the algebra of limits

So,

$\displaystyle\lim_{x \to -2}\left\{\frac{(x+2)^2}{\sqrt{x^2 + 4x + 13} - 3}\right\}$

$= \displaystyle\lim_{x \to -2}\sqrt{(x+2)^2 + 9} + 3$

$= \sqrt{0 + 9} + 3$

$= 6$

Sometimes, however, the problem of '$\frac{0}{0}$' can be removed with much less algebraic manipulation.

Worked example 1.9

Find $\displaystyle\lim_{x\to 2}\frac{x^2-4}{x-2}$.

Since we have a limit of the form '$\frac{0}{0}$', we can't apply the algebra of limits straight away
However, we recognise that the numerator factorises

$$\frac{x^2-4}{x-2}=\frac{(x+2)(x-2)}{x-2}=x+2$$

It is useful to draw the graph at this point to clarify what is happening

Therefore we have the graph:

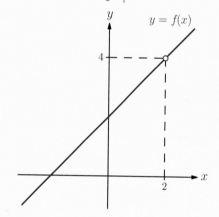

Even though $x=2$ is not in the domain of the function $\frac{x^2-4}{x-2}$, the limit as $x\to 2$ clearly exists

And we can see that:

$$\lim_{x\to 2}\frac{x^2-4}{x-2}=4$$

EXAM HINT

It is always a good idea to see if an algebraic fraction can be simplified before attempting any other methods.

Exercise 1C

1. For each function, find (if they exist):

    * $\displaystyle\lim_{x\to x_0^+} f(x)$

    * $\displaystyle\lim_{x\to x_0^-} f(x)$

    * $\displaystyle\lim_{x\to x_0} f(x)$

    for the given values of x_0:

(a) (i) $f(x) = 2x - 3$, $x_0 = 4$ 　　　(ii) $f(x) = \dfrac{1-4x}{3}$, $x_0 = 0$

(b) (i) $f(x) = \dfrac{2}{x-1}$, $x_0 = 1$ 　　　(ii) $f(x) = \dfrac{x^2+3}{3-x}$, $x_0 = 3$

(c) (i) $f(x) = \ln(x-2)$, $x_0 = 2$ 　　　(ii) $f(x) = \sqrt{x-2}$, $x_0 = 2$

(d) (i) $f(x) = \begin{cases} x^3 - 2x^2 + 3 & x \le 1 \\ 4x - 1 - x^2 & x > 1 \end{cases}$ for $x_0 = 1$

　　(ii) $f(x) = \begin{cases} x^2 + 4x - 5 & x < -1 \\ 2x - 5 & x \ge -1 \end{cases}$ for $x_0 = -1$

(e) (i) $f(x) = \begin{cases} \dfrac{x^2 + 3x - 18}{x^2 - 3x} & x \ne 3 \\ 3 & x = 3 \end{cases}$ for $x_0 = 3$

　　(ii) $f(x) = \begin{cases} \dfrac{x^2 - 25}{x^2 - 5x} & x \ne 5 \\ 2 & x = 5 \end{cases}$ for $x_0 = 5$

2. Let

$$f(x) = \begin{cases} 6 & x \le -5 \\ -2x - 11 & -5 < x \le -3 \\ -x^2 + 4 & -3 < x < 1 \\ -3 & x = 1 \\ x^2 - 4x + 5 & 1 < x < 5 \text{ or } x > 5 \end{cases}$$

(a) Sketch the graph of $f(x)$.

(b) Show that $\lim\limits_{x \to -5} f(x)$ does not exist.

(c) Find $\lim\limits_{x \to -3} f(x)$ if it exists.

(d) $f(5)$ does not exist. Does $\lim\limits_{x \to 5} f(x)$ exist?

(e) List all points, x_0, where $\lim\limits_{x \to x_0} f(x)$ does not exist. *[11 marks]*

3. Find the following limits, if they exist:

(a) $\lim\limits_{x \to -2} \dfrac{2x^2 - 3x + 4}{x^2 - 2x + 1}$

(b) $\lim\limits_{x \to 1} \dfrac{x^2 - 4x + 3}{x^2 - 5x + 4}$ 　　　　　　　*[6 marks]*

4. Let $f(x) = \begin{cases} a & x < -2 \\ 2 & x = -2 \\ x^2 + bx + c & -2 < x < 3 \\ 2x + 16 & x \ge 3 \end{cases}$

Given that $\lim\limits_{x \to x_0} f(x)$ exists for all $x \in \mathbb{R}$, and that $\lim\limits_{x \to -2^+} f(x) = -3$,
find constants a, b and c. 　　　　　　　*[6 marks]*

5. For $f(x) = \dfrac{x - \sqrt{x}}{\sqrt{x}}$:

    (a) Show that $\lim\limits_{x \to 0^+} f(x) = -1$.

    (b) Does $\lim\limits_{x \to 0^\oplus} f(x)$ exist? Explain your answer.   *[5 marks]*

6. (a) Show that $\dfrac{x^2 - 6x + 9}{\sqrt{x^2 - 6x + 13} - 2} = \sqrt{(x-3)^2 + 4} + 2$

    (b) Hence find $\lim\limits_{x \to 3} \dfrac{x^2 - 6x + 9}{\sqrt{x^2 - 6x + 13} - 2}$ *[6 marks]*

7. For the function $f(x) = \begin{cases} \dfrac{x-2}{|x-2|} & x \neq 2 \\ 0 & x = 2 \end{cases}$

    find

    (a) $\lim\limits_{x \to 2^+} f(x)$

    (b) $\lim\limits_{x \to 2^-} f(x)$

    (c) $\lim\limits_{x \to 2} f(x)$ *[6 marks]*

8. Given that $f(x) = \dfrac{\sqrt{1 + 3x} - 2}{\sqrt{x + 8} - 3}$:

    (a) Show that $f(x) = \dfrac{3\left(\sqrt{x+8} + 3\right)}{2 + \sqrt{1 + 3x}}$.

    (b) Hence find $\lim\limits_{x \to 1} \dfrac{\sqrt{1 + 3x} - 2}{\sqrt{x + 8} - 3}$.   *[8 marks]*

9. Find $\lim\limits_{x \to 0} x^3 \sin\left(\dfrac{\pi}{x}\right) \cos\left(\dfrac{\pi}{x}\right)$.   *[9 marks]*

10. Determine whether $\lim\limits_{x \to 3} \dfrac{x^2 - 9}{|x - 3|}$ exists, fully justifying your answer.   *[6 marks]*

1D L'Hôpital's Rule

Worked example 1.8b highlighted the potential difficulty of ending up with $\lim\limits_{x \to a} \dfrac{f(x)}{g(x)}$ where $\lim\limits_{x \to a} f(x) = \lim\limits_{x \to a} g(x) = 0$, i.e. of '$\dfrac{0}{0}$'. In that case we avoided the problem by manipulating the quotient into a different form, but this is not always possible.

Unfortunately there is no general answer to the question, 'What is '$\dfrac{0}{0}$'?' It very much depends on how the numerator and denominator get to 0!

A similar problem is $\lim\limits_{x \to a} \dfrac{f(x)}{g(x)}$ where $\lim\limits_{x \to a} f(x) = \lim\limits_{x \to a} g(x) = \infty$, that is of '$\dfrac{\infty}{\infty}$'. Again the answer is that it depends on the specific functions in the numerator and denominator.

Limits of functions of this type will be looked at again in Section 4E of this option, where we will use an alternative method for calculating them (in certain circumstances) using Maclaurin and Taylor series.

So how do we deal with limits like these when we cannot manipulate the quotient into a more helpful form? The answer is provided by:

KEY POINT 1.6

L'Hôpital's Rule

Given functions $f(x)$ and $g(x)$ such that either

$$\lim_{x \to a} f(x) = \lim_{x \to a} g(x) = 0 \quad \text{or} \quad \lim_{x \to a} f(x) = \lim_{x \to a} g(x) = \infty$$

then $\displaystyle \lim_{x \to a} \frac{f(x)}{g(x)} = \lim_{x \to a} \frac{f'(x)}{g'(x)}$

provided that the latter limit exists.

Worked example 1.10

Find the following limits:

(a) $\displaystyle \lim_{x \to 0} \frac{\sin x}{x}$ (b) $\displaystyle \lim_{x \to e} \frac{1 - \ln x}{x - e}$ (c) $\displaystyle \lim_{x \to \infty} \frac{\ln x}{x}$

Since the limit of this function is of the form $\dfrac{'0'}{0}$ we use l'Hôpital's Rule

(a) $\displaystyle \lim_{x \to 0} \sin x = 0$

and $\displaystyle \lim_{x \to 0} x = 0$

By l'Hôpital's Rule

$$\lim_{x \to 0} \frac{\sin x}{x} = \lim_{x \to 0} \frac{\dfrac{d}{dx}(\sin x)}{\dfrac{d}{dx}(x)}$$

$$= \lim_{x \to 0} \frac{\cos x}{1}$$

$$= \frac{1}{1}$$

$$= 1$$

Since the limit of this function is of the form $\dfrac{'0'}{0}$ we use l'Hôpital's Rule

(b) $\displaystyle \lim_{x \to e} (1 - \ln x) = 0$

and $\displaystyle \lim_{x \to e} (x - e) = 0$

By l'Hôpital's Rule

$$\lim_{x \to e} \frac{1 - \ln x}{x - e} = \lim_{x \to e} \frac{\dfrac{d}{dx}(1 - \ln x)}{\dfrac{d}{dx}(x - e)}$$

$$= \lim_{x \to e} \frac{-\dfrac{1}{x}}{1}$$

$$= \frac{-\dfrac{1}{e}}{1}$$

$$= -\frac{1}{e}$$

continued . . .

Since the limit of this function is of the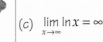
form $\frac{'\infty'}{\infty}$ we use l'Hôpital's Rule

(c) $\lim\limits_{x\to\infty} \ln x = \infty$

and $\lim\limits_{x\to\infty} x = \infty$

By l'Hôpital's Rule

$$\lim_{x\to\infty} \frac{\ln x}{x} = \lim_{x\to\infty} \frac{\dfrac{d}{dx}(\ln x)}{\dfrac{d}{dx}(x)}$$

$$= \lim_{x\to\infty} \frac{\frac{1}{x}}{1}$$

$$= \lim_{x\to\infty} \frac{1}{x} = 0$$

EXAM HINT

You can only apply l'Hôpital's Rule to a quotient that is of the form $\dfrac{'0'}{0}$ or $\dfrac{'\infty'}{\infty}$. It is only valid in these cases.

Sometimes it might be necessary to use l'Hôpital's Rule more than once.

Worked example 1.11

Evaluate $\lim\limits_{x\to 0} \dfrac{1-\cos x}{x^2}$.

Since the limit of this function is of the
form $\dfrac{'0'}{0}$ we use l'Hôpital's Rule

$\lim\limits_{x\to 0}(1-\cos x) = 0$

and $\lim\limits_{x\to 0}(x^2) = 0$

By l'Hôpital's Rule

$$\lim_{x\to 0} \frac{1-\cos x}{x^2} = \lim_{x\to 0} \frac{\dfrac{d}{dx}(1-\cos x)}{\dfrac{d}{dx}(x^2)}$$

$$= \lim_{x\to 0} \frac{\sin x}{2x}$$

In trying to evaluate this limit, we realise
that it is also of the form $\dfrac{'0'}{0}$ so we can
apply l'Hôpital's Rule again

$\lim\limits_{x\to 0}(\sin x) = 0$

and $\lim\limits_{x\to 0}(2x) = 0$

Applying l'Hôpital's Rule again

$$\lim_{x\to 0} \frac{1-\cos x}{x^2} = \lim_{x\to 0} \frac{\dfrac{d}{dx}(\sin x)}{\dfrac{d}{dx}(2x)}$$

$$= \lim_{x\to 0} \frac{\cos x}{2}$$

$$= \frac{1}{2}$$

We met limits of the form '$\infty - \infty$' for sequences when we commented that this was not generally 0. Indeed Worked example 1.2 had $\infty - \infty = \dfrac{1}{2}$.

L'Hôpital's rule can also be used to find limits of the form '$0 \times \infty$' or '$\infty - \infty$'. First it is necessary to rearrange these expressions into a quotient which is the of the form '$\dfrac{0}{0}$' or '$\dfrac{\infty}{\infty}$'.

Worked example 1.12

Evaluate the following:

(a) $\lim\limits_{x \to 0} (x \ln x)$

(b) $\lim\limits_{x \to 0} \left(\dfrac{1}{x} - \dfrac{1}{e^x - 1} \right)$

We have a limit of the form $0 \times (-\infty)$ and so again think of l'Hôpital's Rule. However, to apply it here we need to write this product as a quotient and hope that the conditions for the rule are then satisfied

(a) $x \ln x = \dfrac{\ln x}{\frac{1}{x}}$

The limit of the quotient is now of the form '$\dfrac{\infty}{\infty}$' and so we can apply l'Hôpital's Rule

By l'Hôpital's Rule:

$$\lim_{x \to 0} x \ln x = \lim_{x \to 0} \frac{\frac{d}{dx}(\ln x)}{\frac{d}{dx}\left(\frac{1}{x}\right)}$$

$$= \lim_{x \to 0} \frac{\frac{1}{x}}{-\frac{1}{x^2}}$$

$$= \lim_{x \to 0} -\frac{x^2}{x}$$

$$= \lim_{x \to 0} -x$$

$$= 0$$

The limit this time is of the form '$\infty - \infty$' and with no other obvious way of proceeding we combine the two quotients. This may lead to some cancellation or to the possibility of using l'Hôpital's Rule

(b) $\dfrac{1}{x} - \dfrac{1}{e^x - 1} = \dfrac{e^x - 1 - x}{x(e^x - 1)}$

$$= \dfrac{e^x - 1 - x}{xe^x - x}$$

The limit of the single quotient is of the form '$\dfrac{0}{0}$' and so l'Hôpital's Rule is needed

By l'Hôpital's rule:

$$\lim_{x \to 0} \left(\frac{1}{x} - \frac{1}{e^x - 1} \right) = \lim_{x \to 0} \left(\frac{\frac{d}{dx}(e^x - 1 - x)}{\frac{d}{dx}(xe^x - x)} \right)$$

$$= \lim_{x \to 0} \frac{e^x - 1}{e^x + xe^x - 1}$$

continued . . .

The limit is still of the
form $\frac{'0'}{0}$ and so we need
l'Hôpital's Rule again

$$= \lim_{x\to 0} \frac{e^x}{e^x + e^x + xe^x}$$

$$= \frac{1}{1+1+0}$$

$$= \frac{1}{2}$$

Exercise 1D

1. Evaluate the following using l'Hôpital's Rule:

(a) (i) $\displaystyle\lim_{x\to 0} \frac{e^x - e^{-x}}{\sin x}$
    (ii) $\displaystyle\lim_{x\to 1} \frac{\ln x}{x-1}$

(b) (i) $\displaystyle\lim_{x\to \pi} \frac{\pi^2 - x^2}{\cos\left(\dfrac{x}{2}\right)}$
    (ii) $\displaystyle\lim_{x\to 3} \frac{x^2 - 9}{\sin(x-3)}$

(c) (i) $\displaystyle\lim_{x\to 0} \frac{x^2 + x}{\tan x}$
    (ii) $\displaystyle\lim_{x\to 1} \frac{\sqrt[4]{x} - 1}{\sqrt[3]{x} - 1}$

2. Evaluate the following by using l'Hôpital's Rule more than once:

(a) $\displaystyle\lim_{x\to 0} \frac{(x+1)^2 - e^{2x}}{1 - \cos x}$

(b) $\displaystyle\lim_{x\to 1} \frac{(\ln x)^2}{x^3 + x^2 - 5x + 3}$

(c) $\displaystyle\lim_{x\to 0} \frac{1 - \cos x}{3x^2}$

(d) $\displaystyle\lim_{x\to 0} \frac{\tan x - x}{x - \sin x}$

(e) $\displaystyle\lim_{x\to \infty} \frac{e^x}{x^2}$

(f) $\displaystyle\lim_{x\to \frac{\pi}{4}} \frac{1 + \sin 6x}{1 + \cos 4x}$

3. By rearranging into a quotient and applying l'Hôpital's Rule, find the following:

(a) $\displaystyle\lim_{x\to 0} x^2 \ln x$

(b) $\displaystyle\lim_{x\to \frac{\pi}{2}} (\sec x - \tan x)$

(c) $\displaystyle\lim_{x\to 1} \left(\frac{1}{x-1} - \frac{1}{\ln x}\right)$

4. Find the following limits:

(a) $\displaystyle\lim_{x\to 0} \frac{x - \cos x}{x + \cos x}$

(b) $\displaystyle\lim_{x\to 0} \frac{x + \sin x}{x - \sin x}$

(c) $\displaystyle\lim_{x\to 0} \frac{x - \cos x}{x + \sin x}$

[5 marks]

5. (a) What is wrong with the following 'proof'?

$$\lim_{x\to 1}\frac{x^3+x-2}{x^2-3x+2}=\lim_{x\to 1}\frac{3x^2+1}{2x-3}=\lim_{x\to 1}\frac{6x}{2}=3$$

(b) Find the correct limit. [4 marks]

6. Find $\displaystyle\lim_{x\to 0}\frac{1-\cos(x^5)}{2x^{10}}$. [6 marks]

7. Find $\displaystyle\lim_{x\to\frac{\pi}{2}}\frac{\cos^2(3x)}{\cos^2 x}$. [6 marks]

8. Find $\displaystyle\lim_{x\to 0}\left(\frac{1}{x}-\frac{1}{\sin x}\right)$. [8 marks]

9. Find $\displaystyle\lim_{x\to\infty}x^2\left(\arctan(x^2)-\frac{\pi}{2}\right)$. [8 marks]

1E Continuous functions

Once we have established that the limit of a function exists at a point x_0, the next question is whether that function is continuous at x_0. This idea of being continuous is as you might expect: if the function does not have a 'gap' or 'jump' at a point then it is continuous there (as long as the limit exists in the first place). We can think of continuous as being able to sketch the function without taking our pen off the paper.

For a function to be continuous at a certain point, it has to be defined there. For example, it makes no sense to talk about
$y=\dfrac{1}{(x-1)^2}$ being continuous at $x=1$, as it has an asymptote there so $x=1$ is not in its domain.

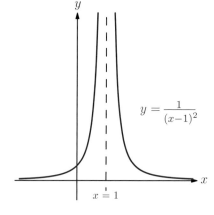

$y=\dfrac{1}{(x-1)^2}$

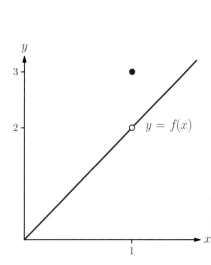

$y=f(x)$

A function such as $f(x)=\begin{cases}2x & x\neq 1\\ 3 & x=1\end{cases}$ that we met in Section 1C
is not continuous at $x=1$.

Here, although $x = 1$ is in the domain and the limit exists ($\lim\limits_{x \to 1} f(x) = 2$), there is a 'jump' and we cannot draw the function without taking our pen from the paper.

This requirement of there not being a 'jump' for a function to be continuous is stated more formally as:

KEY POINT 1.7

A function $f(x)$ is **continuous** at the point x_0 if
$$\lim_{x \to x_0} f(x) = f(x_0)$$
Both the limit and the value $f(x_0)$ must exist for $f(x)$ to be continuous there.

The function is said to be continuous if it is continuous at all points of its domain.

Notice that, according to this definition, $y = \dfrac{1}{(1-x)^2}$ is actually a continuous function, as it is continuous at all points of its domain (which is $x \neq 1$). Sometimes an apparently sensible definition leads to results that contradict our intuition.

We now look at further examples of the idea of 'jumps' or 'gaps' causing discontinuity, with reference to the formal definition.

Worked example 1.13

Determine where the following functions are continuous.

(a) $f(x) = |x|$

(b) $g(x) = \begin{cases} -2x - 6 & x < -1 \\ 2 & x = -1 \\ \dfrac{x^2 + 2x - 3}{x - 1} & x > -1, x \neq 1 \end{cases}$

We only need to consider any points where there may be a problem. With $|x|$ the only such point is $x = 0$

(a) $|x| = x$ $x > 0$
so is clearly continuous here and similarly
$|x| = -x$ $x < 0$
so is clearly continuous here too.

Check whether $\lim\limits_{x \to 0} |x|$ exists

$\lim\limits_{x \to 0^-} |x| = \lim\limits_{x \to 0^+} |x| = 0$

$\therefore \lim\limits_{x \to 0} |x| = 0$

Check whether $f(0) = \lim\limits_{x \to 0} f(x)$

And $|0| = 0$
So $\lim\limits_{x \to 0} |x| = |0|$

and therefore $|x|$ is continuous at $x = 0$ and hence continuous everywhere.

continued . . .

As with the more complicated piecewise functions that we met in Section 1C, it is a good idea to sketch the function first. The only potentially awkward piece to sketch is the quotient $\dfrac{x^2+2x-3}{x-1}$, but just as when looking for limits, we start by considering whether it can be simplified.

We do need to note here, however, that $f(1)$ is not defined

(b) $\dfrac{x^2+2x-3}{x-1} = \dfrac{(x+3)(x-1)}{x-1}$

$= x+3 \quad x > -1, x \neq 1$

So, we have:

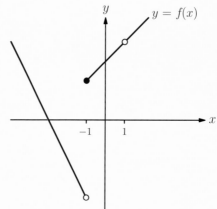

Again, we only need to consider any points where there may be a problem. Here these points are $x = -1$ and 1

Clearly $f(x)$ is continuous for:

$x < -1$

$-1 < x < 1$

$x > 1$

Although the limit exists at $x = -1$, there is a 'jump' so the function isn't continuous

For $x = -1$

$\lim_{x \to -1^-} f(x) = -4$

but $f(-1) = 2$

Therefore $\lim_{x \to -1} f(x) \neq f(-1)$

and so $f(x)$ is not continuous at $x = -1$

Although, again, the limits exists both from above and from below at $x = 1$, this time there is a 'gap' in the function as it is not defined at $x = 1$

For $x = 1$ $\lim_{x \to -1} f(x) = 4$

but $f(1)$ is not defined.

Therefore $f(x)$ is not continuous at $x = 1$

EXAM HINT

As with the definition of limit, the definition of continuity at a point is often used to show that a function is not continuous. For this purpose it is only necessary to find a sequence $x_n \to x_0$ such that $f(x_n) \nrightarrow f(x_0)$.

The following example demonstrates a standard method for showing that a function is not continuous at a point.

Worked example 1.14

Show that:

$$f(x) = \begin{cases} \cos\left(\dfrac{1}{x}\right) & x > 0 \\ 0 & x \le 0 \end{cases}$$

is not continuous at $x = 0$.

> We would like to find a sequence $x_k \to 0$, such that $f(x_k) \nrightarrow f(0)$. Then $f(x)$ cannot be continuous

Take $x_k = \dfrac{1}{2\pi k}$

Then $x_k \to 0$
but

$$f(x_k) = \cos\dfrac{1}{\left(\dfrac{1}{2\pi k}\right)}$$

$$= \cos(2\pi k)$$

$$= 1$$

i.e. $x_k \to 0$ but $f(x_k) \nrightarrow f(0)$

so $f(x)$ is not continuous.

In Worked example 1.6 we showed that $\displaystyle\lim_{x \to 0} \cos\left(\dfrac{1}{x}\right)$ does not exist, so we knew it could not be continuous at $x = 0$. However,

the above example is included to show that it is easier to prove that it is discontinuous at $x = 0$ than it is to establish that the limit does not exist.

Exercise 1E

1. Determine whether the following functions are continuous at the given points (it may help to sketch the graphs in some cases).

   (a) (i) $f(x) = x^3 - 3x^2 + 5x - 2$ at $x = 2$

   (ii) $g(x) = x^4 - 16$ at $x = -2$

   (b) (i) $f(x) = \dfrac{x^2 - 1}{x + 1}$ at $x = 1$

   (ii) $f(x) = \begin{cases} \dfrac{x^2 - 1}{x + 1} & x \ne -1 \\ -2 & x = -1 \end{cases}$ at $x = -1$

   (c) (i) $f(x) = \dfrac{x^2 + 2x - 15}{x - 4}$ at $x = 4$

   (ii) $g(x) = \dfrac{x - 3}{x^2 - x + 12}$ at $x = -3$

(d) (i) $f(x) = \begin{cases} 4x-1 & x \geq 2 \\ x+3 & x < 2 \end{cases}$ at $x = 2$

(ii) $g(x) = \begin{cases} x^2-1 & x \leq -1 \\ x-1 & x > -1 \end{cases}$ at $x = -1$

(e) (i) $f(x) = e^{-2x+1}$ at $x = \dfrac{1}{2}$

(ii) $g(x) = \sec x$ at $x = \dfrac{\pi}{2}$

(f) (i) $f(x) = \begin{cases} \dfrac{x^2-16}{x-4}, & x \neq 4 \\ 8, & x = 4 \end{cases}$ at $x = 4$

(ii) $g(x) = \begin{cases} \dfrac{x-1}{x^2+x-2}, & x \neq 1, -2 \\ 3, & x = 1, -2 \end{cases}$ at $x = 1$

2. For

$$f(x) = \begin{cases} x & x < 0 \\ 1 & x = 0 \\ 1+x & 0 < x < 1 \\ 3 & x = 1 \\ 2x^2 & x > 1 \end{cases}$$

(a) Determine whether the following limits exist and find them if they do:

(i) $\lim\limits_{x \to 0^+} f(x)$ (ii) $\lim\limits_{x \to 0^-} f(x)$

(iii) $\lim\limits_{x \to 0} f(x)$ (iv) $\lim\limits_{x \to 1^+} f(x)$

(v) $\lim\limits_{x \to 1^-} f(x)$ (vi) $\lim\limits_{x \to 1} f(x)$

(b) At which points is $f(x)$ continuous?   [7 marks]

3. Find the value(s) of $k \neq 0$ for which the function

$$f(x) = \begin{cases} kx+2 & x \leq 1 \\ -\dfrac{1}{kx} & x > 1 \end{cases}$$

is continuous at $x = 1$.   [4 marks]

4. (a) Given that $\lim\limits_{x \to x_0} f(x)$ exist for all $x \in \mathbb{R}$ for the function

$$f(x) = \begin{cases} -2x-3 & x < -4 \\ 7 & x = -4 \\ ax^2+bx+13 & -4 < x \leq 1 \\ x+9 & x > 1 \end{cases}$$

find the constants a and b.

(b) Where is $f(x)$ continuous?   [6 marks]

5. Show that the function

$$f(x) = \begin{cases} x\cos\left(\dfrac{1}{x^2}\right), & x \neq 0 \\ 0, & x = 0 \end{cases}$$

is continuous at $x = 0$. *[7 marks]*

6. For

$$f(x) = \begin{cases} x & x \in \mathbb{Q} \\ 0 & x \notin \mathbb{Q} \end{cases}$$

show that $f(x)$ is only continuous at $x = 0$.

1F Differentiable functions

Once we have established that the limit of a function exists at a point x_0 and that the function is continuous there, we might then want to ask whether the function can be differentiated at that point.

In the core course you should have studied differentiation from first principles and used the definition of the derivative at a point x_0:

$$f'(x_0) = \lim_{h \to 0} \frac{f(x_0 + h) - f(x_0)}{h}$$

We can also find an alternative definition, which will sometimes be more useful to work with, by a simple manipulation of the variables.

If we let $h = x - x_0$, then we get:

$$f'(x_0) = \lim_{(x - x_0) \to 0} \frac{f(x_0 + (x - x_0)) - f(x_0)}{x - x_0} = \lim_{x \to x_0} \frac{f(x) - f(x_0)}{x - x_0}$$

KEY POINT 1.8

The derivative of a function $f(x)$ at the point x_0 is given by:

$$f'(x_0) = \lim_{h \to 0} \frac{f(x_0 + h) - f(x_0)}{h}$$

or equivalently by

$$f'(x_0) = \lim_{x \to x_0} \frac{f(x) - f(x_0)}{x - x_0}$$

if the limit exists.

If it does not, then the function is not differentiable at that point.

It follows from the definitions of continuity and differentiability that any function that is differentiable at a point x_0 must be continuous at that point:

If $f(x)$ is differentiable, we have $\lim\limits_{x \to x_0} \left(\dfrac{f(x) - f(x_0)}{x - x_0} \right) = f'(x_0)$

Then $\lim\limits_{x \to x_0} \left(f(x) - f(x_0) \right) = \lim\limits_{x \to x_0} \left(\dfrac{\left(f(x) - f(x_0) \right)(x - x_0)}{x - x_0} \right)$

$$= \left[\lim\limits_{x \to x_0} \left(\dfrac{f(x) - f(x_0)}{x - x_0} \right) \right] \left[\lim\limits_{x \to x_0} \left(x - x_0 \right) \right]$$

$$= f'(x_0) \times 0$$

$$= 0$$

$\therefore \lim\limits_{x \to x_0} f(x) = f(x_0) \qquad$ and so $f(x)$ is continuous.

It follows that a function that is not continuous at a point cannot be differentiable at that point.

However, it is also perfectly possible for a function that is continuous at a point not to be differentiable there. This can happen due to two main factors.

- There may be a 'sharp point':

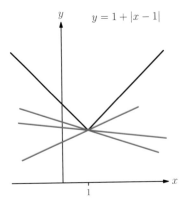

At such a point it is not clear how the tangent should be drawn; in fact it could be drawn in infinitely many different ways and so the derivative is simply said not to exist at this point.

- The tangent may be vertical:

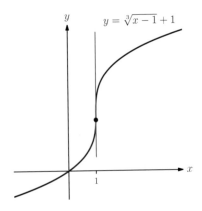

In this case x_0 could not be in the domain of the gradient function $f'(x)$, so again the derivative cannot exist at this point.

For a function $f(x)$ to be differentiable at a point x_0:

- $f(x)$ must be continuous at x_0 (and hence $\lim_{x \to x_0} f(x)$ must already exist)

- $f(x)$ must not have a 'sharp point' at x_0

- the tangent to $f(x)$ at x_0 must not be vertical.

As well as just identifying points where a function is not differentiable, you may also be required to use the definition to show that it is not differentiable.

In the case of continuous functions, this will mean you will need to show that $\lim_{h \to 0} \dfrac{f(x+h)-f(x)}{h}$ does not exist.

Remember that one way to do this is to find the limits when $h \to 0$ from above and from below.

KEY POINT 1.10

If a continuous function $f(x)$ is differentiable at $x = x_0$ then the limits:

$$\lim_{h \to 0^-} \frac{f(x_0+h)-f(x_0)}{h} \text{ and } \lim_{h \to 0^+} \frac{f(x_0+h)-f(x_0)}{h}$$

exist and are equal.

If one of the limits does not exist, or if they are not equal, then the function is not differentiable.

Worked example 1.15

Show that:

(a) $f(x) = (x-1)^{\frac{1}{3}}$ is not differentiable at $x = 1$.

(b) $g(x) = |x|$ is not differentiable at $x = 0$.

We need to show that $\lim_{h \to 0} \dfrac{f(1+h)-f(1)}{h}$ does not exist, so first we find $\dfrac{f(1+h)-f(1)}{h}$

(a) $\dfrac{f(1+h)-f(1)}{h} = \dfrac{(1+h-1)^{\frac{1}{3}}-(1-1)^{\frac{1}{3}}}{h}$

$$= \dfrac{h^{\frac{1}{3}}}{h}$$

$$= \dfrac{1}{h^{\frac{2}{3}}}$$

It is now clear that the limit is not finite and so $x = 1$ is not in the domain of the function $f'(x)$

$\therefore \lim_{h \to 0} \dfrac{f(1+h)-f(1)}{h} = \infty$

And hence $f(x)$ is not differentiable at $x = 1$

We need to show that $\lim_{h \to 0} \dfrac{g(x+h)-g(x)}{h}$ does not exist, so first we find $\dfrac{g(x+h)-g(x)}{h}$

(b) $\dfrac{g(x+h)-g(x)}{h} = \dfrac{|0+h|-|0|}{h}$

$$= \dfrac{|h|}{h}$$

continued . . .

This time the behaviour of the limit is not so obvious, but we suspect that the limit might not exist due to the limits from above and below being different. So we find each of these limits

$$\lim_{h\to 0^-}\frac{|h|}{h}=\lim_{h\to 0^-}\left(\frac{-h}{h}\right)$$
$$=\lim_{h\to 0^-}(-1)$$
$$=-1$$

And similarly,

$$\lim_{h\to 0^+}\frac{|h|}{h}=\lim_{h\to 0^+}\frac{h}{h}$$
$$=\lim_{h\to 0^+}1$$
$$=1$$

Therefore $\lim_{h\to 0}\dfrac{|h|}{h}$ does not exist and $g(x)=|x|$ is not differentiable at $x=0$

If we have a piecewise function, we may want to join the pieces so that the resulting function is differentiable. For example, if the function represents displacement, it needs to be differentiable so that the velocity is defined.

Worked example 1.16

Find constants a and b so that the function

$$f(x)=\begin{cases}\ln x & x\leq 3\\ ax+b & x>3\end{cases}$$

is differentiable for all $x>0$.

For a function to be differentiable, it must first be continuous. This means that the limits when $x\to 3$ from above and below must be the same and equal to $f(3)$

f has to be continuous:
$$\lim_{x\to 3^-}f(x)=\lim_{x\to 3^+}f(x)=f(3)$$

So
$$a(3)+b=\ln 3$$
$$\Rightarrow 3a+b=\ln 3$$

Also, the limit in the definition of the derivative has to exist. We need to look at the limits above and below 3 again

Also,
$$\lim_{h\to 3^-}\frac{f(3+h)-f(3)}{h}=\lim_{h\to 3^+}\frac{f(3+h)-f(3)}{h}$$

As $x=3$ is in the first part of the domain, the limit from below is just the derivative of $\ln x$ at $x=3$

From below:
$$\frac{d}{dx}(\ln x)=\frac{1}{3}\text{ at }x=3$$

From above:
$$\frac{d}{dx}(ax+b)=a\to a\text{ as }x\to 3$$

Hence,
$$a=\frac{1}{3}$$
$$\therefore b=3a-\ln 3$$
$$=1-\ln 3$$

Exercise 1F

1. Sketch each of the following functions and then find all points (if there are any) where the function is not differentiable.

(a) $f(x) = \sqrt[3]{x-2} + 3$

(b) $f(x) = \begin{cases} \dfrac{|x-1|}{x-1} & x \neq 1 \\ 1 & x = 1 \end{cases}$

(c) $f(x) = \begin{cases} \dfrac{x^2-9}{x-3} & x \neq 3 \\ 6 & x = 3 \end{cases}$

(d) $f(x) = |2x+1|$

(e) $f(x) = \begin{cases} x^2 & x < 0 \\ x & x \geq 0 \end{cases}$

(f) $f(x) = \dfrac{1}{(x-1)^2}$

(g) $f(x) = \sqrt{x}$

2. (a) Sketch the function:

$$f(x) = \begin{cases} 0 & x \leq 0 \\ \sqrt{x} & 0 < x \leq 4 \\ \dfrac{x}{4} + 1 & x > 4 \end{cases}$$

(b) Determine where the function is continuous.

(c) Determine where the function is differentiable, fully justifying your answer. *[7 marks]*

3. (a) Sketch the function:

$$f(x) = \begin{cases} -\dfrac{x}{2} + 1 & x \leq 0 \\ -x^2 + 6x + 1 & 0 < x < 2 \\ x^3 + 1 & x \geq 2 \end{cases}$$

(b) Determine where the function is continuous.

(c) Determine where the function is differentiable, fully justifying your answer. *[7 marks]*

4. Determine where the function

$$f(x) = \begin{cases} x^3 + 3x^2 - x - 3, & x \leq -3 \\ |x^2 + 2x - 3|, & -3 < x < 3 \\ 8x - 10, & x \geq 3 \end{cases}$$

is differentiable. *[6 marks]*

5. The function f is defined for $x \in \mathbb{R}$ by:

$$f(x) = \begin{cases} x^3 & x \le 2 \\ -x^2 + bx + c & x > 2 \end{cases}$$

Find the values of b and c so that f is differentiable for all $x \in \mathbb{R}$.

[6 marks]

6. For:

$$f(x) = \begin{cases} x \sin \dfrac{1}{x} & x \ne 0 \\ 0 & x = 0 \end{cases}$$

(a) Show that $f(x)$ is continuous at $x = 0$.

(b) Find $f'(x)$ when $x \ne 0$.

(c) Show that $f(x)$ is not differentiable at $x = 0$. [10 marks]

7. Assuming that $f''(a)$ exists, show that:

$$f''(a) = \lim_{h \to 0} \frac{f(a+h) - 2f(a) + f(a-h)}{h^2}$$

8. Show that $f(x) = \sin|x|$ is not differentiable at $x = 0$. [5 marks]

9. (a) Given that

$$f(x) = \begin{cases} \sqrt[3]{ax + b} & x \le 1 \\ x & x > 1 \end{cases}$$

is differentiable at $x = 1$, find a and b.

(b) State the range of values of x for which $f(x)$ is differentiable.

[7 marks]

10. For $f(x) = \begin{cases} x^2 \sin \dfrac{1}{x} & x \ne 0 \\ 0 & x = 0 \end{cases}$

(a) Show that $f'(x)$ exists for all x.

(b) Find $f'(0)$.

(c) Find $f'(x)$ when $x \ne 0$.

(d) Show that $f'(x)$ is not continuous at $x = 0$. [13 marks]

11. Using the function in the previous question, construct a function $f(x)$ for which $f'(0) > 0$ but there is no interval $]-a, a[$ in which $f(x)$ is an increasing function.

1G Rolle's Theorem and the Mean Value Theorem

There are two important results that follow from our understanding of continuity and differentiability.

For a non-constant function on an interval $[a, b]$, if we know that function is continuous and differentiable and it starts and finishes at the same *y*-value, then it is clear that there must be at least one turning point somewhere in the interval.

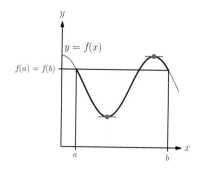

KEY POINT 1.11

Rolle's Theorem

For a function, $f(x)$, that is continuous on an interval $[a,b]$ and differentiable on $]a,b[$,

if $f(a) = f(b)$ then there must exist a point $c \in]a,b[$ such that $f'(c) = 0$.

Obviously continuity is important here as otherwise we could have a function such as:

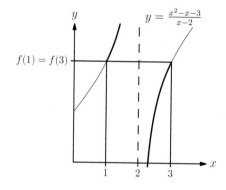

for which $f(a) = f(b)$ but there is no point *c* where $f'(c) = 0$.

However, we also need differentiability, otherwise we could have a continuous function that does not have a turning point, such as:

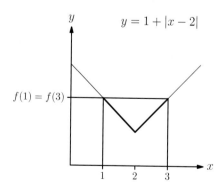

EXAM HINT

Remember that a sharp point such as in this modulus function is not the same as a turning point. At a turning point, $f'(x) = 0$ but at the sharp point ($x = 2$) the derivative does not even exist.

The most common application of Rolle's Theorem is to establish a maximum number of possible roots of a polynomial.

Worked example 1.17

Prove that the polynomial $f(x) = x^3 + 3x^2 + 6x + 1$ has exactly one root.

Since $f(x)$ is continuous, we only need to find an interval on which the sign of $f(x)$ changes to conclude that there must be a value, x_0, in that interval such that $f(x_0) = 0$, i.e. at least one root

$f(-1) = -3 < 0$

$f(1) = 11 > 0$

Since $f(x)$ is continuous, there must exist an $x_0 \in \left]-1,1\right[$ such that $f(x_0) = 0$

$\therefore f(x)$ has at least one root.

We now need to show that there is only one root, so suppose there are two and look for a contradiction

Suppose that there exists a second root, $x_1 > x_0$

Then $f(x_0) = f(x_1)$

This suggests that we could apply Rolle's Theorem to conclude there is a turning point in the interval $\left]x_0,x_1\right[$, which might produce the contradiction we are looking for

Since $f(x)$ is continuous and differentiable, by Rolle's Theorem there exists a $c \in \left]x_0,x_1\right[$ such that $f'(c) = 0$.

However,
$$f'(x) = 3x^2 + 6x + 6$$
$$= 3(x^2 + 2x + 2)$$
$$= 3\left[(x+1)^2 + 3\right] \neq 0$$

Therefore we have a contradiction and so there is only the one root x_0.

Rolle's Theorem can be useful for these kinds of question but it is rather restrictive to require the function to have the same value at both end points of the interval. If we remove this restriction then we see that there must still be a point $c \in \left]a,b\right[$ at which the tangent is parallel to the line joining $f(a)$ to $f(b)$, but now of course that tangent does not have 0 gradient.

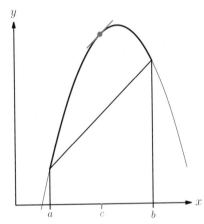

This leads to the following generalisation of Rolle's Theorem.

KEY POINT 1.12

Mean Value Theorem

For a function, $f(x)$, that is continuous on an interval $[a,b]$ and differentiable on $\left]a,b\right[$, there must exist a point $c \in \left]a,b\right[$ such that $f'(c) = \dfrac{f(b) - f(a)}{b - a}$.

This result clearly follows from the diagram above, but we can prove it formally using Rolle's Theorem. We must choose a function based on $f(x)$ that fulfils the conditions at the end points of the interval needed for Rolle's Theorem.

Let $\quad g(x) = f(x) - \left(\dfrac{f(b) - f(a)}{b-a} \right)(x-a).$

Clearly $g(x)$ is continuous and differentiable since $f(x)$ is, and moreover,

$$g(a) = f(a) - \left(\frac{f(b) - f(a)}{b-a} \right)(a-a)$$
$$= f(a)$$

and

$$g(b) = f(b) - \left(\frac{f(b) - f(a)}{b-a} \right)(b-a)$$
$$= f(b) - (f(b) - f(a))$$
$$= f(a)$$

that is, $\quad g(a) = g(b).$

Therefore, by Rolle's Theorem, there exists a point $c \in \,]a,b[$ such that $g'(c) = 0$.

So

$$g'(c) = f'(c) - \frac{f(b) - f(a)}{b-a} = 0$$
$$\Rightarrow f'(c) = \frac{f(b) - f(a)}{b-a}$$

There are a number of possible applications of the Mean Value Theorem (MVT).

Worked example 1.18

Prove that $|\sin a - \sin b| \le |a-b|$.

It looks like we can just apply the MVT on $f(x) = \sin x$

Since $f(x) = \sin x$ is continuous and differentiable for all $x \in \mathbb{R}$, by the Mean Value Theorem there exists $c \in \,]a,b[$ such that

$$\frac{f(b) - f(a)}{b-a} = f'(c)$$

$$\Rightarrow \frac{\sin b - \sin a}{b-a} = \cos c$$

We now need to take mod of both sides and observe that $|\cos x| \le 1$.

$$\Rightarrow \left| \frac{\sin b - \sin a}{b-a} \right| = |\cos c| \le 1$$

$$\Rightarrow |\sin a - \sin b| \le |a-b|$$

Worked example 1.19

If $f(x)$ is such that $f(2) = -4$ and $f'(x) \geq -2$ for all $x \in]2,7[$, find the smallest possible value for $f(7)$.

$f'(x) \geq -2$ so we know $f(x)$ is differentiable and hence continuous. We have information on one end point of the interval and want to find out something about the function at the other end point, so MVT might be useful

Since the derivative exists for all $x \in]2,7[$ we know that $f(x)$ is differentiable and hence continuous and so by the Mean Value Theorem, there exists $c \in]2,7[$ such that

$$\frac{f(7) - f(2)}{7 - 2} = f'(c)$$

$$\Rightarrow \frac{f(7) - (-4)}{5} = f'(c)$$

Use the fact that $f'(c) \geq -2$ and rearrange

Since $f'(x) \geq -2$ for all $x \in]2,7[$,

$$\frac{f(7) - (-4)}{5} \geq -2$$

$$\Rightarrow f(7) + 4 \geq -10$$

$$\Rightarrow f(7) \geq -14$$

i.e. the smallest possible value for $f(7)$ is -14

The Mean Value Theorem can also be used in more practical settings.

Worked example 1.20

A car driving along the motorway and travelling below the speed limit of 70 mph passes a police officer at 12:00. At 12:20 the same car passes another police officer 24 miles further along the motorway; again it was travelling at less than 70 mph. The driver is pulled over by the second policeman and given a speeding ticket.

Use the Mean Value Theorem to show how the police knew the driver had exceeded the speed limit during his journey.

We need a function that will model the car's journey

Let $f(t)$ be the function that gives the car's position at time t hours after 12:00

We need time to be measured in hours and can take distance moved from initial position when $t = 0$ (at 12:00) to be 0, i.e. $f(0) = 0$

Assuming this function to be continuous and differentiable, by the Mean Value Theorem there is a time t_0 at which:

$$f'(t_0) = \frac{f\left(\frac{1}{3}\right) - f(0)}{\frac{1}{3} - 0}$$

$$= \frac{24 - 0}{\frac{1}{3} - 0}$$

$$= 72$$

continued . . .

$f'(t) = v(t)$, the car's velocity

However, $f'(t_0)$ is the car's velocity at some time t_0 and so the car was travelling at 72 mph during its journey.

Note: In this context the Mean Value Theorem is saying that at some point on the journey, the car must have attained its average speed.

Exercise 1G

1. Find the value(s) of c in the given intervals whose existence is guaranteed by Rolle's Theorem:

   (a) (i) $x^2 - 5x + 8$ $x \in [0,5]$ (ii) $5 - 2x - x^2$ $x \in [-5,3]$

   (b) (i) $\cos(2x)$ $x \in [0,\pi]$ (ii) $\sin\left(\dfrac{x}{4}\right)$ $x \in [0,8\pi]$

   (c) (i) $x^3 - x + 1$ $x \in [-1,1]$ (ii) $\sqrt{2x - x^2}$ $x \in [0,2]$

2. Find the value(s) of c in the given intervals, whose existence is guaranteed by the Mean Value Theorem:

   (a) (i) $3x^2 + x - 7$ $x \in [1,3]$ (ii) $x^2 - 5x + 3$ $x \in [-2,2]$

   (b) (i) $\sin x$ $x \in \left[0, \dfrac{\pi}{2}\right]$ (ii) $\tan x$ $x \in \left[0, \dfrac{\pi}{3}\right]$

   (c) (i) $x^3 - 3x + 4$ $x \in [0,2]$ (ii) $7 - \sqrt{x}$ $x \in [4,36]$

3. The function $f(x)$ is defined for $x \in [1,10]$ and has $f(1) = 12$, and $f'(x) \le 2$.

   Use the Mean Value Theorem to find the largest possible value for $f(10)$.   *[4 marks]*

4. For $f(x) = Ax^2 + Bx + C$, $x \in [a,b]$ show that:

   $$f'\left(\dfrac{a+b}{2}\right) = \dfrac{f(b) - f(a)}{b - a}$$ *[4 marks]*

5. Let $f(x) = \dfrac{2x}{3} - \sqrt{x}$.

   (a) Show that there does not exist a $c \in \,]1,4[$ such that, $f'(c) = 0$.

   (b) Why does this not contradict Rolle's Theorem?   *[4 marks]*

6. At 9 a.m. a car is travelling at 39 mph. 15 minutes later it is travelling at 45 mph. Use the Mean Value Theorem to show that at some point between 9 a.m. and 9.15 a.m., the car's acceleration was exactly 24 mh^{-2}.   *[5 marks]*

7. In a race, a hare and a tortoise both start at the same time and, unexpectedly, pass the finish line at the same time as well. Show that at some point during the race, they were moving with the same speed. *[6 marks]*

8. Prove that $x = 1$ is the only real solution of the equation
$$x^3 - 3x^2 + 9x - 7 = 0.$$ *[6 marks]*

9. Prove that there are exactly two positive real numbers x such that $e^x = 3x$. *[9 marks]*

10. (a) Given that $f(x) = \sqrt{1+x}$, show that $f'(c) < \dfrac{1}{2}$ for all $c > 0$.

(b) Use the Mean Value Theorem to prove that
$$\sqrt{1+x} < 1 + \frac{x}{2} \quad \text{for } x > 0$$ *[6 marks]*

11. Show that:
$$\left| \cos^2 a - \sin^2 a + \sin^2 b - \cos^2 b \right| \le 2 \left| a - b \right|$$ *[7 marks]*

12. (a) By considering the function $f(x) = e^x - (1+x)$, use the Mean Value Theorem to prove that $e^x > 1 + x$.

(b) Use a similar argument to prove that
$$e^x > 1 + x + \frac{x^2}{2} \quad \text{for } x > 0.$$

(c) Use you answer to part (b) to place an upper bound on $\ln 2$, giving your answer to 3DP. *[11 marks]*

13. Let $p(x)$ be a polynomial of degree n. Prove that there are at most n distinct $x \in \mathbb{R}$ with $p(x) = 0$.

14. (a) If $f(x)$ and $g(x)$ are continuous and differentiable and $g'(x) \ne 0$, show that by using a function of the form $h(x) = f(x) - kg(x)$ where k is some appropriately chosen constant, there exists $c \in \left]a,b\right[$ such that:
$$\frac{f'(c)}{g'(c)} = \frac{f(b) - f(a)}{g(b) - g(a)}$$

(b) If $f(a) = g(a) = 0$, prove that
$$\lim_{x \to a} \frac{f(x)}{g(x)} = \lim_{x \to a} \frac{f'(x)}{g'(x)}$$
providing the latter limit exists.

15. Establish the number of roots of the equation $\cos x = x$ $(x \in \mathbb{R})$ fully justifying your answer.

Summary

- Limits behave as expected algebraically; that is if the sequence $\{a_n\}$ **converges** to a limit a and the sequence $\{b_n\}$ to a limit b, then:

$$\lim_{n\to\infty}(pa_n + qb_n) = p\lim_{n\to\infty}a_n + q\lim_{n\to\infty}b_n = pa + qb \quad (p, q \in \mathbb{R})$$

$$\lim_{n\to\infty}(a_n b_n) = \left(\lim_{n\to\infty}a_n\right)\left(\lim_{n\to\infty}b_n\right) = ab$$

$$\lim_{n\to\infty}\left(\frac{a_n}{b_n}\right) = \frac{\lim_{n\to\infty}a_n}{\lim_{n\to\infty}b_n} = \frac{a}{b} \quad (b \neq 0)$$

- If the sequence $\{a_n\}$ **diverges**, then for some constant $c \in \mathbb{R}$,

$$\lim_{n\to\infty}\left(\frac{c}{a_n}\right) = 0 \qquad \lim_{n\to\infty}\left(\frac{a_n}{c}\right) = \infty$$

- It is usually necessary to manipulate a_n into a form where the numerator and denominator both have finite limits so that the algebra of limits can be applied. This can often be achieved by dividing through by the highest power of n.

- If a sequence is sandwiched between two other sequences, both of which converge to the same limit, then that sequence is squeezed and must converge to the limit too.

  The Squeeze Theorem: if we have sequences $\{a_n\}, \{b_n\}$ and $\{c_n\}$ such that

$$a_n \leq b_n \leq c_n \text{ for all } n \in \mathbb{Z}^+ \text{ and } \lim_{n\to\infty}a_n = \lim_{n\to\infty}c_n = L < \infty$$

then $\lim_{n\to\infty}b_n = L$.

- If for any sequence $\{x_n\}$ such that $x_n \to x_0$ we have that $f(x_n) \to L$, then $L \in \mathbb{R}$ is said to be the limit of the function.

- To show that the limit of a function does not exist at a point x_0, find two sequences $x_n \to x_0$ and $y_n \to x_0$, but for which $f(x_n)$ and $f(y_n)$ do not tend to the same limit.

- If we find the limit of a function at point x_0 by having a sequence that approaches from below, we write $\lim_{x\to x_0^-}f(x)$.

  If we do so by having a sequence that approaches from above we write $\lim_{x\to x_0^+}f(x)$.

  We need both the limit from above and the limit from below to exist and coincide for the limit to exist at that point. If they do then:

$$\lim_{x\to x_0}f(x) = \lim_{x\to x_0^+}f(x) = \lim_{x\to x_0^-}f(x)$$

- The Squeeze Theorem and the algebra of limits hold for functions as well.

- We can use **l'Hôpital's Rule** to find limits of functions of the form $\dfrac{`0`}{0}$ and $\dfrac{`\infty`}{\infty}$:

  Given functions $f(x)$ and $g(x)$ that are differentiable in the neighbourhood of a point a and $g(x) \neq 0$, if either

$$\lim_{x\to a}f(x) = \lim_{x\to a}g(x) = 0 \quad \text{or} \quad \lim_{x\to a}f(x) = \lim_{x\to a}g(x) = \infty$$

then $\lim_{x\to a}\dfrac{f(x)}{g(x)} = \lim_{x\to a}\dfrac{f'(x)}{g'(x)}$ provided that the latter exists.

- It may be necessary to manipulate functions that have limits of the form '$0 \times \infty$' or '$\infty - \infty$' into quotients so that l'Hôpital's Rule can then be applied.

- A function $f(x)$ is **continuous** at the point x_0 if $\lim\limits_{x \to x_0} f(x) = f(x_0)$.

  Both the limit and the value $f(x_0)$ must exist for $f(x)$ to be continuous there.

- To show that a function is not continuous at a point x_0, find a sequence $x_n \to x_0$ but for which $f(x_n) \nrightarrow f(x_0)$.

  The function is said to be continuous if it is continuous at all points of its domain.

- The derivative of a function $f(x)$ at the point x_0 is given by $f'(x_0) = \lim\limits_{h \to 0} \dfrac{f(x_0 + h) - f(x_0)}{h}$

  Or equivalently by $f'(x_0) = \lim\limits_{x \to x_0} \dfrac{f(x) - f(x_0)}{x - x_0}$ if the limit exists.

  If it does not, then the function is not differentiable at that point.

- For a function $f(x)$ to be differentiable at a point x_0:

  - $f(x)$ must be continuous at x_0 (and hence $\lim\limits_{x \to x_0} f(x)$ must already exist)

  - $f(x)$ must not have a 'sharp point' at x_0

  - The tangent to $f(x)$ at x_0 must not be vertical.

- A function that is differentiable at a point is continuous at that point.

- **Rolle's Theorem** for differentiable functions states that:

  For a function, $f(x)$, that is continuous on an interval $[a,b]$ and differentiable on $]a,b[$, if $f(a) = f(b)$ then there must exist a point $c \in]a,b[$ such that $f'(c) = 0$.

- The **Mean Value Theorem** is a generalisation of Rolle's Theorem that states that:

  For a function, $f(x)$, that is continuous on an interval $[a,b]$ and differentiable on $]a,b[$, there must exist a point $c \in]a,b[$ such that $f'(c) = \dfrac{f(b) - f(a)}{b - a}$.

1. (a) Find a and b so that the function

$$f(x) = \begin{cases} -(x+1)^3 - 1 & x < -1 \\ ax + b & -1 \le x \le 1 \\ -2x^2 + 6x - 1 & x > 1 \end{cases}$$

is continuous everywhere.

(b) Where is $f(x)$ differentiable?   *[6 marks]*

2. By letting $m = \dfrac{1}{n}$, evaluate $\lim\limits_{n \to \infty} n \tan\left(\dfrac{1}{n}\right)$.   *[6 marks]*

3. Prove that there is exactly one real solution to the equation
$\sin x = 3x - 2$.   *[6 marks]*

4. The general term of a sequence is given by the formula:

$$a_n = \frac{n^2 + 3n}{2n^2 - 1} \qquad n \in \mathbb{Z}^+$$

(a) Given that $\lim\limits_{n \to \infty} a_n = L$ where $L \in \mathbb{R}$, find the value of L.

(b) Find the smallest value of $N \in \mathbb{Z}^+$ such that

$|a_n - L| < 10^{-3}$ for all $n \ge N$ *[9 marks]*

(© *IB Organization 2006*)

5. (a) Write x^x in the form e^k.

(b) Using l'Hôpital's Rule, evaluate $\lim\limits_{x \to 0} x^x$.

(c) What assumption have you made?   *[10 marks]*

6. Consider the sequence $\left\{ \dfrac{x^n}{n!} \right\}$ for any $x \in \mathbb{R}^+$

(a) By choosing an integer $m > x$ and letting $n \ge m$, show that:

$$\frac{x^n}{n!} \le \frac{x^n}{m^n} \times \frac{m^m}{(m-1)!}$$

(b) By using the Squeeze Theorem show that $\lim\limits_{n \to \infty} \dfrac{x^n}{n!} = 0$.

                               [10 marks]

7. Find:

(a) $\lim\limits_{s \to 4} \left(\dfrac{s - \sqrt{3s + 4}}{4 - s} \right)$.

(b) $\lim\limits_{x \to 0} \left(\dfrac{\cos x - 1}{x \sin x} \right)$.   *[9 marks]*

8. Suppose that $f(x)$ is an odd function that is differentiable on $\mathbb{R}$.

(a) Show that there is some $a \in]-x, x[$ such that $\dfrac{f(x)}{x} = f'(a)$

(b) Hence show that $-|x| \le \sin x \le |x|$ [8 marks]

9. Given that $\lim\limits_{n \to \infty} \left(1 + \dfrac{1}{n}\right)^n = e$:

(a) Show that $\lim\limits_{n \to \infty} \left(1 - \dfrac{1}{n}\right)^n = \lim\limits_{k \to \infty} \left(\dfrac{k}{k+1}\right)^{k+1}$

(b) Hence, show that $\lim\limits_{n \to \infty} \left(1 - \dfrac{1}{n}\right)^n = \dfrac{1}{e}$.

(c) Therefore, using the Squeeze Theorem, find $\lim\limits_{n \to \infty} \dfrac{n!}{n^n}$.   [13 marks]

10. (a) Show that $(1 + x)^n > nx$ for all $n \in \mathbb{Z}^+$.

(b) Prove that $\lim\limits_{n \to \infty} 2^{1/n} = 1$

(c) Hence find the limit of the sequence whose general term is given by

$$a_n = \left(4^n + 5^n\right)^{1/n}.$$ [14 marks]

11. (a) Find $\lim\limits_{x \to \infty} \dfrac{\ln\left(e^x + x\right)}{x}$

(b) Hence find $\lim\limits_{x \to \infty} \left(e^x + x\right)^{\frac{1}{x}}$

(c) What assumption have you made in part (b)?   [9 marks]

2 Improper integrals

You should be familiar, from the Core syllabus, with finding the probability of a continuous random variable falling between a and b by integrating the pdf between these limits.

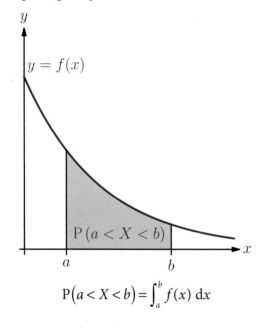

$$P(a < X < b) = \int_a^b f(x)\,dx$$

But what if we want $P(X > a)$, where the pdf is non-zero for all real numbers?

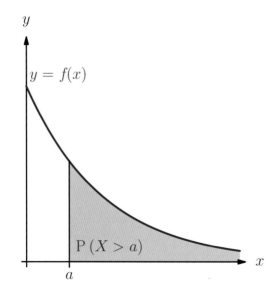

$$P(X > a) = \int_a^\infty f(x)\,dx$$

Here we would like to take ∞ as the upper limit on our integral, but this raises questions about whether or not the value of the integral will now be finite and, if so, how we can find it.

In this chapter we concentrate on integrals of this form. We will use our knowledge of limits from chapter 1 to determine when we get a finite value for the integral and in some cases find the value. First, however, we analyse the link between differentiation and definite integration more closely using the Fundamental Theorem of Calculus.

2A The Fundamental Theorem of Calculus

You will have seen that the area under a continuous curve $f(x)$ between the limits $x = a$ and $x = b$ is found by calculating the definite integral:

$$A = \int_a^b f(x) \, dx$$

If we allow the upper limit to vary then the area will be a function of this upper limit.

Denoting this limit by x we can write:

$$A(x) = \int_a^x f(t) \, dt$$

Notice here that, as x is a limit, we cannot use x as the variable we are integrating with respect to, so we simply use another variable t (this could be anything as once the integration is done we are going to replace it with the limits x and a anyway). We refer to this as a 'dummy variable'.

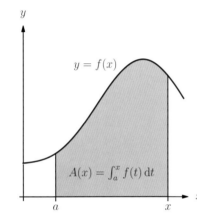

Now consider the area under the graph $y = f(x)$ between a and x. By changing the upper limit, x, we will change the area as shown in the graph opposite.

If the change in x is very small, the new area can be approximated by a rectangle with area:

$$\Delta A \approx f(x) \times \Delta x$$

$$\Leftrightarrow \frac{\Delta A}{\Delta x} \approx f(x)$$

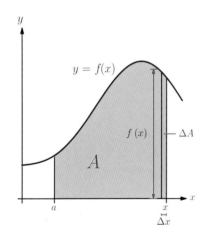

In the limit, $f(x) = \lim_{\Delta x \to 0} \frac{\Delta A}{\Delta x} = \frac{dA}{dx}$.

or alternatively:

$$\frac{d}{dx} \int_a^x f(t) \, dt = f(x)$$

This shows that $f(x)$ is the derivative of the area function $A(x)$ with respect to x. Hence, the process of integration (finding the area under a curve) is the reverse of differentiation.

But the function $A(x)$ is not the only function whose derivative is $f(x)$.

For any function $g(x)$ such that $g'(x) = f(x)$, we must have $A(x) = g(x) + c$ for some constant c.

This is clear from our understanding of differentiation, but it can be proved formally using the Mean Value Theorem.

Then, since
$$A(a) = \int_a^a f(t)\, dt = 0$$

we also have
$$g(a) + c = 0$$
$$\Rightarrow c = -g(a)$$
$$\therefore A(x) = g(x) - g(a)$$

Letting $x = b$, we have
$$A(b) = g(b) - g(a)$$

and
$$A(b) = \int_a^b f(x)\, dx$$

Therefore
$$\int_a^b f(x)\, dx = g(b) - g(a)$$

This is all summarised in Key Point 2.1.

KEY POINT 2.1

Fundamental Theorem of Calculus

For a continuous function $f(x)$ on the interval $[a, b]$:
$$\frac{d}{dx} \int_a^x f(t)\, dt = f(x)$$

And for any function $g(x)$ such that $g'(x) = f(x)$:
$$\int_a^b f(x)\, dx = g(b) - g(a)$$

Although we can already find definite integrals and evaluate integrated functions at given limits, the idea of differentiating through with respect to the upper limit as in the first statement of the Fundamental Theorem of Calculus (FTC) is new. The following example illustrates a straightforward application of this idea.

Worked example 2.1

Find $\dfrac{d}{dx} \displaystyle\int_a^x \cos(t^2)\, dt$.

At first sight this might appear difficult; indeed we cannot integrate the function $\cos(t^2)$. However, the FTC says we don't need to. We apply the theorem with
$$f(t) = \cos(t^2)$$

By the Fundamental Theorem of Calculus:
$$\frac{d}{dx} \int_a^x \cos(t^2)\, dt = \cos(x^2)$$

The variable with respect to which the differentiation is taking place and the dummy variable do not have to be x and t.

Worked example 2.2

Find:

(a) $\dfrac{\mathrm{d}}{\mathrm{d}a} \displaystyle\int_a^b f(y)\,\mathrm{d}y$ (b) $\dfrac{\mathrm{d}}{\mathrm{d}x} \displaystyle\int_a^b f(z)\,\mathrm{d}z$

This is similar to the statement in Key point 2.1, except that the differentiation is w.r.t. the variable in the lower limit. Therefore we use the relationship

$$\int_a^b = -\int_b^a$$

(a)

$$\frac{\mathrm{d}}{\mathrm{d}a}\int_a^b f(y)\,\mathrm{d}y = \frac{\mathrm{d}}{\mathrm{d}a}\left(-\int_b^a f(y)\,\mathrm{d}y\right)$$

$$= -\frac{\mathrm{d}}{\mathrm{d}a}\int_b^a f(y)\,\mathrm{d}y$$

$$= -f(a)$$

by the Fundamental Theorem of Calculus

Here the differentiation is w.r.t. x but x is not one of the limits. Therefore proceed with an expression for just $\int_a^b f(z)\,\mathrm{d}z$

(b)

Let $g'(z) = f(z)$

Then $\displaystyle\int_a^b f(z)\,\mathrm{d}z = g(b) - g(a)$

Differentiate w.r.t. x, noting that $g(b)$ and $g(a)$ are not functions of x

$$\frac{\mathrm{d}}{\mathrm{d}x}\int_a^b f(z)\,\mathrm{d}z = \frac{\mathrm{d}}{\mathrm{d}x}\big(g(b) - g(a)\big)$$

$$= 0$$

We could also apply the Fundamental Theorem of Calculus to a function with two variables, $f(x,y)$. In such cases we need to make sure that we integrate (or differentiate) with respect to just one of these variables, and treat the other as a constant. The following example looks at this and also the idea of differentiating the function before we integrate it; sometimes known as differentiating under the integral sign.

Worked example 2.3

Find:

(a) $\dfrac{\mathrm{d}}{\mathrm{d}x} \displaystyle\int_a^b x^2 \cos y\,\mathrm{d}y$ (b) $\displaystyle\int_a^b \dfrac{\mathrm{d}}{\mathrm{d}x}\left(x^2 \cos y\right)\mathrm{d}y$

The integration here is w.r.t. y, so we treat the x^2 as a constant, unaffected by the integration

(a)

$$\int_a^b x^2 \cos y\,\mathrm{d}y = x^2 \int_a^b \cos y\,\mathrm{d}y$$

$$= x^2 \big[\sin y\big]_a^b$$

$$= x^2 (\sin b - \sin a)$$

continued ...

Then differentiate w.r.t. x, remembering that $\sin a$ and $\sin b$ are just constants

$$\therefore \frac{d}{dx}\int_a^b x^2 \cos y \, dy = \frac{d}{dx}\left(x^2(\sin b - \sin a)\right)$$

$$= 2x(\sin b - \sin a)$$

(b)

This time we need to differentiate before we integrate. As the differentiation is w.r.t. x, $\cos y$ is unaffected

$$\frac{d}{dx}(x^2 \cos y) = 2x \cos y$$

Now integrate w.r.t. y, noting that x is now unaffected

$$\therefore \int_a^b \frac{d}{dx}(x^2 \cos y)\,dy = \int_a^b 2x \cos y \, dy$$

$$= 2x\int_a^b \cos y \, dy$$

$$= 2x\left[\sin x\right]_a^b$$

$$= 2x(\sin b - \sin a)$$

We see that we get the same answer, whether we do the integration or the differentiation first. This is true using any function.

Exercise 2A

1. Find the following:

   (a) (i) $\dfrac{d}{dx}\displaystyle\int_0^x e^{t^2}\,dt$ (ii) $\dfrac{d}{dx}\displaystyle\int_2^x 2\cos^5 t\,dt$

   (b) (i) $\dfrac{d}{dx}\displaystyle\int_x^3 2\sin(2t^3)\,dt$ (ii) $\dfrac{d}{dx}\displaystyle\int_x^1 5\sqrt{t^2+3}\,dt$

   (c) (i) $\dfrac{d}{dt}\displaystyle\int_a^t \dfrac{x^3+3}{x^2+2x+5}\,dx$ (ii) $\dfrac{d}{dt}\displaystyle\int_b^t \dfrac{e^x}{x^2+7}\,dx$

   (d) (i) $\dfrac{d}{db}\displaystyle\int_a^b e^{-y^3}\,dy$ (ii) $\dfrac{d}{da}\displaystyle\int_a^b 3\cos^2(2t^2)\,dt$

2. Find the following:

   (a) (i) $\dfrac{d}{dx}\displaystyle\int_a^x f(t)\,dt$ (ii) $\dfrac{d}{dy}\displaystyle\int_c^y g(t)\,dt$

   (b) (i) $\dfrac{d}{db}\displaystyle\int_a^b f(x)\,dx$ (ii) $\dfrac{d}{da}\displaystyle\int_a^b g(x)\,dx$

   (c) (i) $\dfrac{d}{dx}\displaystyle\int_a^b f(x)\,dx$ (ii) $\dfrac{d}{dt}\displaystyle\int_a^b g(x)\,dx$

(d) (i) $\displaystyle\int_a^b \frac{d}{dx} f(x)\, dx$ (ii) $\displaystyle\int_a^b \frac{d}{dt} g(x)\, dx$

(e) (i) $\displaystyle\frac{d}{dx}\int_a^x \big(f(c)\big)^2\, dc$ (ii) $\displaystyle\frac{d}{dt}\int_t^a \big(f(c)\big)^{\frac{1}{3}}\, dc$

3. Find:

(a) $\displaystyle\frac{d}{dx}\int_a^x \frac{d}{dt}\ln t\, dt$ (b) $\displaystyle\frac{d}{dx}\int_a^x \frac{d}{dt} f(t)\, dt$ [4 marks]

4. (a) Find:

(i) $\displaystyle\frac{d}{dx}\int_a^b \frac{x^3}{t}\, dt$ (ii) $\displaystyle\int_a^b \frac{d}{dx}\left(\frac{x^3}{t}\right) dt$

(b) Is $\displaystyle\frac{d}{dt}\int_a^b f(x,t)\, dt = \int_a^b \frac{d}{dt} f(x,t)\, dt$ for any function $f(x,t)$?

[6 marks]

5. Using the chain rule, find:

(a) $\displaystyle\frac{d}{dx}\int_x^{x^2} \sin(t^2)\, dt$

(b) $\displaystyle\frac{d}{dy}\int_{y^{1/4}}^{y^{1/2}} e^{-x^4}\, dx$ [5 marks]

6. Let $f(t)$ be continuous on $[a,b]$ and $F(x)=\displaystyle\int_a^x f(t)\, dt$.
Use the Mean Value Theorem to show that there exists $c \in\,]a,b[$
such that:

$$\int_a^b f(t)\, dt = f(c)(b-a) \qquad \text{[7 marks]}$$

2B Convergent and divergent improper integrals

We now return to the familiar part of the FTC:

$$\int_a^b f(x)\, dx = g(b) - g(a) \quad \text{where } g'(x) = f(x)$$

In the core course, the limits of integration were often convenient, relatively small numbers such as 0, 1, π. However, limits can also be very large and this makes no difference to the method used to evaluating the integral.

See Sections 1A and 1B for convergence of sequences.

What if we continue along this line of reasoning and let $b \to \infty$? Can we still evaluate the integral?

Well, an integral can either converge to a finite limit or diverge to ∞, in much the same way that we saw with sequences in chapter 1.

Integrals of the form $\int_a^\infty f(x)\,dx$ are known as **improper integrals**.

The improper integral $\int_a^\infty f(x)\,dx$ is convergent if the limit

$$\lim_{b\to\infty}\int_a^b f(x)\,dx = \lim_{b\to\infty}\{I(b)\} - I(a)$$

exists and is finite. Otherwise the integral diverges.

When we work with improper integrals, we often use the following limits of functions (familiar to us from the previous chapter):

- $\displaystyle\lim_{x\to\infty} e^{-x} = 0$

- $\displaystyle\lim_{x\to\infty} x^{-p} = 0 \qquad (p > 0)$

Worked example 2.4

Evaluate $\displaystyle\int_0^\infty e^{-3x}\,dx$.

Integrate as normal but replace the upper limit with b and take the limit as $b \to \infty$ after the integration is completed

$$\int_0^\infty e^{-3x}\,dx = \lim_{b\to\infty}\int_0^b e^{-3x}\,dx$$

$$= \lim_{b\to\infty}\left[-\frac{1}{3}e^{-3x}\right]_0^b$$

$$= \lim_{b\to\infty}\left(-\frac{1}{3}e^{-3b} + \frac{1}{3}\right)$$

$$= \lim_{b\to\infty}\left(-\frac{1}{3}e^{-3b}\right) + \frac{1}{3}$$

As $b \to \infty$, $e^{-3b} \to 0$. Therefore the integral is convergent

$$= \frac{1}{3}$$

Worked example 2.5

Determine for which values of $p \in \mathbb{R}$, $\displaystyle\int_1^\infty x^p\,dx$ is convergent.

Replace the upper limit with b and take the limit as $b \to \infty$ after the integration is completed

$$\int_1^\infty x^p\,dx = \lim_{b\to\infty}\int_1^b x^p\,dx$$

We realise that there will be two different cases: if $p = -1$ we need to integrate with $\ln x$

$$= \begin{cases} \displaystyle\lim_{b\to\infty}\left[\dfrac{x^{p+1}}{p+1}\right]_1^b & \text{if } p \neq -1 \\[2ex] \displaystyle\lim_{b\to\infty}\left[\ln x\right]_1^b & \text{if } p = -1 \end{cases}$$

continued ...

$$
= \begin{cases} \lim_{b \to \infty} \left(\dfrac{b^{p+1}}{p+1} - \dfrac{1^{p+1}}{p+1} \right) & \text{if } p \neq -1 \\[2ex] \lim_{b \to \infty} (\ln b - \ln 1) & \text{if } p = -1 \end{cases}
$$

$$
= \begin{cases} \lim_{b \to \infty} \left(\dfrac{b^{p+1} - 1}{p+1} \right) & \text{if } p \neq -1 \\[2ex] \lim_{b \to \infty} \ln b & \text{if } p = -1 \end{cases}
$$

At this stage we can see that the case $p \neq -1$ needs to be split into two separate cases. When $p+1 > 0$, $b^{p+1} \to \infty$ but when $p+1 < 0$, $b^{p+1} \to 0$

$$
= \begin{cases} \infty & \text{if } p > -1 \\[1ex] -\dfrac{1}{p+1} & \text{if } p < -1 \\[2ex] \infty & \text{if } p = -1 \end{cases}
$$

i.e.

$\displaystyle \int_1^\infty x^p \, dx$ converges only for $p < -1$

Or equivalently

$\displaystyle \int_1^\infty \frac{1}{x^p} \, dx$ converges only for $p > 1$

There are many integrals that cannot be expressed in terms of standard functions (an indefinite integral cannot be found) and yet look at first sight as if they should be susceptible to one of the many integration methods. Examples that we will meet in this Option, either in this chapter or in Section 4E, include

$$
\int \sin(x^2) \, dx, \int \cos(x^2) \, dx, \int \frac{\sin x}{x} \, dx, \int e^{x^2} \, dx, \int e^{-x^2} \, dx
$$

Of these, the last (the Gaussian function e^{-x^2}) is perhaps the most important as it forms the basis for the pdf for the normal distribution. Although it is impossible to find an indefinite integral, it can be shown that

$$
\int_{-\infty}^{\infty} e^{-x^2} \, dx = \sqrt{\pi}
$$

When we said above that these integrals cannot be expressed in terms of standard functions, they can be expressed in terms of special functions defined just for this purpose; for example, the sine integral function $\mathrm{Si}(x)$ defined as

$$
\mathrm{Si}(x) = \int_0^x \frac{\sin t}{t} \, dt
$$

or the error function $\mathrm{erf}(x)$ defined as

$$
\mathrm{erf}(x) = \int_0^x e^{-t^2} \, dt
$$

Does using this kind of specially defined function aid our understanding here at all?

We will see a method for approximating integrals that we cannot find otherwise, and quantifying the error in estimation, in Section 4E.

Sometimes the integration is difficult (if not impossible in terms of standard functions, see Exercise 2B, question 2(a)) and so we need another way of determining whether or not an integral is convergent without actually attempting to evaluate it explicitly. The following is one way this can be achieved:

KEY POINT 2.3

Comparison Test for improper integrals

If $0 \le f(x) \le g(x)$ for all $x \ge a$ then:

$\int_a^\infty f(x)\,dx$ is convergent if $\int_a^\infty g(x)\,dx$ is convergent.

$\int_a^\infty g(x)\,dx$ is divergent if $\int_a^\infty f(x)\,dx$ is divergent.

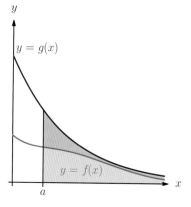

This result is intuitive: if we know that $\int_a^\infty g(x)\,dx$ is convergent (has finite area bounded by the x-axis) and that $f(x)$ is always below $g(x)$, then of course $\int_a^\infty f(x)\,dx$ must also be convergent (and have a smaller area bounded by the x-axis).

Worked example 2.6

Show that $\int_0^\infty \dfrac{\sqrt{x}}{1+x^2}\,dx$ is convergent.

The integration here is complicated so we consider using the above result and try to find a function $g(x) \ge \dfrac{\sqrt{x}}{1+x^2}$ such that $\int_0^\infty g(x)$ converges

$1 + x^2 \ge x^2$ for all $x \in \mathbb{R}$

$$\Rightarrow \frac{\sqrt{x}}{1+x^2} \le \frac{\sqrt{x}}{x^2} = \frac{1}{x^{3/2}}$$

We know that $\int_0^\infty \dfrac{1}{x^{3/2}}\,dx$ converges (Worked example 2.5) and so we apply the above result

Then, since $\int_0^\infty \dfrac{1}{x^{3/2}}\,dx$ converges,

$$\int_0^\infty \frac{\sqrt{x}}{1+x^2}\,dx$$

converges by the Comparison Test for improper integrals.

The following result is also useful, often in conjunction with the Comparison Test:

KEY POINT 2.4

If $\int_a^\infty |f(x)|\,dx$ converges, then so does $\int_a^\infty f(x)\,dx$.

As with the Comparison Test for improper integrals, this result is just what we might expect: $|f(x)|$ is always above the x-axis whereas $f(x)$ might go below the x-axis. Therefore, $\int_a^\infty |f(x)|\,dx$

will always have a value at least as large as $\int_a^\infty f(x)\,dx$, as for the latter there might be cancellation due to 'negative areas'.

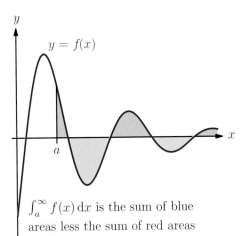

$\int_a^\infty f(x)\,dx$ is the sum of blue areas less the sum of red areas

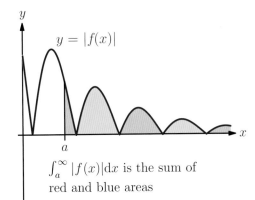

$\int_a^\infty |f(x)|dx$ is the sum of red and blue areas

Of course if $\int_a^\infty |f(x)|\,dx$ is finite, then so must be the smaller value of $\int_a^\infty f(x)\,dx$.

Worked example 2.7

Show that $\displaystyle\int_1^\infty \frac{\cos x}{1+x^3}\,dx$ converges.

We want to use the Comparison Test but $\cos x$ can be negative and so we can't apply the test directly

However, we can remove this problem by taking the modulus and attempting to show that $\displaystyle\int_1^\infty \left|\frac{\cos x}{1+x^3}\right|\,dx$ converges (and hence, using the above result, that $\displaystyle\int_1^\infty \frac{\cos x}{1+x^3}\,dx$ converges)

$|\cos x| \leq 1$ and $1+x^3 \geq x^3$

$\therefore \left|\dfrac{\cos x}{1+x^3}\right| \leq \dfrac{1}{x^3}$

From Worked example 2.5 $\displaystyle\int_1^\infty \frac{1}{x^3}\,dx$ converges and so we can apply the Comparison Test

Since $\displaystyle\int_1^\infty \frac{1}{x^3}\,dx$ converges, so does

$$\int_1^\infty \left|\frac{\cos x}{1+x^3}\right|\,dx$$

by the Comparison Test for improper integrals.

Hence, $\displaystyle\int_1^\infty \frac{\cos x}{1+x^3}\,dx$ converges.

If we need to find the limit of a convergent improper integral we may need to use any of the integration methods encountered in the Core syllabus, such as integration by parts and substitution, and also the methods from the previous chapter.

Worked example 2.8

Evaluate the convergent improper integral $\int_1^\infty xe^{-x}\,dx$.

Integrate by parts, remembering the use of $\lim_{b\to\infty}$ to deal with the upper limit

$$\int_1^\infty xe^{-x}\,dx = \lim_{b\to\infty}\int_1^b xe^{-x}\,dx$$

$$= \lim_{b\to\infty}\left(\left[-xe^{-x}\right]_1^b - \int_1^b -e^{-x}\,dx\right)$$

$$= \lim_{b\to\infty}\left(\left[-xe^{-x}\right]_1^b - \left[e^{-x}\right]_1^b\right)$$

$$= \lim_{b\to\infty}\left\{\left(-be^{-b}+e^{-1}\right)-\left(e^{-b}-e^{-1}\right)\right\}$$

$$= 2e^{-1} - \lim_{b\to\infty}\left(\frac{1+b}{e^b}\right)$$

We are now faced with a limit of the type $\dfrac{\infty}{\infty}$ and so apply l'Hôpital's Rule

By l'Hôpital's Rule:

$$\lim_{b\to\infty}\left(\frac{1+b}{e^b}\right) = \lim_{b\to\infty}\frac{1}{e^b} = 0$$

$$\therefore \int_1^\infty xe^{-x}\,dx = 2e^{-1}$$

In the above example we established $\lim_{x\to\infty}\dfrac{x}{e^x}=0$, using l'Hôpital's Rule. This and the following standard results can just be quoted in the exam in cases such as Worked example 2.8.

◁ *See Section 1D for l'Hôpital's Rule.* ◁

KEY POINT 2.5

- $\lim_{x\to\infty}\dfrac{x^p}{e^x} = 0$

- $\lim_{x\to\infty}\dfrac{x^p}{\ln x} = \infty$

Exercise 2B

1. Test the following for convergence. For those that do converge, give the value of the improper integral.

   (a) $\displaystyle\int_0^\infty \frac{1}{(1+x)^2}\,dx$

   (b) $\displaystyle\int_0^\infty e^{-\frac{x}{4}}\,dx$

   (c) $\displaystyle\int_0^\infty \frac{1}{\sqrt{1+x}}\,dx$

   (d) $\displaystyle\int_0^\infty xe^{-x^2}\,dx$

2. Find which of the following converge using the Comparison Test for improper integrals:

(a) $\int_2^\infty \dfrac{1}{\sqrt{x-1}}\, dx$

(b) $\int_1^\infty e^{-x^2}\, dx$

(c) $\int_1^\infty \dfrac{2x}{x^3+5}\, dx$

(d) $\int_1^\infty \dfrac{\cos\frac{x}{2}}{x^2+4x}\, dx$

(e) $\int_3^\infty \dfrac{x+2}{x^2-3x+1}\, dx$

(f) $\int_1^\infty \dfrac{\sin 2x}{x^4+x^2+2}\, dx$

3. Find for what values of p the following improper integrals converge:

(a) $\int_0^\infty e^{px}\, dx$

(b) $\int_1^\infty \dfrac{\ln x}{x^p}\, dx$

4. Evaluate $\int_0^\infty e^{-x}\, dx$. *[3 marks]*

5. Evaluate $\int_0^\infty \dfrac{1}{x^2+1}\, dx$. *[3 marks]*

6. (a) Show that

$$x^4+6x^2+14=(x^2+3)^2+5 \text{ for all } x\in\mathbb{R}$$

(b) Hence show that

$$\int_1^\infty \dfrac{x^2+3}{x^4+6x^2+14}\, dx \text{ converges} \qquad [5\ marks]$$

7. (a) Show that

$$\int_a^4 \dfrac{1}{\sqrt{x}}\, dx = 4 - 2\sqrt{a}$$

for $0 < a < 4$.

(b) Hence explain why $\int_0^4 \dfrac{1}{\sqrt{x}}\, dx$ converges and find its value.

[5 marks]

8. (a) Show that $\dfrac{3}{x^2+x-2} = \dfrac{1}{x-1} - \dfrac{1}{x+2}$.

(b) Hence find the exact value of:

$$\int_3^\infty \dfrac{3}{x^2+x-2}\, dx \qquad [6\ marks]$$

9. Evaluate the improper integral: $\int_{1/\pi}^\infty \dfrac{1}{x^2}\sin\left(\dfrac{1}{x}\right)\, dx$ *[6 marks]*

10. Show that $\int_0^\infty \dfrac{\sin(\lambda x)}{e^x}\, dx = \dfrac{\lambda}{1+\lambda^2}$. *[10 marks]*

11. Show by induction that $\int_0^\infty x^n e^{-x}\, dx = n!$ *[11 marks]*

12. Does the improper integral $\int_1^\infty \dfrac{\sin x}{x}\, dx$ converge? *[9 marks]*

2C Approximation of improper integrals

We saw in the last section that there are some improper integrals that we can prove are convergent but that we cannot evaluate exactly. It makes sense to see whether we can at least find an approximate value of the integral in such cases.

Using the geometrical interpretation of integration as the area between a curve and the x-axis, we shall try to place bounds on a convergent improper integral; that is, to find values L (the lower bound) and U (the upper bound) such that:

$$L < \int_a^\infty f(x)\, dx < U$$

To achieve this, we consider a function $f(x)$ and construct rectangles of width 1 at each integer value of $x \geq a$. The height of the rectangle is determined by the height of the function $f(a)$ at the left hand end of the interval.

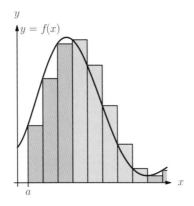

As we can see, some rectangles will overestimate the area under the function and some will underestimate. In general it is not clear whether the total area of the rectangles is an over- or underestimate of the area under the function (and hence of the value of the integral $\int_a^\infty f(x)\, dx$).

We can see from the diagram that the area of the rectangles is an overestimate where the function is decreasing and an underestimate where it is increasing. Therefore, if we restrict ourselves to the specific case of either an increasing or a decreasing function, we can use the area of these rectangles to form the bounds we are looking for on the integral.

So, consider firstly a *decreasing function* $f(x)$ for all $x > a$.

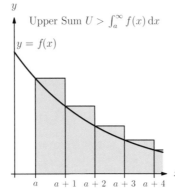

The total area of the rectangles is

$$\left(f(a)\times 1\right)+\left(f(a+1)\times 1\right)+\left(f(a+2)\times 1\right)+\cdots$$

$$=f(a)+f(a+1)+f(a+2)+\ldots$$

$$=\sum_{k=a}^{\infty}f(k)$$

And the diagram shows that this is an overestimate, giving

$$\int_{a}^{\infty}f(x)\,\mathrm{d}x<\sum_{k=a}^{\infty}f(k)$$

which is the upper bound U mentioned above, usually referred to as the **upper sum** of $\int_{a}^{\infty}f(x)\,\mathrm{d}x$.

To form a lower bound L, usually referred to as the **lower sum**, consider the rectangles formed by using the right-hand end of each interval; that is starting with the rectangle of height $f(a+1)$.

EXAM HINT

The upper and lower sums are also known as Riemann sums.

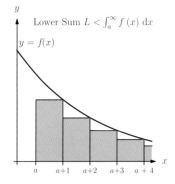

The total area of these rectangles is:

$$\left(f(a+1)\times 1\right)+\left(f(a+2)\times 1\right)+\left(f(a+3)\times 1\right)+\cdots$$

$$=f(a+1)+f(a+2)+f(a+3)+\cdots$$

$$=\sum_{k=a+1}^{\infty}f(k)$$

And this is an understimate, giving:

$$\sum_{k=a+1}^{\infty}f(k)<\int_{a}^{\infty}f(x)\,\mathrm{d}x$$

If we were to now consider an *increasing function* we would have exactly the same bounds but the other way round. However, note that in order for an increasing function to have a convergent improper integral (if it is divergent there is no point us trying to put bounds on it), the function must be below the x-axis.

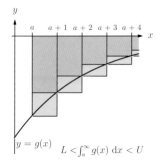

For a decreasing function $f(x)$ for all $x > a$, we have an upper and lower sum such that:

$$\sum_{k=a+1}^{\infty} f(k) < \int_{a}^{\infty} f(x)\, dx < \sum_{k=a}^{\infty} f(k)$$

For an increasing function $g(x)$ for all $x > a$, we have an upper and lower sum such that:

$$\sum_{k=a}^{\infty} g(k) < \int_{a}^{\infty} g(x)\, dx < \sum_{k=a+1}^{\infty} g(k)$$

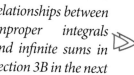

We will use these relationships between improper integrals and infinite sums in Section 3B in the next chapter.

When the upper and lower sums are geometric series we will actually be able to evaluate them and give numerical bounds on the value of the improper integral.

Worked example 2.9

Find constants L and U such that $L < \int_{1}^{\infty} -\left(\dfrac{1}{3}\right)^{x} dx < U$.

We first need to establish whether $-\left(\dfrac{1}{3}\right)^{x}$ is increasing or decreasing in order to get our expressions for the lower and upper sum the right way round. We can do this either by reference to the graph or by differentiating

$-\left(\dfrac{1}{3}\right)^{x} = -(3^{-x})$

$y = -(3^{-x})$ is a reflection in the x-axis of $y = 3^{-x}$

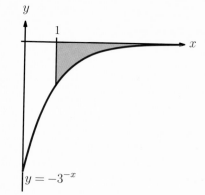

$y = -3^{-x}$

Therefore, $-(3^{-x})$ is increasing for all x

Now apply the result for upper and lower sums of an increasing function

Hence:

$$\sum_{k=1}^{\infty} -\left(\frac{1}{3}\right)^{k} < \int_{1}^{\infty} -\left(\frac{1}{3}\right)^{x} dx < \sum_{k=2}^{\infty} -\left(\frac{1}{3}\right)^{k}$$

We now have geometric series forming the upper and lower bounds so we can evaluate these using $S_{\infty} = \dfrac{a}{1-r}$

Both have $r = \dfrac{1}{3}$; the lower sum has $a = \dfrac{1}{3}$ and the upper sum $a = \dfrac{1}{9}$

But $\displaystyle\sum_{k=1}^{\infty} -\left(\frac{1}{3}\right)^{k} = -\frac{\frac{1}{3}}{1-\frac{1}{3}} = -\frac{1}{2}$

and $\displaystyle\sum_{k=2}^{\infty} -\left(\frac{1}{3}\right)^{k} = -\frac{\frac{1}{9}}{1-\frac{1}{3}} = -\frac{1}{6}$

Therefore:

$$-\frac{1}{2} < \int_{1}^{\infty} -\left(\frac{1}{3}\right)^{x} dx < -\frac{1}{6}$$

Often we will not be able to evaluate the infinite sums and we will only be able to give expressions for the upper and lower bounds. In such cases, however, we may be able to evaluate the integral itself and thereby form bounds on the value of the infinite sum. We shall look at this approach in the next chapter which deals with infinite series; but the following example gives an introduction to the idea.

Worked example 2.10

(a) Find upper and lower sums for the improper integral $\int_3^\infty \frac{1}{x^2} \, dx$.

(b) Hence place upper and lower bounds on $\sum_{k=3}^\infty \frac{1}{k^2}$.

To get the expressions for the lower and upper sum the right way round we need to establish whether $\frac{1}{x^2}$ is increasing or decreasing

We can do this either by reference to the graph or by differentiating

(a) $\frac{d}{dx}\left(\frac{1}{x^2}\right) = -\frac{2}{x^3}$

As $-\frac{2}{x^3} < 0$ for all $x \geq 3$, $\frac{1}{x^2}$ is decreasing for all $x \geq 3$

Now apply the result for upper and lower sums of a decreasing function, noting the lower limit of $x = 3$ on the integral

Hence $\sum_{k=4}^\infty \frac{1}{k^2} < \int_3^\infty \frac{1}{x^2} \, dx < \sum_{k=3}^\infty \frac{1}{k^2}$

We can't evaluate the infinite sums, but this time we can evaluate the improper integral itself

(b)

$\int_3^\infty \frac{1}{x^2} \, dx = \lim_{b \to \infty} \int_3^b x^{-2} \, dx$

$= \lim_{b \to \infty} \left[-x^{-1}\right]_3^b$

$= \lim_{b \to \infty} \left(-b^{-1} + 3^{-1}\right)$

$= \frac{1}{3}$

This gives us a lower bound of $\frac{1}{3}$ immediately

$\therefore \sum_{k=4}^\infty \frac{1}{k^2} < \frac{1}{3} < \sum_{k=3}^\infty \frac{1}{k^2}$

which gives a lower bound for $\sum_{k=3}^\infty \frac{1}{k^2}$

To form an upper bound we need to change $\sum_{k=4}^\infty \frac{1}{k^2}$ into $\sum_{k=3}^\infty \frac{1}{k^2}$ by adding the previous term of the series, $\frac{1}{3^2}$

But

$\sum_{k=4}^\infty \frac{1}{k^2} < \frac{1}{3} \Rightarrow \frac{1}{3^2} + \sum_{k=4}^\infty \frac{1}{k^2} < \frac{1}{3^2} + \frac{1}{3}$

$\Rightarrow \sum_{k=3}^\infty \frac{1}{k^2} < \frac{4}{9}$

which gives an upper bound

Put these bounds together

Therefore $\frac{1}{3} < \sum_{k=3}^\infty \frac{1}{k^2} < \frac{4}{9}$

Exercise 2C

1. Find the upper and lower sums for the following integrals (the functions are decreasing):

(a) $\displaystyle\int_1^\infty e^{-x^2}\,dx$

(b) $\displaystyle\int_5^\infty \frac{1}{\sqrt{x+2}}\,dx$

(c) $\displaystyle\int_2^\infty \frac{\ln x}{x^2}\,dx$

2. Find the upper and lower sums for the following integrals (the functions are increasing):

(a) $\displaystyle\int_{10}^\infty -\frac{1}{x^2}\,dx$

(b) $\displaystyle\int_1^\infty \ln\left(\frac{x^2}{x^2+1}\right)\,dx$

(c) $\displaystyle\int_2^\infty \frac{1}{e^{-x}-e^x}\,dx$

3. Find upper and lower sums of:

(a) $\displaystyle\int_0^\infty -\frac{1}{(x+2)^3}\,dx$

(b) $\displaystyle\int_0^\infty \frac{1}{x^2+8x+17}\,dx$ *[6 marks]*

4. (a) Show that the improper integral $\displaystyle\int_3^\infty \frac{1}{e^x+e^{-x}}\,dx$ exists.

(b) Show that $f(x)=\dfrac{1}{e^x+e^{-x}}$ is decreasing for all $x>0$.

(c) Find the upper and lower sums of $\displaystyle\int_3^\infty \frac{1}{e^x+e^{-x}}\,dx$. *[7 marks]*

5. (a) Find the upper and lower sums of:
$$\int_{10}^\infty 2^{-x}\,dx$$

(b) By evaluating the two series, find two constants a and b such that:
$$a<\int_{10}^\infty 2^{-x}\,dx<b$$
Give exact values of a and b.

(c) Using the result that
$$\int a^x\,dx = \frac{a^x}{\ln a}+C$$
and your answer from part (b), show that:
$$\frac{1}{2}<\ln 2<1 \qquad\qquad \text{[10 marks]}$$

Summary

- The **Fundamental Theorem of Calculus** links the concepts of differentiation and integration (to find the area under a curve). For a continuous function $f(x)$ on the interval $[a,b]$,

$$\frac{d}{dx}\int_a^x f(t)\,dt = f(x)$$

and for any function $g(x)$ such that $g'(x) = f(x)$

$$\int_a^b f(x)\,dx = g(b) - g(a).$$

- The **improper integral**

$$\int_a^\infty f(x)\,dx = \lim_{b\to\infty}\int_a^b f(x)\,dx$$

is convergent (exists) if the limit is finite. Otherwise the integral is divergent (does not exist).

- Convergence or divergence of improper integrals can be established *by comparison* with other known convergent or divergent integrals; that is, if $0 \le f(x) \le g(x)$ for all $x \ge a$ then:

  - $\int_a^\infty f(x)\,dx$ is convergent if $\int_a^\infty g(x)\,dx$ is convergent.

  - $\int_a^\infty g(x)\,dx$ is divergent if $\int_a^\infty f(x)\,dx$ is divergent.

- $\int_a^\infty \dfrac{1}{x^p}\,dx$ converges only for $p > 1$.

- If $\int_a^\infty |f(x)|\,dx$ converges, then so does $\int_a^\infty f(x)\,dx$.

- Improper integrals of increasing functions or decreasing functions can be approximated by the sum of infinitely many rectangles of width 1.

  - For a *decreasing function* $f(x)$ for all $x > a$, we have an **upper** and **lower (Reimann) sum** such that:

$$\sum_{k=a+1}^{\infty} f(k) < \int_a^\infty f(x)\,dx < \sum_{k=a}^{\infty} f(k)$$

  - For an *increasing function* $g(x)$ for all $x > a$, we have an **upper** and **lower (Reimann) sum** such that:

$$\sum_{k=a}^{\infty} g(k) < \int_a^\infty g(x)\,dx < \sum_{k=a+1}^{\infty} g(k)$$

Mixed examination practice 2

1. Evaluate the following improper integrals:

   (a) $\displaystyle\int_0^\infty \frac{3}{(2x+3)^2}\,dx$

   (b) $\displaystyle\int_2^\infty \frac{x+4}{\left(x^2+8x+5\right)^{\frac{3}{2}}}\,dx$ *[6 marks]*

2. Find the following:

   (a) $\displaystyle\frac{d}{db}\int_a^b \ln\left(\cos^2 3x+1\right)\,dx$

   (b) $\displaystyle\frac{d}{db}\int_a^b \ln\left(\cos^2 3x+1\right)\,dt$ *[4 marks]*

3. (a) Write $\ln n$ in the form $\ln n = \displaystyle\int_a^b f(x)\,dx$

   where a, b and $f(x)$ are to be found.

   (b) For $x \ge 1$ and $c > 0$, show that $\dfrac{1}{x} \le x^{c-1}$.

   (c) By choosing a suitable value for c, find the limit of the sequence whose general term is:
   $$u_n = \frac{\ln n}{n}$$ *[9 marks]*

4. (a) Using integration by parts, show that:
   $$\int_0^\infty e^{-x}\cos x\,dx = \int_0^\infty e^{-x}\sin x\,dx$$

   (b) Find the value of these two integrals.   *[11 marks]*

   (© IB Organization 2007)

5. Show that the improper integral $\displaystyle\int_1^\infty \frac{\sin x}{x^\alpha}\,dx$ exists for all $\alpha > 1$.   *[8 marks]*

6. (a) Show that $\displaystyle\int_0^\infty e^{-x^2}\,dx$ converges.

   (b) Find upper and lower sums for the integral.   *[7 marks]*

7. (a) Show that $x > \sqrt{x} - 1$ for $x \ge 2$

   (b) Find $\displaystyle\lim_{x\to\infty} \frac{e^x}{x}$

   (c) Determine whether or not $\displaystyle\int_2^\infty \frac{e^x}{\sqrt{x}-1}\,dx$ converges.   *[8 marks]*

8. (a) Show that $2x - \sqrt{4x^2 + 21} = \dfrac{-k}{2x + \sqrt{4x^2 + 21}}$, where k is a constant to be determined.

(b) Evaluate $\displaystyle\int_1^\infty 2 - \frac{4x}{\sqrt{4x^2 + 21}}\ dx$. 　　　　　　　　　　　　　*[9 marks]*

9. (a) Use a sketch to illustrate that $\ln x < x$ for $x \geq 1$.

(b) Hence, determine whether the following converges or diverges.

$$\int_1^\infty \frac{(\ln x)^2 \cos x}{x^{\frac{7}{2}}}\ dx.$$ 　　　　　　　　　　　　　*[6 marks]*

3 Infinite series

In this chapter you will learn:

- how to relate the convergence of infinite series to the convergence of sequences from chapter 1 of this option

- to determine whether positive series converge or diverge using a number of tests

- to determine whether series with both positive and negative terms converge or diverge

- to put bounds on the limits of some convergent series

- to find the values of x for which infinite series in increasing integer powers of x converge.

In the main course you studied infinite series where the terms of a geometric sequence were summed. Under certain conditions ($|r| < 1$) the series was said to converge to a limit; that is, as we added more and more terms of the sequence, the sum approached nearer and nearer to a finite number but could never reach that number.

For example, for the geometric series

$$2 + \frac{3}{2} + \frac{9}{8} + \frac{27}{32} + \ldots = \sum_{k=1}^{\infty} 2\left(\frac{3}{4}\right)^k$$

the sum converges to (its sum to infinity is)

$$S_\infty = \frac{a}{1-r} = \frac{2}{1 - \dfrac{3}{4}} = 8$$

If $|r| \geq 1$ for a geometric series there is no such finite limit.

There are other types of series that we can categorise as convergent or divergent very easily.

For example the series $1 + 2 + 3 + 4 + \cdots = \sum_{k=1}^{\infty} k$ clearly does not converge.

But what of a series such as $1 + \dfrac{1}{2} + \dfrac{1}{3} + \dfrac{1}{4} + \cdots = \sum_{k=1}^{\infty} \dfrac{1}{k}$?

This looks as if it could be convergent; each term is getting smaller and indeed we know from chapter 1 of this option that the sequence $\left\{\dfrac{1}{k}\right\}$ converges to 0, so perhaps our sum will converge too?

Unsurprisingly, the idea of the convergence of series is very closely related to that of the convergence of sequences. We will start by defining convergence of series generally with reference to convergence of sequences and then look at ways in which we can determine whether series (including the above!) converge or diverge and in some cases what their limits are too.

See Section 1A and 1B for convergence of sequences.

3A Convergence of series

From an infinite sequence $u_1, u_2, u_3, u_4, \ldots$ we have the infinite series given by

$$S = u_1 + u_2 + u_3 + u_4 + \ldots$$

In order to make sense of the idea of a convergent $(S < \infty)$ or divergent $(S = \infty)$ infinite series, we will relate this to the now familiar idea of a convergent or divergent sequence by setting up the sequence $\quad S_1, S_2, S_3, S_4, \ldots$

where
$$S_1 = u_1$$
$$S_2 = u_1 + u_2$$
$$S_3 = u_1 + u_2 + u_3$$
$$\vdots$$
$$S_n = u_1 + u_2 + \ldots + u_n$$

Here each S_n, $n \in \mathbb{Z}^+$, is known as the **nth partial sum**. We then have the following definition:

KEY POINT 3.1

If the sequence $S_1, S_2, S_3, S_4, \ldots$ of partial sums converges to a limit S, then the infinite series is convergent (to S).

$$S = \lim_{n \to \infty} S_n = \sum_{k=1}^{\infty} u_k$$

Otherwise it is divergent.

Worked example 3.1

By finding the nth partial sum of the following series, determine whether the series converge or diverge.

(a) $\displaystyle\sum_{k=1}^{\infty} 2 \times \left(\frac{2}{3}\right)^k$

(b) $\displaystyle\sum_{k=1}^{\infty} \frac{3-k}{4}$

We recognise this as a geometric series with $a = 2$ and $r = \dfrac{2}{3}$ and can therefore use the formula for the sum of the first n terms to get the nth partial sum

(a) This is a geometric series with
$$a = 2 \text{ and } r = \frac{2}{3}$$

So the nth partial sum is given by
$$S_n = \frac{a(1 - r^n)}{1 - r}$$

$$= \frac{2\left(1 - \left(\frac{2}{3}\right)^n\right)}{1 - \frac{2}{3}}$$

$$= 6\left(1 - \left(\frac{2}{3}\right)^n\right)$$

continued ...

If this sequence of partial sums converges, then the series converges

Letting $n \to \infty$, $\left(\dfrac{2}{3}\right)^n \to 0$ and therefore

$$S_n \to 6(1-0) = 6$$

Since S_n converges, so does $\displaystyle\sum_{k=1}^{\infty} 2 \times \left(\frac{2}{3}\right)^k$

This series isn't perhaps so immediately recognisable, so find the first few terms

(b) $\dfrac{1}{2} + \dfrac{1}{4} + 0 - \dfrac{1}{4} - \dfrac{1}{2} - \cdots$

We now see it is an arithmetic series

This is an arithmetic series with

$$a = \frac{1}{2} \text{ and } d = -\frac{1}{4}$$

We can use a known formula for the sum of the first n terms to get the nth partial sum

So, the nth partial sum is given by:

$$S_n = \frac{n}{2}\left[2a + (n-1)d\right]$$

$$= \frac{n}{2}\left[2 \times \frac{1}{2} + (n-1)\left(-\frac{1}{4}\right)\right]$$

$$= \frac{n}{2}\left[1 - \left(\frac{n-1}{4}\right)\right]$$

$$= \frac{n}{2} - \frac{n^2}{8} + \frac{n}{8}$$

$$= \frac{5n - n^2}{8}$$

If this sequence of partial sums converges, then the series converges

Letting $n \to \infty$

$$S_n = \frac{5n - n^2}{8} \to -\infty$$

Since S_n diverges, so does $\displaystyle\sum_{k=1}^{\infty} \frac{3-k}{4}$

With the definition of convergence of infinite series, we can now use our work on convergence of sequences to help us establish when certain series (which are after all just sequences of partial sums) converge. The first step is to think about what we know about u_k for a convergent series $\displaystyle\sum_{k=1}^{\infty} u_k$.

If $\displaystyle\sum_{k=1}^{\infty} u_k$ converges then we know that the sequence of partial sums $\{S_n\}$ converges to a limit S; that is, $\displaystyle\lim_{n\to\infty} S_n = S$.

We also have that: $u_n = (u_1 + u_2 + \cdots + u_n) - (u_1 + u_2 + \cdots + u_{n-1})$

$$= S_n - S_{n-1}$$

So, $\lim\limits_{n\to\infty} u_n = \lim\limits_{n\to\infty}(S_n - S_{n-1})$

$\qquad\qquad = \lim\limits_{n\to\infty} S_n - \lim\limits_{n\to\infty} S_{n-1}$

$\qquad\qquad = S - S$

$\qquad\qquad = 0.$

This gives us the important result that:

KEY POINT 3.2

If the series $\displaystyle\sum_{k=1}^{\infty} u_k$ is convergent then $\lim\limits_{k\to\infty} u_k = 0$.

The converse, however, is not true: just because $\lim\limits_{k\to\infty} u_k = 0$

it is not necessarily the case that $\displaystyle\sum_{k=1}^{\infty} u_k$ is convergent.

In the next section we will use Key point 3.2 to determine the divergence of some series.

An example of the latter is $\displaystyle\sum_{k=1}^{\infty} \frac{1}{k}$. Here $\lim\limits_{k\to\infty} u_k = 0$ but, as we will see in the next section $\displaystyle\sum_{k=1}^{\infty} \frac{1}{k}$ diverges.

Exercise 3A

1. Evaluate (correct to 3SF) the first four partial sums for the series $\displaystyle\sum_{k=1}^{\infty} u_k$ where:

   (a) $u_k = \dfrac{1}{k^2}$

   (b) $u_k = \sin\left(\dfrac{k\pi}{3}\right)$

   (c) $u_k = \dfrac{1}{k+5}$

   (d) $u_k = e^{-k}$

2. Write an expression (in terms of n) for the nth partial sum of the given series, and hence decide whether the series is convergent or divergent.

   (a) $\displaystyle\sum_{k=1}^{\infty} 3k+1$

   (b) $\displaystyle\sum_{k=1}^{\infty} 2 - \dfrac{k}{5}$

   (c) $\displaystyle\sum_{k=1}^{\infty} \dfrac{1}{3^k}$

   (d) $\displaystyle\sum_{k=1}^{\infty} 1.2^k$

   (e) $\displaystyle\sum_{k=1}^{\infty} \left(-\dfrac{1}{2}\right)^{4k}$

3. Given the expression for the nth partial sum of the series $\displaystyle\sum_{k=1}^{\infty} u_k$, find (and simplify) u_k:

   (a) $S_n = 3n^2 - 1$

   (b) $S_n = 3^n - 1$

   (c) $S_n = \dfrac{5}{4^n} - 5$

   (d) $S_n = \ln n$

   (e) $S_n = \dfrac{2^n - 1}{3 \times 2^n}$

3B Tests for convergence and divergence

Divergence Test

From Key point 3.2 we note that if $\lim_{k \to \infty} u_k \neq 0$ the series cannot be convergent. We therefore have a possible way of checking whether a series diverges.

KEY POINT 3.3

Divergence Test

If $\lim_{k \to \infty} u_k \neq 0$ or if the limit does not exist, the series $\sum_{k=1}^{\infty} u_k$ is divergent.

Of course this will not always identify a divergent series ($\lim_{k \to \infty} u_k$ might be 0 and the series could diverge as mentioned above), but it is often the first thing to check.

Worked example 3.2

Show that the series $\sum_{k=1}^{\infty} \dfrac{k^2 + 3k + 1}{4k^2 + 3}$ diverges.

To show that $\lim_{k \to \infty} u_k \neq 0$ we need to manipulate u_k into a form that enables us to find its limit as $k \to \infty$

$$u_k = \frac{k^2 + 3k + 1}{4k^2 + 3}$$

$$= \frac{1 + \frac{3}{k} + \frac{1}{k^2}}{4 + \frac{3}{k^2}}$$

$$\therefore \lim_{k \to \infty} u_k = \frac{1}{4} \neq 0$$

Hence $\sum_{k=1}^{\infty} \dfrac{k^2 + 3k + 1}{4k^2 + 3}$ diverges.

We will now present a number of tests for determining convergence or divergence of series, which can be established using the principles discussed in Section 3A.

Comparison Test

The first of these tests is similar to the Comparison Test for improper integrals used in chapter 2 of this option.

We would like to know whether the following series converges or not.

EXAM HINT

In the exam it is a good idea to check the Divergence Test before considering any of the other tests from this chapter.

See Section 2B (Key point 2.3) for the Comparison Test for improper integrals.

$$1 + \frac{1}{4} + \frac{1}{10} + \frac{1}{28} + \frac{1}{82} + \frac{1}{244} + \cdots$$

While we cannot say much about this series immediately, we do recognise that it is similar to the geometric series:

$$1 + \frac{1}{3} + \frac{1}{9} + \frac{1}{27} + \frac{1}{81} + \frac{1}{243} + \cdots$$

which we know converges because $r = \frac{1}{3}$ ($S_\infty = \frac{3}{2}$). We also note that each term of our series is less than or equal to the corresponding term of the geometric series:

$$1 \leq 1$$

$$\frac{1}{4} \leq \frac{1}{3}$$

$$\frac{1}{10} \leq \frac{1}{9}$$

$$\frac{1}{28} \leq \frac{1}{27}$$

$$\vdots$$

Hence, each partial sum (after the first one) is less than the corresponding partial sum of the geometric series and our series must therefore converge (to a limit less than $\frac{3}{2}$).

This idea is generalised by the following result:

Comparison Test

Given two series of positive terms $\sum\limits_{k=1}^{\infty} a_k$ and $\sum\limits_{k=1}^{\infty} b_k$ such that $a_k \leq b_k$ for all $k \in \mathbb{Z}^+$, then if:

- $\sum\limits_{k=1}^{\infty} b_k$ is convergent to a limit S, $\sum\limits_{k=1}^{\infty} a_k$ is also convergent to a limit T where $T \leq S$

- $\sum\limits_{k=1}^{\infty} a_k$ is divergent, so is $\sum\limits_{k=1}^{\infty} b_k$.

Just as with the Comparison Test for improper integrals in chapter 2 of this option, this result is intuitive. Now, instead of comparing areas under functions, we are comparing a sequence of partial sums.

If $\sum_{k=1}^{\infty} b_k$ converges to S and $a_k \le b_k$ for all $k \in \mathbb{Z}^+$ we have the following for the partial sums of each series:

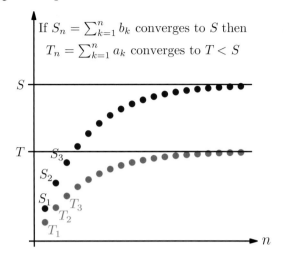

If $S_n = \sum_{k=1}^{n} b_k$ converges to S then
$T_n = \sum_{k=1}^{n} a_k$ converges to $T < S$

and if $\sum_{k=1}^{\infty} a_k$ diverges, we have:

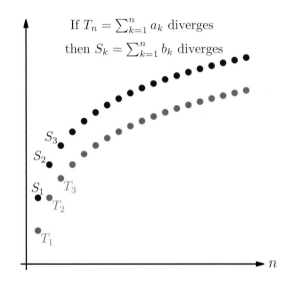

If $T_n = \sum_{k=1}^{n} a_k$ diverges
then $S_k = \sum_{k=1}^{n} b_k$ diverges

EXAM HINT

In looking for a convergent $\sum_{k=1}^{\infty} b_k$ such that $a_k \le b_k$ for all k, first it is often worth considering geometric series.

We will see shortly that the p-series is ▷ *also commonly used* ▷ *in the Comparison Test.*

Worked example 3.3

Establish whether or not the series $\displaystyle\sum_{k=1}^{\infty} \frac{1}{2^k + 3}$ converges.

 We will try first of all to show that the series converges by finding a series we know converges and which satisfies the conditions of the Comparison Test
If we do not have any success with this approach we will then consider trying to establish divergence by finding a known divergent series

continued . . .

The series is similar to $\sum_{k=1}^{\infty} \dfrac{1}{2^k}$ which we know converges (it is a geometric series with $r = \dfrac{1}{2}$), so let's start by considering this

$2^k > 0$ for all k

and

$2^k + 3 > 2^k$ for all k

$\therefore \dfrac{1}{2^k + 3} < \dfrac{1}{2^k}$ for all $k \in \mathbb{Z}^+$

and since $\sum_{k=1}^{\infty} \dfrac{1}{2^k}$ converges, so does $\sum_{k=1}^{\infty} \dfrac{1}{2^k + 3}$ by the Comparison test.

Limit Comparison Test

Sometimes we meet a series which is very similar to a known convergent (or divergent) series, but which does not fulfil the conditions of the Comparison Test.

For example the series $\sum_{k=1}^{\infty} \dfrac{1}{2^k - 1} = 1 + \dfrac{1}{3} + \dfrac{1}{7} + \dfrac{1}{15} + \dfrac{1}{31} + \dfrac{1}{63} + \cdots$

has terms similar to our known convergent series $\sum_{k=1}^{\infty} \dfrac{1}{2^k}$ but

each of its terms are larger than those of the known convergent series and not smaller. Although the standard Comparison Test is therefore no use, the following extension of the test is.

KEY POINT 3.5

Limit Comparison Test

Given two series of positive terms $\sum_{k=1}^{\infty} a_k$ and $\sum_{k=1}^{\infty} b_k$, where

$\lim_{k \to \infty} \dfrac{a_k}{b_k} = l > 0$, then if one series converges so does the other and if one series diverges so does the other.

EXAM HINT

Choose as b_k the general term of the series to which you had hoped to apply the Comparison Test.

Show that the series $\displaystyle\sum_{k=1}^{\infty} \frac{1}{2^k - 1}$ is convergent.

We know that this series isn't suitable for the Comparison Test with $\displaystyle\sum_{k=1}^{\infty} \frac{1}{2^k}$ but we hope it satisfies the conditions of the Limit Comparison Test

Let

$$a_k = \frac{1}{2^k - 1} \quad \text{and} \quad b_k = \frac{1}{2^k}$$

Then

$$\frac{a_k}{b_k} = \frac{1}{2^k - 1} \times \frac{2^k}{1}$$

$$= \frac{2^k}{2^k - 1}$$

$$= \frac{1}{1 - \left(\dfrac{1}{2}\right)^k}$$

and so

$$\lim_{k \to \infty} \frac{a_k}{b_k} = 1$$

Hence $\displaystyle\sum_{k=1}^{\infty} \frac{1}{2^k - 1}$ converges by the Limit Comparison Test.

Integral Test

In the previous chapter we found upper and lower bounds (sums) for the improper integral $\displaystyle\int_a^{\infty} f(x)\,dx$ in the separate cases where $f(x)$ was increasing and decreasing. Here we will use this result for the case where $f(x)$ is a decreasing positive function and $a = 1$, but now put bounds on the infinite sum and not the improper integral.

So, from chapter 2 we have:

$$\sum_{k=a+1}^{\infty} f(k) < \int_a^{\infty} f(x)\,dx < \sum_{k=a}^{\infty} f(k)$$

For the lower sum, letting $a = 1$ and noting that $f(1)$ is positive:

$$\sum_{k=1+1}^{\infty} f(k) < \int_1^{\infty} f(x)\,dx$$

$$\Rightarrow \sum_{k=1}^{\infty} \big(f(k)\big) - f(1) < \int_1^{\infty} f(x)\,dx$$

$$\Rightarrow \sum_{k=1}^{\infty} f(k) < f(1) + \int_1^{\infty} f(x)\,dx$$

Combining this with the upper sum $\displaystyle\int_1^{\infty} f(x)\,dx < \sum_{k=1}^{\infty} f(k)$

we now have: $\displaystyle\int_1^{\infty} f(x)\,dx < \sum_{k=1}^{\infty} f(k) < f(1) + \int_1^{\infty} f(x)\,dx$

Look back at the graphical method used in Section 2C to establish the upper and lower sums, and at Worked example 2.10 where we placed bounds on the sum $\displaystyle\sum_{k=3}^{\infty} \frac{1}{k^2}$.

EXAM HINT

In the exam, you may be required to use this method to place bounds on an infinite sum that cannot be evaluated directly.

Then, if the improper integral $\int_1^\infty f(x)\,dx$ converges to a limit

L, the sum is bounded between the two constants L and $f(1) + L$:

$$L < \sum_{k=1}^{\infty} f(k) < f(1) + L$$

Also, as $f(x)$ is positive, the sum increases as more and more terms are added. It seems clear that an increasing series that is bounded above (here by the constant $f(1) + L$) must converge to a limit that is less than or equal to this bound:

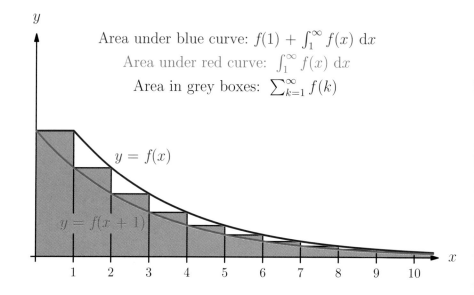

Area under blue curve: $f(1) + \int_1^\infty f(x)\ dx$
Area under red curve: $\int_1^\infty f(x)\ dx$
Area in grey boxes: $\sum_{k=1}^\infty f(k)$

$y = f(x)$

$y = f(x+1)$

The general result that any increasing series bounded above or decreasing series bounded below has a limit is known as the Monotone Convergence Theorem. Although this result is not part of the syllabus it helps us understand the following test for convergence of series:

Do we need to have a formal proof of a result like the Monotone Convergence Theorem when it seems so clear that it is true? Does a proof add to our understanding?

KEY POINT 3.6

Integral Test

Given a positive decreasing function $f(x)$, $x \geq 1$,

if $\int_1^\infty f(x)\,dx$ is:

• convergent then $\sum_{k=1}^{\infty} f(k)$ is convergent

• divergent then $\sum_{k=1}^{\infty} f(k)$ is divergent.

The following example of the use of the Integral Test resembles closely the method of Worked example 2.5 when we examined the convergence of the improper integral $\int_1^\infty x^p\,dx$.

Determine for which values of p the series $\displaystyle\sum_{k=1}^{\infty} k^p$ converges.

We note that when $p \geq 0$ it looks like the series must be divergent so use the Divergence Test to confirm this

For $p > 0$

$$\lim_{k\to\infty} u_k = \lim_{k\to\infty} k^p = \infty \neq 0$$

For $p = 0$

$$\lim_{k\to\infty} u_k = \lim_{k\to\infty} 1 = 1 \neq 0$$

In both cases the series diverges by the Divergence Test.

Now we turn our attention to $p < 0$. We see that k^p is positive and decreasing for $k > 1$ so we can use the Integral Test. We realise that there will be two different cases: if $p = -1$ we need to integrate with $\ln x$

$$\int_1^{\infty} x^p \, dx = \lim_{b\to\infty} \int_1^{b} x^p \, dx$$

$$= \begin{cases} \lim_{b\to\infty} \left[\dfrac{x^{p+1}}{p+1} \right]_1^b & \text{if } p \neq -1 \\[2mm] \lim_{b\to\infty} \left[\ln x \right]_1^b & \text{if } p = -1 \end{cases}$$

$$= \begin{cases} \lim_{b\to\infty} \left(\dfrac{b^{p+1} - 1}{p+1} \right) & \text{if } p \neq -1 \\[2mm] \lim_{b\to\infty} \ln b & \text{if } p \neq -1 \end{cases}$$

At this stage we can see that the case $p \neq -1$ needs to be split into two separate cases. When $p + 1 > 0$, $b^{p+1} \to \infty$ but when $p + 1 < 0$, $b^{p+1} \to 0$

$$= \begin{cases} \infty & \text{if } -1 < p < 0 \\[2mm] -\dfrac{1}{p+1} & \text{if } p < -1 \\[2mm] \infty & \text{if } p = -1 \end{cases}$$

$\therefore$ by the Integral Test $\displaystyle\sum_{k=1}^{\infty} k^p$ is:

- divergent for $-1 \leq p < 0$
- convergent for $p < -1$

So, $\displaystyle\sum_{k=1}^{\infty} k^p$ is convergent only when $p < -1$ or equivalently,

$$\sum_{k=1}^{\infty} \frac{1}{k^p}$$

is convergent only when $p > 1$.

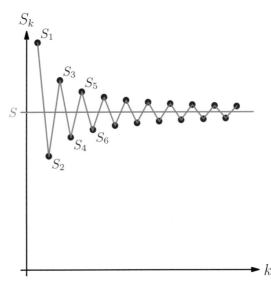

EXAM HINT

The result for convergence of the p-series is very useful and will often be used in conjunction with other tests such as the Comparison Test to establish the convergence (or otherwise) of a number of other series.

The series $\displaystyle\sum_{k=1}^{\infty} \frac{1}{k^p}$ will be referred to as the **p-series**. When $p = 1$ this is the **harmonic series**.

Alternating series

We have just seen that the harmonic series $\displaystyle\sum_{k=1}^{\infty} \frac{1}{k}$ diverges, but what about the same series with alternating positive and negative terms?

$$\sum_{k=1}^{\infty} (-1)^{k+1} \frac{1}{k} = 1 - \frac{1}{2} + \frac{1}{3} - \frac{1}{4} + \cdots$$

It certainly has a greater chance of being convergent due to the negative terms but we cannot use any of the tests we have seen thus far as these all require positive terms. Any series with alternately positive and negative signs is known as an **alternating series**. The following result allows us to analyse the convergence of this kind of series.

KEY POINT 3.7

Alternating Series Test

If for an alternating series $\displaystyle\sum_{k=1}^{\infty} u_k$:

- $|u_{k+1}| < |u_k|$ for sufficiently large k

- $\displaystyle\lim_{k \to \infty} |u_k| = 0$

then the series is convergent.

The fact that the magnitude of each u_k is decreasing to 0 (while the signs are alternately positive and negative) means that the sequence of partial sums S_k alternates either side of its eventual limit:

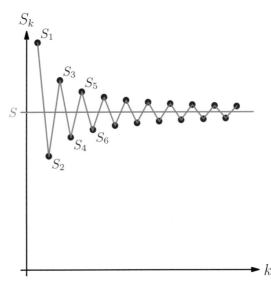

In the case of our alternating harmonic series (in Worked example 3.6 below we will show this is convergent by the Alternating Series Test) we have the first few partial sums:

$$S_1 = 1 > S$$

$$S_2 = 1 - \frac{1}{2} = \frac{1}{2} < S$$

$$S_3 = 1 - \frac{1}{2} + \frac{1}{3} = \frac{5}{6} > S$$

$$S_4 = 1 - \frac{1}{2} + \frac{1}{3} - \frac{1}{4} = \frac{7}{12} < S$$

▷ *In fact $S = \ln 2$ and while we will not be required to find this exactly, we can approximate the limit using ▷ Key point 3.8.*

It is stated in the conditions of the Alternating Series Test that $|u_{k+1}| < |u_k|$ for sufficiently large k. This does not actually need to be true for all $k \in \mathbb{Z}^+$ (although it often will be) as we will just have some finite sum from the finitely many terms before this situation occurs. This clearly does not affect the convergence of the series.

EXAM HINT

Alternating positive and negative terms are usually generated by $(-1)^k$ but you may also see $\cos(kx)$ used for the same purpose.

Worked example 3.6

Determine whether $\displaystyle\sum_{k=1}^{\infty}(-1)^{k+1}\frac{1}{k}$ is convergent.

Establish expressions for u_k and u_{k+1} in readiness to apply the Alternating Series Test

$$|u_k| = \frac{1}{k} \text{ and } |u_{k+1}| = \frac{1}{k+1}$$

We now need to check that the conditions of the test are satisfied

$$0 < \frac{1}{k+1} < \frac{1}{k} \quad \text{for all } k \in \mathbb{Z}^+$$

i.e. $\quad |u_{k+1}| < |u_k| \quad$ for all $k \in \mathbb{Z}^+$

and $\quad \displaystyle\lim_{k \to \infty}|u_k| = \lim_{k \to \infty}\frac{1}{k} = 0$

Therefore, by the Alternating Series Test

$\displaystyle\sum_{k=1}^{\infty}(-1)^{k+1}\frac{1}{k}$ is convergent.

Once we know we have a convergent alternating series, we can go on to think about an approximation for the limit.

If we were to stop, or truncate, the series at the nth partial sum, how accurate would this approximation be to the true limit S? The distance between the nth partial sum and S, $|S - S_n|$, known as the **truncation error**, is less than the distance between the $(n + 1)$th partial sum and the nth partial sum $|S_{n+1} - S_n|$.

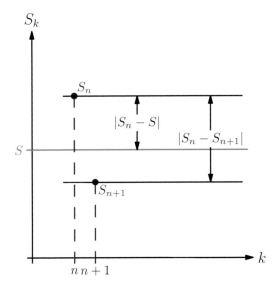

But

$$S_{n+1} - S_n = \left(u_1 + u_2 + \cdots + u_n + u_{n+1}\right) - \left(u_1 + u_2 + \cdots + u_n\right) = u_{n+1}$$

and therefore:

$$|S - S_n| < |S_{n+1} - S_n| = |u_{n+1}|$$

That is, we have the following:

KEY POINT 3.8

If $S = \displaystyle\sum_{k=1}^{\infty} u_k$ is the sum of an alternating series that satisfies:

- $|u_{k+1}| < |u_k|$ for all $k \in \mathbb{Z}^+$
- $\displaystyle\lim_{k \to \infty} |u_k| = 0$

then the error in taking the first n terms as an approximation to S (the truncation error) is less than the absolute value of the $(n + 1)$th term:

$$|S - S_n| < |u_{n+1}|$$

For example, taking the first 9 terms of our alternating harmonic series will give an error of less than the 10th term for an approximation of the limit:

$$|S - S_9| < |u_{10}| = \left| -\frac{1}{10} \right| = 0.1$$

If we increase the number of terms in our approximation to 99, the error is less than $\dfrac{1}{100} = 0.01$.

Worked example 3.7

How many terms of the series $\sum_{k=1}^{\infty}(-1)^{k-1}\dfrac{1}{k^2}$
is it necessary to take to find an approximation that is accurate to within 0.001?

First see what this series actually is:

$$\sum_{k=1}^{\infty}(-1)^{k-1}\dfrac{1}{k^2} = 1 - \dfrac{1}{2^2} + \dfrac{1}{3^2} - \dfrac{1}{4^2} + \cdots$$

$\sum_{k=1}^{\infty}(-1)^{k-1}\dfrac{1}{k^2}$ is an alternating series with

$$|u_{k+1}| = \dfrac{1}{(k+1)^2} < \dfrac{1}{k^2} = |u_k|$$

and $\lim_{k\to\infty}|u_k| = \lim_{k\to\infty}\dfrac{1}{k^2} = 0$

So, we have an alternating series and can consider using the previous result if the conditions are satisfied

Therefore, by the Alternating Series Test

$$\sum_{k=1}^{\infty}(-1)^{k-1}\dfrac{1}{k^2} \text{ converges to } S$$

Use Key point 3.8 to find an expression for the truncation error

The truncation error of using the first n terms to approximate S satisfies

$$|S - S_n| < |u_{n+1}| = \dfrac{1}{(n+1)^2}$$

We need the error to be less than 0.001

We therefore require

$$\dfrac{1}{(n+1)^2} < 0.001$$

$$\Rightarrow (n+1)^2 > 1000$$

$$\Rightarrow \quad n > \sqrt{1000} - 1$$

$$= 30.62$$

Therefore, we need to take 31 terms.

Absolute and conditional convergence

We have seen that the harmonic series

$$\sum_{k=1}^{\infty}\dfrac{1}{k} = 1 + \dfrac{1}{2} + \dfrac{1}{3} + \dfrac{1}{4} + \dfrac{1}{5} + \cdots$$

diverges, while the alternating version of the series

$$\sum_{k=1}^{\infty}(-1)^{k-1}\dfrac{1}{k} = 1 - \dfrac{1}{2} + \dfrac{1}{3} - \dfrac{1}{4} + \dfrac{1}{5} - \cdots$$

converges.

Series like this that only become convergent when some of their terms are negative are known as **conditionally convergent**,

whereas those such as $\sum_{k=1}^{\infty}\dfrac{1}{k^2} = 1 + \dfrac{1}{2^2} + \dfrac{1}{3^2} + \dfrac{1}{4^2} + \dfrac{1}{5^2} + \cdots$

which are convergent already before making any of the terms negative, are known as **absolutely convergent**.

KEY POINT 3.9

A series $\sum_{k=1}^{\infty} u_k$ is absolutely convergent if the series $\sum_{k=1}^{\infty} |u_k|$ is convergent.

If a series $\sum_{k=1}^{\infty} u_k$ is convergent but $\sum_{k=1}^{\infty} |u_k|$ is divergent, then the series is conditionally convergent.

If $u_k \geq 0$ for all k then absolute convergence and convergence are the same thing.

We also have the analogous result to that for improper integrals in chapter 2 of this option (Key point 2.4).

KEY POINT 3.10

If a series is absolutely convergent, then it is convergent, i.e.

if $\sum_{k=1}^{\infty} |u_k|$ is convergent then so is $\sum_{k=1}^{\infty} u_k$

This result follows immediately from the Comparison Test, as clearly $u_k \leq |u_k|$ for all $k \in \mathbb{Z}^+$.

While this might not seem that useful, it can allow us to establish the convergence of some series with terms that are not all positive but which are *not* alternating series either.

Worked example 3.8

Show that $\displaystyle\sum_{k=1}^{\infty} \frac{\sin k}{k^2}$ is convergent.

We note that this is not a series with only positive terms or an alternating series as the terms are not alternately positive and negative:

$$\sum_{k=1}^{\infty} \frac{\sin k}{k^2} = 0.841 + 0.227 + 0.0156 - 0.0473 + \cdots$$

In order to prove convergence, we are therefore hoping that it is absolutely convergent (and therefore convergent)

$$|u_k| = \left| \frac{\sin k}{k^2} \right|$$

continued . . .

In reviewing the other tests at our disposal now that we have taken the modulus and therefore have all positive terms, we recognise that the convergent series $\sum_{k=1}^{\infty} \frac{1}{k^2}$ would be suitable for use with the Comparison Test

$\therefore |u_k| \leq \frac{1}{k^2}$ (since $|\sin k| \leq 1$)

and as $\sum_{k=1}^{\infty} \frac{1}{k^2}$ is convergent, by the

Comparison Test so is $\sum_{k=1}^{\infty} \left| \frac{\sin k}{k^2} \right|$.

Finally, since $\sum_{k=1}^{\infty} \frac{\sin k}{k^2}$ has been shown to be absolutely convergent, it is also convergent.

Why does it matter whether a series is absolutely convergent or conditionally convergent?

The answer is that for absolutely convergent series we can re-order the terms in any way we like without affecting the sum (in just the same way that we could for any finite series). But, surprisingly, we cannot do this for conditionally convergent series; that is, different arrangements of the same terms of a conditionally convergent series can result in different values for the sum of the series!

For example, consider the conditionally convergent series

$\sum_{k=1}^{\infty} (-1)^{k+1} \frac{1}{k}$ again and let $S \neq 0$ be its sum, i.e.

$$S = 1 - \frac{1}{2} + \frac{1}{3} - \frac{1}{4} + \frac{1}{5} - \frac{1}{6} + \frac{1}{7} - \frac{1}{8} + \cdots$$

And then consider the following rearrangement of the terms into a pattern that ensures each occurs still just the once and with the correct sign:

$$\left(1 - \frac{1}{2}\right) - \frac{1}{4} + \left(\frac{1}{3} - \frac{1}{6}\right) - \frac{1}{8} + \left(\frac{1}{5} - \frac{1}{10}\right) - \frac{1}{12} + \left(\frac{1}{7} - \frac{1}{14}\right) - \frac{1}{16} + \cdots$$

$$= \frac{1}{2} - \frac{1}{4} + \frac{1}{6} - \frac{1}{8} + \frac{1}{10} - \frac{1}{12} + \frac{1}{14} - \frac{1}{16} + \cdots$$

$$= \frac{1}{2}\left(1 - \frac{1}{2} + \frac{1}{3} - \frac{1}{4} + \frac{1}{5} - \frac{1}{6} + \frac{1}{7} - \frac{1}{8} + \cdots\right)$$

$$= \frac{1}{2}S$$

Thus, since $S \neq 0$, we have a different value for the sum depending on how we choose to order the terms, which is clearly absurd; hence we cannot re-order the terms of a conditionally convergent series.

The case where the Ratio Test is inconclusive will be examined in more detail in the next section. When this occurs you will have to resort to one of the other tests to determine convergence/divergence.

▷ ▷

EXAM HINT

The Ratio Test is often useful when the u_k involves $k!$ or a^k.

Ratio Test

The final test for convergence is particularly useful and will be central in our study of power series in the next section.

KEY POINT 3.11

Ratio Test

Given a series $\sum_{k=1}^{\infty} u_k$, if:

- $\lim\limits_{k\to\infty}\left|\dfrac{u_{k+1}}{u_k}\right| < 1$, then the series is absolutely convergent

  (and hence convergent)

- $\lim\limits_{k\to\infty}\left|\dfrac{u_{k+1}}{u_k}\right| > 1$, then the series is divergent

- $\lim\limits_{k\to\infty}\left|\dfrac{u_{k+1}}{u_k}\right| = 1$, then the Ratio Test is inconclusive.

Worked example 3.9

Using the Ratio Test, establish whether or not the following series converge (absolutely):

(a) $\displaystyle\sum_{k=1}^{\infty} \frac{(-3)^k k^{10}}{10^k}$

(b) $\displaystyle\sum_{k=1}^{\infty} (-1)^{k+1} \frac{k!}{k^k}$

(c) $\displaystyle\sum_{k=1}^{\infty} \frac{(2k)!}{(k!)^2}$

In part (b) you may assume that $\lim\limits_{n\to\infty}\left(1+\dfrac{1}{n}\right)^n = e$

Establish expressions for u_k and u_{k+1} in readiness to apply the Ratio Test

(a) $a_k = \dfrac{(-3)^k k^{10}}{10^k}$ and

$$a_{k+1} = \frac{(-3)^{k+1}(k+1)^{10}}{10^{k+1}}$$

Find $\left|\dfrac{u_{k+1}}{u_k}\right|$ ensuring that the expression is rearranged into a convenient form to enable the limit to be found

So,

$$\left|\frac{u_{k+1}}{u_k}\right| = \left|\frac{(-3)^{k+1}(k+1)^{10}}{10^{k+1}} \times \frac{10^k}{(-3)^k k^{10}}\right|$$

$$= \left|\frac{(-3)^{k+1}(k+1)^{10}}{(-3)^k k^{10}} \times \frac{10^k}{10^{k+1}}\right|$$

$$= \left|-3\left(\frac{k+1}{k}\right)^{10} \times \frac{1}{10}\right|$$

$$= \frac{3}{10}\left(\frac{k+1}{k}\right)^{10}$$

$$= \frac{3}{10}\left(\frac{1+\dfrac{1}{k}}{1}\right)^{10}$$

continued . . .

Take the limit as $k \rightarrow \infty$ and compare with the criteria of the Ratio Test

Hence,

$$\lim_{k \to \infty} \left| \frac{u_{k+1}}{u_k} \right| = \frac{3}{10} \left(\frac{1+0}{1} \right)^{10} = \frac{3}{10} < 1$$

Therefore by the Ratio Test the series converges absolutely.

Establish expressions for u_k and u_{k+1} to apply the Ratio Test

(b) $u_k = \dfrac{k!}{k^k}$ and $u_{k+1} = \dfrac{(k+1)!}{(k+1)^{k+1}}$

Find $\left| \dfrac{u_{k+1}}{u_k} \right|$ ensuring that the expression is rearranged into a convenient form to enable the limit to be found

So,

$$\left| \frac{u_{k+1}}{u_k} \right| = \left| \frac{(k+1)!}{(k+1)^{k+1}} \times \frac{k^k}{k!} \right|$$

$$= \frac{(k+1)!}{k!} \times \frac{k^k}{(k+1)^{k+1}}$$

$$= (k+1) \times \left(\frac{k}{k+1} \right)^k \times \frac{1}{k+1}$$

$$= \left(\frac{k}{k+1} \right)^k$$

$$= \frac{1}{\left(1 + \dfrac{1}{k} \right)^k}$$

We are given in the question that

$$\lim_{k \to \infty} \left(1 + \frac{1}{k} \right)^k = e$$

Hence,

$$\lim_{k \to \infty} \left| \frac{u_{k+1}}{u_k} \right| = \frac{1}{e} < 1$$

Therefore by the Ratio Test the series converges absolutely.

Establish expressions for u_k and u_{k+1} in readiness to apply the Ratio Test

(c) $u_k = \dfrac{(2k)!}{(k!)^2}$ and $u_{k+1} = \dfrac{(2(k+1))!}{((k+1)!)^2}$

Find $\dfrac{u_{k+1}}{u_k}$ ensuring that the expression is rearranged into a convenient form to enable the limit to be found.
Note that as all the terms are positive there is no need for the modulus sign

So, $\dfrac{u_{k+1}}{u_k} = \dfrac{(2(k+1))!}{((k+1)!)^2} \times \dfrac{(k!)^2}{(2k)!}$

$$= \frac{(2(k+1))!}{(2k)!} \times \left(\frac{k!}{(k+1)!} \right)^2$$

$$= \frac{(2k+2)(2k+1)}{(k+1)^2}$$

$$= \frac{4k^2 + 6k + 2}{k^2 + 2k + 1}$$

$$= \frac{4 + \dfrac{6}{k} + \dfrac{2}{k^2}}{1 + \dfrac{2}{k} + \dfrac{1}{k^2}}$$

Take the limit as $k \rightarrow \infty$ and compare with the criteria of the Ratio Test

Hence, $\displaystyle \lim_{k \to \infty} \frac{u_{k+1}}{u_k} = 4 > 1$

Therefore by the Ratio Test the series diverges.

The result $\lim_{n\to\infty}\left(1+\dfrac{1}{n}\right)^n$, used in Worked example 3.9, was established in Exercise 1B, question 7.

Exercise 3B

1. Show that the following converge using the Comparison Test:

(a) (i) $\displaystyle\sum_{k=1}^{\infty}\frac{1}{k^2+5}$ (ii) $\displaystyle\sum_{k=1}^{\infty}\frac{1}{k(k+3)}$

(b) (i) $\displaystyle\sum_{k=1}^{\infty}\frac{\sqrt{k}}{k^2+1}$ (ii) $\displaystyle\sum_{k=1}^{\infty}\frac{k}{k^4+2k+4}$

(c) (i) $\displaystyle\sum_{k=3}^{\infty}\frac{k-2}{k^3+3}$ (ii) $\displaystyle\sum_{k=2}^{\infty}\frac{\sqrt{k-1}}{k^2+3k+5}$

(d) (i) $\displaystyle\sum_{k=1}^{\infty}\frac{1}{k^k}$ (ii) $\displaystyle\sum_{k=1}^{\infty}\frac{1}{k!}$

(e) (i) $\displaystyle\sum_{k=1}^{\infty}\frac{2^k+3^k}{4^k+5^k}$ (ii) $\displaystyle\sum_{k=1}^{\infty}\frac{2^k}{e^{2k}}$

(f) (i) $\displaystyle\sum_{k=1}^{\infty}\frac{\cos^2 k}{k^2}$ (ii) $\displaystyle\sum_{k=1}^{\infty}\frac{|\sin k|}{k^2+2}$

2. Show that the following diverge using the Comparison Test or Divergence Test:

(a) (i) $\displaystyle\sum_{k=4}^{\infty}\frac{1}{k-3}$ (ii) $\displaystyle\sum_{k=2}^{\infty}\frac{1}{\sqrt{k-1}}$

(b) (i) $\displaystyle\sum_{k=1}^{\infty}\frac{k^2}{2k^2+7k+4}$ (ii) $\displaystyle\sum_{k=1}^{\infty}\frac{3k+2}{2k+1}$

(c) (i) $\displaystyle\sum_{k=2}^{\infty}\frac{k+1}{\sqrt{k^4-2}}$ (ii) $\displaystyle\sum_{k=2}^{\infty}\frac{k^2+3}{k^3-2}$

(d) (i) $\displaystyle\sum_{k=1}^{\infty}\frac{4^{k+2}}{3^k}$ (ii) $\displaystyle\sum_{k=1}^{\infty}\frac{(\pi+k)^{k+1}}{3^k}$

(e) (i) $\displaystyle\sum_{k=1}^{\infty}\frac{\sqrt{k^2+1}}{k}$ (ii) $\displaystyle\sum_{k=1}^{\infty}\frac{\sqrt{k^4+1}}{k}$

(f) (i) $\displaystyle\sum_{k=1}^{\infty}\left(\frac{x+k}{k}\right)^k$ (ii) $\displaystyle\sum_{k=1}^{\infty}\left(\frac{k}{x+k}\right)^k$

3. Determine whether the following converge or diverge using the Limit Comparison Test.

(a) (i) $\displaystyle\sum_{k=2}^{\infty}\frac{4}{k^3-2}$ (ii) $\displaystyle\sum_{k=1}^{\infty}\frac{1}{k+3}$

(b) (i) $\displaystyle\sum_{k=1}^{\infty}\frac{1}{5^k-4}$ (ii) $\displaystyle\sum_{k=1}^{\infty}\frac{2^k}{3^k-1}$

(c) (i) $\displaystyle\sum_{k=1}^{\infty}\frac{1}{2k+\sqrt{k}+3}$ (ii) $\displaystyle\sum_{k=2}^{\infty}\frac{1}{4k^2-k-1}$

> **EXAM HINT**
>
> If a question in the exam requires use of $\lim_{n\to\infty}\left(1+\dfrac{1}{n}\right)^n = e$, you will be given this – you are not expected to know it. However, this limit will be used occasionally in this exercise, so look out for it!

(d) (i) $\displaystyle\sum_{k=2}^{\infty} \frac{k^2+5}{k^4-2}$ (ii) $\displaystyle\sum_{k=1}^{\infty} \frac{4k^2-k+5}{k^5+k^4+2k-2}$

(e) (i) $\displaystyle\sum_{k=1}^{\infty} \frac{4k^2-3k}{\sqrt{3+k^5}}$ (ii) $\displaystyle\sum_{k=1}^{\infty} \frac{3k+2}{\sqrt[3]{4k^7-3}}$

4. Using the Integral Test, determine whether the following converge or diverge.

(a) (i) $\displaystyle\sum_{k=1}^{\infty} \frac{1}{k+2}$ (ii) $\displaystyle\sum_{k=1}^{\infty} \frac{1}{\sqrt[3]{k+3}}$

(b) (i) $\displaystyle\sum_{k=4}^{\infty} \frac{k}{\left(k^2+9\right)^{\frac{3}{2}}}$ (ii) $\displaystyle\sum_{k=4}^{\infty} \frac{k}{k^2+9}$

(c) (i) $\displaystyle\sum_{k=1}^{\infty} \frac{1}{k^2+1}$ (ii) $\displaystyle\sum_{k=1}^{\infty} \frac{3}{2k^2+5}$

(d) (i) $\displaystyle\sum_{k=1}^{\infty} \frac{1}{k^2}\cos\left(\frac{1}{k}\right)$ (ii) $\displaystyle\sum_{k=1}^{\infty} \frac{1}{k^3}\sin\left(\frac{1}{k^2}\right)$

(e) (i) $\displaystyle\sum_{k=2}^{\infty} \frac{\ln k}{k}$ (ii) $\displaystyle\sum_{k=1}^{\infty} ke^{-k^2}$

5. Use the Alternating Series Test to determine whether the following series converge or not. Where they do, find an upper bound (to 3SF) on the error in taking the first 10 terms of the series as an approximation.

(a) (i) $\displaystyle\sum_{k=1}^{\infty} \frac{(-1)^{k+1}}{k^{\frac{2}{3}}}$ (ii) $\displaystyle\sum_{k=1}^{\infty} \frac{(-1)^k}{\sqrt{k}}$

(b) (i) $\displaystyle\sum_{k=1}^{\infty} (-1)^k \frac{2k+3}{3k+4}$ (ii) $\displaystyle\sum_{k=1}^{\infty} (-1)^{k+1} \frac{k-1}{k}$

(c) (i) $\displaystyle\sum_{k=2}^{\infty} \frac{(-2)^k}{3^k}$ (ii) $\displaystyle\sum_{k=2}^{\infty} \frac{(-3)^k}{2^k}$

(d) (i) $\displaystyle\sum_{k=2}^{\infty} \frac{\cos(k\pi)}{\ln k}$ (ii) $\displaystyle\sum_{k=1}^{\infty} \frac{\cos(k\pi)k}{k!}$

(e) (i) $\displaystyle\sum_{k=1}^{\infty} \frac{(-k)^{k+1}}{k^2}$ (ii) $\displaystyle\sum_{k=1}^{\infty} \frac{(-k)^{k+1}}{k^{3k}}$

6. Determine whether the following converge absolutely, conditionally or diverge.

(a) (i) $\displaystyle\sum_{k=1}^{\infty} \frac{\cos k}{k^2}$ (ii) $\displaystyle\sum_{k=1}^{\infty} \frac{\sin k}{k^3+1}$

(b) (i) $\displaystyle\sum_{k=1}^{\infty} (-1)^{k+1} \frac{k}{2k+1}$ (ii) $\displaystyle\sum_{k=1}^{\infty} (-1)^k \frac{4k^2+3}{3k-1}$

(c) (i) $\displaystyle\sum_{k=2}^{\infty} \frac{(-1)^k k}{k^2+1}$ (ii) $\displaystyle\sum_{k=2}^{\infty} \frac{(-1)^k}{k^2-1}$

(d) (i) $\displaystyle\sum_{k=1}^{\infty} \frac{\cos(k\pi)}{\sqrt{k}+3k-1}$ (ii) $\displaystyle\sum_{k=1}^{\infty} \frac{(-1)^k}{\sqrt[4]{k^2+2k+1}}$

(e) (i) $\displaystyle\sum_{k=1}^{\infty} \frac{(-2)^{k+1}}{(2k+1)!}$ (ii) $\displaystyle\sum_{k=2}^{\infty} (-1)^k \frac{k^4}{e^k}$

7. Use the Ratio Test to establish whether the following series converge or diverge.

(a) (i) $\displaystyle\sum_{k=0}^{\infty}\frac{1}{(2k+1)!}$ (ii) $\displaystyle\sum_{k=1}^{\infty}\frac{k!}{\sqrt{k!}}$

(b) (i) $\displaystyle\sum_{k=1}^{\infty}\frac{k!}{k^2 e^k}$ (ii) $\displaystyle\sum_{k=1}^{\infty}\frac{k^4}{2^k}$

(c) (i) $\displaystyle\sum_{k=1}^{\infty}\frac{(2k)!}{(k!)^3}$ (ii) $\displaystyle\sum_{k=1}^{\infty}\frac{2^k}{k!}$

(d) (i) $\displaystyle\sum_{k=1}^{\infty}\frac{(2k)!}{k^k}$ (ii) $\displaystyle\sum_{k=1}^{\infty}\frac{2^k k!}{k^k}$

(e) (i) $\displaystyle\sum_{k=1}^{\infty}\frac{2^k+5}{3^k}$ (ii) $\displaystyle\sum_{k=1}^{\infty}\frac{k3^k}{k+4}$

8. Determine whether each of the following series converges or diverges.

(a) $\displaystyle\sum_{k=1}^{\infty}\frac{k+1}{k^2+2}$ (b) $\displaystyle\sum_{k=1}^{\infty}\frac{\arctan k}{\sqrt{k^5+3}}$

(c) $\displaystyle\sum_{k=1}^{\infty}(-1)^{k+1}\frac{k^2}{k^3+1}$ *[8 marks]*

9. (a) Find the values of x for which

$$x^{\ln x} \geq x^2$$

(b) Determine whether the series

$$\sum_{k=1}^{\infty}\frac{1}{k^{\ln k}}$$ *[5 marks]*

converges or diverges.

10. Determine whether the series

$$\sum_{k=1}^{\infty}\frac{\cos(k\pi)4^k}{k!}$$

diverges, converges conditionally or converges absolutely.
    [6 marks]

11. (a) Show that the series

$$\sum_{k=1}^{\infty}\frac{(-1)^k}{(k!)^2}$$

converges.

(b) Determine how many terms of the series need be taken to approximate the sum to within $\dfrac{1}{1000}$.   *[6 marks]*

12. Determine whether the following series converge or diverge, clearly stating your reasoning.

(a) $\displaystyle\sum_{k=1}^{\infty}\left\{\sqrt{k^3+1}-\sqrt{k^3-1}\right\}$

(b) $\displaystyle\sum_{k=0}^{\infty}(-1)^k\frac{(2k)!}{3^k k!}$ *[9 marks]*

13. (a) Show that the series

$$\sum_{k=1}^{\infty} \frac{k-1}{k!}$$

is convergent.

(b) Find the sum of the series. *[7 marks]*

14. (a) Show that the sequence with general term

$$u_k = \frac{4k^2}{k^3 + 9}$$

is decreasing for $k > n$ stating the value of the integer n.

(b) Show that the series

$$\sum_{k=1}^{\infty} (-1)^{k+1} \frac{4k^2}{k^3 + 9}$$

converges.

(c) Determine whether this convergence is conditional or absolute. *[8 marks]*

15. For the series

$$\sum_{k=1}^{\infty} \frac{(3k)!}{(k!)^3 c^k} \qquad c > 0$$

determine for which values of the constant c the Ratio Test gives convergence. *[7 marks]*

16. Show that the series

$$\sum_{k=2}^{\infty} \frac{\sin k}{\sqrt{k^3 - 1}}$$

converges. *[6 marks]*

17. (a) Given a positive, decreasing function $f(x)$ for all $x \geq 1$,

write down the upper and lower sums for $\int_n^{\infty} f(x)\,dx$.

(b) Hence give an upper bound for the error in using the *n*th

partial sum as an approximation to $\sum_{k=1}^{\infty} f(k)$.

(c) Find an upper bound on the error in using the 5th partial

sum to estimate $\sum_{k=1}^{\infty} \frac{1}{k^5}$.

(d) How many terms of the series is it necessary to take to

approximate $\sum_{k=1}^{\infty} \frac{1}{k^5}$ within 10^{-6}? *[9 marks]*

18. (a) Show that

$$\sum_{k=1}^{\infty} \frac{4^{k+1}}{(3k+1)!}$$

converges.

(b) Test for convergence:

$$\sum_{k=1}^{\infty} \frac{(3k)! + 4^{k+1}}{(3k+1)!} \qquad \text{[10 marks]}$$

19. (a) For the series

$$\sum_{k=2}^{\infty} \frac{1}{k(\ln k)^a}$$

determine for which values a the series converges and for which it diverges.

(b) Determine whether the following converge or diverge. If they converge state whether convergence is conditional or absolute.

(i) $\displaystyle\sum_{k=2}^{\infty} \frac{(-1)^k}{k \ln k}$ (ii) $\displaystyle\sum_{k=2}^{\infty} \frac{(-1)^k}{k(\ln k)^2}$ *[12 marks]*

20. Show that if $\displaystyle\sum_{k=1}^{\infty} a_k$ is absolutely convergent, then

$$\sum_{k=1}^{\infty}\left(a_k + |a_k|\right) \text{ is convergent.}$$ *[6 marks]*

21. Show that the Ratio Test is inconclusive for

$$\sum_{k=1}^{\infty} \frac{1\times3\times5\times\ldots\times(2k-1)}{4\times6\times8\times\ldots\times(2k+2)}$$ *[5 marks]*

We can think of a power series as a function of x. We will see in the next ▷ *chapter that power* ▷ *series are used to represent a wide variety of common functions.*

3C Power series

In this chapter so far, we have seen infinite series generated by substituting positive integers into a general term; when such a series has been convergent, the sum has been a number. Now we will consider series whose terms also include powers of a variable $x \in \mathbb{R}$; if convergent, the value of the sum will therefore depend on x.

KEY POINT 3.12

A **power series** is an infinite series of the form:

$$\sum_{k=0}^{\infty} a_k (x-b)^k = a_0 + a_1(x-b) + a_2(x-b)^2 + a_3(x-b)^3 + \cdots$$

Often $b = 0$ and this reduces to

$$\sum_{k=0}^{\infty} a_k x^k = a_0 + a_1 x + a_2 x^2 + a_3 x^3 + \cdots$$

As for the other infinite series in this chapter, we would like to know when (for which values of x) a power series converges. We are certainly familiar with this in some cases already, for example the geometric series:

$$\sum_{k=0}^{\infty}(cx)^k = 1 + cx + c^2x^2 + c^3x^3 + \cdots \quad \text{for some constant } c \in \mathbb{R}$$

which we know to be convergent only when $|cx| < 1$, i.e.

when $-\dfrac{1}{c} < x < \dfrac{1}{c}$.

More generally, it may be the case that a power series,

$$\sum_{k=0}^{\infty} a_k(x-b)^k, \text{ converges:}$$

- for all $x \in \mathbb{R}$

- only for a single value $b \in \mathbb{R}$

- for all $x \in \mathbb{R}$ such that $|x-b| < R$, where $R \in \mathbb{R}^+$.

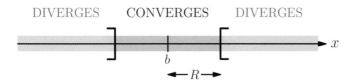

The latter is the case for our geometric series above, with $b = 0$

and $R = \dfrac{1}{c}$.

KEY POINT 3.13

The largest number $R \in \mathbb{R}^+$ such that a power series converges for $|x-b| < R$ and diverges for $|x-b| > R$ is called the **radius of convergence** of the power series. It may be determined by the Ratio Test. If:

- $R = \infty$ then the series converges for all $x \in \mathbb{R}$.

- $R = 0$ then the series converges only when $x = b$.

This is nearly a complete description of the range of values for which a power series will converge but since the Ratio Test does not help at the points $x = -R$ and $x = R$ we need to consider these separately each time.

KEY POINT 3.14

The **interval of convergence** of a power series is the set of all points for which the series converges. It always includes all points such that $|x-b| < R$ but may also include end point(s) of this interval.

For what values of x is $\displaystyle\sum_{k=0}^{\infty} \frac{(x-2)^k}{\sqrt{k+1}}$ convergent?

We start by applying the Ratio Test to find the radius of convergence

Let $u_k = \dfrac{(x-2)^k}{\sqrt{k+1}}$

Then $\left|\dfrac{u_{k+1}}{u_k}\right| = \left|\dfrac{(x-2)^{k+1}}{\sqrt{k+2}} \times \dfrac{\sqrt{k+1}}{(x-2)^k}\right|$

$= (x-2) \times \sqrt{\dfrac{k+1}{k+2}}$

$= (x-2) \times \sqrt{\dfrac{1+\dfrac{1}{k}}{1+\dfrac{2}{k}}}$

So, $\displaystyle\lim_{k\to\infty} \left|\dfrac{u_{k+1}}{u_k}\right| = |x-2|$

By the Ratio Test, $\displaystyle\sum_{k=0}^{\infty} u_k$ is convergent for

$|x-2| < 1$

$\Rightarrow 1 < x < 3$

We know that the Ratio Test is inconclusive when $|x-2|=1$, i.e. when $x=1$ and $x=3$, so we now need to examine these two possibilities separately

When $x = 1$:

$\displaystyle\sum_{k=0}^{\infty} u_k = \sum_{k=0}^{\infty} \frac{(-1)^k}{\sqrt{k+1}}$

We have an alternating series, so we hope this will be convergent by the Alternating Series Test

This is an alternating series with:

$|u_{k+1}| = \left|\dfrac{(-1)^{k+1}}{\sqrt{k+2}}\right|$

$= \dfrac{1}{\sqrt{k+2}}$

$< \dfrac{1}{\sqrt{k+1}} = |u_k|$

Apply result that $\dfrac{1}{\infty} = 0$

and $\displaystyle\lim_{k\to\infty} |u_k| = \lim_{k\to\infty} \frac{1}{\sqrt{k+1}} = 0$

Therefore, it is convergent by the Alternating Series Test.

Now consider what happens to the power series when $x = 3$

When $x = 3$:

$\displaystyle\sum_{k=0}^{\infty} u_k = \sum_{k=0}^{\infty} \frac{1}{\sqrt{k+1}}$

continued . . .

This is very similar to the *p*-series with $p = \dfrac{1}{2}$. We know $\displaystyle\sum_{k=1}^{\infty} \dfrac{1}{p^{\frac{1}{2}}}$ is divergent and so would like to show that each term of our series is larger than each corresponding term of this *p*-series, therefore making our series divergent by the Comparison Test. However, each term of our series is actually smaller than that of the *p*-series. We therefore attempt to use the Limit Comparison Test

Apply algebra of limits

Put this information together with that from the radius of convergence

---

Let $u_k = \dfrac{1}{\sqrt{k+1}}$ and $v_k = \dfrac{1}{\sqrt{k}}$

Then

$$\lim_{k \to \infty} \frac{u_k}{v_k} = \lim_{k \to \infty}\left(\frac{1}{\sqrt{k+1}} \times \frac{\sqrt{k}}{1} \right)$$

$$= \lim_{k \to \infty} \sqrt{\frac{k}{k+1}}$$

$$= \lim_{k \to \infty} \sqrt{\frac{1}{1 + \frac{1}{k}}}$$

$$= \sqrt{\frac{1}{1 + 0}} = 1 > 0$$

Therefore, by the Limit Comparison Test,

since $\displaystyle\sum_{k=1}^{\infty} \dfrac{1}{\sqrt{k}}$ diverges, so does $\displaystyle\sum_{k=1}^{\infty} \dfrac{1}{\sqrt{k+1}}$

So, the series is convergent for $1 \le x < 3$

Why then is it so important to know the interval of convergence of a power series? In part, the answer to this is:

KEY POINT 3.15

A power series can be differentiated or integrated term by term over any interval contained within its interval of convergence (and possibly at the end points of the interval).

Outside of this interval we cannot differentiate or integrate in this way.

Worked example 3.11

Find an expression for $\displaystyle\int_{2}^{5/2} \sum_{k=0}^{\infty} \dfrac{(x-2)^k}{\sqrt{k+1}}\, dx$.

Since we established in Worked example 3.10 that the interval of convergence for this power series is [1, 3[and the interval over which we are asked to integrate here lies entirely within the interval of convergence, we are able to integrate term by term, i.e. pass the integral sign inside the sum

$$\int_{2}^{5/2} \sum_{k=0}^{\infty} \frac{(x-2)^k}{\sqrt{k+1}}\, dx = \sum_{k=0}^{\infty} \int_{2}^{5/2} \frac{(x-2)^k}{\sqrt{k+1}}\, dx$$

$$= \sum_{k=0}^{\infty} \left[\frac{(x-2)^{k+1}}{(k+1)\sqrt{k+1}} \right]_{2}^{5/2}$$

$$= \sum_{k=0}^{\infty} \frac{1}{(k+1)^{3/2}} \left(\left(\frac{5}{2} - 2\right)^{k+1} - 0 \right)$$

$$= \sum_{k=0}^{\infty} \frac{\left(\frac{1}{2}\right)^{k+1}}{(k+1)^{3/2}}$$

- An **alternating series** is one with alternately positive and negative terms.

- **Alternating Series Test**

   If for an alternating series $\sum_{k=1}^{\infty} u_k$:

   - $|u_{k+1}| < |u_k|$ for all $k \in \mathbb{Z}^+$ and $\lim_{k \to \infty} |u_k| = 0$

     then the series is convergent.

- If $S = \sum_{k=1}^{\infty} u_k$ is the sum of an alternating series that satisfies:

$$|u_{k+1}| < |u_k| \text{ for all } k \in \mathbb{Z}^+ \text{ and } \lim_{k \to \infty} |u_k| = 0$$

   then the error in taking the first n terms as an approximation to S (the **truncation error**) is less than the absolute value of the $(n + 1)$th term:

$$|S - S_n| < |u_{n+1}|$$

- A series $\sum_{k=1}^{\infty} u_k$ is **absolutely convergent** if the series $\sum_{k=1}^{\infty} |u_k|$ is convergent.

   If a series $\sum_{k=1}^{\infty} u_k$ is convergent but $\sum_{k=1}^{\infty} |u_k|$ is divergent, then the series is **conditionally convergent**.

   An absolutely convergent series is convergent.

- **Ratio Test**

   Given a series $\sum_{k=1}^{\infty} u_k$, if:

   - $\lim_{k \to \infty} \left| \dfrac{u_{k+1}}{u_k} \right| < 1$, then the series is absolutely convergent (and hence convergent).

   - $\lim_{k \to \infty} \left| \dfrac{u_{k+1}}{u_k} \right| > 1$, then the series is divergent.

   - $\lim_{k \to \infty} \left| \dfrac{u_{k+1}}{u_k} \right| = 1$, then the Ratio test is inconclusive.

- A **power series** is an infinite series of the form:

$$\sum_{k=0}^{\infty} a_k (x - b)^k = a_0 + a_1(x - b) + a_2(x - b)^2 + a_3(x - b)^3 + \cdots$$

   It may converge:

   - for all $x \in \mathbb{R}$

   - only for a single value $b \in \mathbb{R}$

   - for all $x \in \mathbb{R}$ such that $|x - b| < R$, where $R \in \mathbb{R}^+$.

- The largest number $R \in \mathbb{R}^+$ such that a power series converges for $|x - b| < R$ and diverges for $|x - b| > R$ is called the **radius of convergence** of the power series. It may be determined by the Ratio Test. If:

  - $R = \infty$ then the series converges for all $x \in \mathbb{R}$.

  - $R = 0$ then the series converges only when $x = b$.

- The **interval of convergence** of a power series is the set of all points for which the series converges. It always includes all points such that $|x - b| < R$ but may also include end point(s) of this interval.

  A power series can be differentiated or integrated term by term over any interval contained within its interval of convergence.

1. Establish whether the following converge or diverge:

(a) $\displaystyle\sum_{k=1}^{\infty} \frac{3k}{k^2 - 1}$

(b) $\displaystyle\sum_{k=1}^{\infty} \frac{5\sqrt{k} + 81}{3k^2\sqrt{k} + 7\sqrt{k}}$　　　　　　　　　*[7 marks]*

2. Find the radius of convergence of the following:

(a) $\displaystyle\sum_{k=0}^{\infty} \frac{k^3 x^k}{k!}$

(b) $\displaystyle\sum_{k=0}^{\infty} \frac{(k!)^2 x^{2k}}{(2k)!}$　　　　　　　　　*[6 marks]*

3. (a) Show that $f(x) = x^2 e^{-x}$ is decreasing for all $x > 2$.

(b) Determine whether

$$\sum_{k=2}^{\infty} k^2 e^{-k}$$

converges or diverges.　　　　　　　　　*[8 marks]*

4.

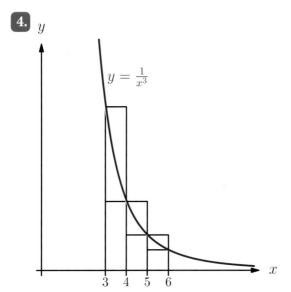

The diagram shows part of the graph of $y = \dfrac{1}{x^3}$ together with line segments parallel to the coordinate axes.

(a) Using the diagram show that,

$$\frac{1}{4^3} + \frac{1}{5^3} + \frac{1}{6^3} + \cdots < \int_3^{\infty} \frac{1}{x^3}\,dx < \frac{1}{3^3} + \frac{1}{4^3} + \frac{1}{5^3} + \cdots$$

(b) Hence find upper and lower bounds for the sum $\displaystyle\sum_{n=1}^{\infty} \frac{1}{n^3}$　　*[15 marks]*

(© *IB Organization 2008*)

5. Consider the sequence of partial sums $\{S_n\}$ given by

$$S_n = \sum_{k=1}^{n} \frac{1}{k}$$

(a) Show that for all positive integers n

$$S_{2n} \geq S_n + \frac{1}{2}$$

(b) Hence prove that the sequence $\{S_n\}$ is not convergent. *[7 marks]*

(© *IB Organization 2002*)

6. (a) Use the Integral Test to show that the series

$$S = 1 + \frac{1}{2^2} + \frac{1}{3^2} + \frac{1}{4^2} + \frac{1}{5^2} + \dots \text{ converges.}$$

(b) Let

$$A = 1 - \frac{1}{2^2} + \frac{1}{3^2} - \frac{1}{4^2} + \frac{1}{5^2} - \dots$$

Show that

$$S - A = 2\left(\frac{1}{2^2} + \frac{1}{4^2} + \frac{1}{6^2} + \dots \right)$$

(c) Hence find the sum A, given that S converges to $\frac{\pi^2}{6}$. *[9 marks]*

7. Determine whether $\displaystyle\sum_{k=1}^{\infty} x\left(\arctan x - \frac{\pi}{2} \right)$ converges or diverges. *[6 marks]*

8. (a) Show that, $\displaystyle\sum_{k=1}^{\infty} \frac{1}{k^2 + 5k + 6}$ converges.

(b) Show that $\dfrac{2}{k^2 + 5k + 6} = \dfrac{A}{k+2} - \dfrac{B}{k+3}$

where A and B are constants to be found.

(c) By writing down successive terms of the series,

$$\sum_{k=1}^{n} \left(\frac{A}{k+2} - \frac{B}{k+3} \right)$$

show that, $\displaystyle\sum_{k=1}^{n} \frac{2}{k^2 + 5k + 6} = \frac{2}{3} - \frac{2}{n+3}$

(d) Hence find,

$$\sum_{k=1}^{\infty} \frac{2}{k^2 + 5k + 6}$$

[11 marks]

9. Test the convergence or divergence of the following, explaining your reasoning fully.

(a) $\displaystyle\sum_{n=0}^{\infty}(-1)^{n}\frac{3^{n-2}}{e^{n}}$

(b) $\displaystyle\sum_{n=1}^{\infty}\frac{\cos(n\pi)}{\sqrt[3]{n}}$

(c) $\displaystyle\sum_{n=2}^{\infty}(-1)^{n-1}\frac{5}{n(\ln n)^{2}}$ *[13 marks]*

10. The coefficients of the power series $\displaystyle\sum_{k=0}^{\infty}a_{k}x^{k}$ satisfy the relation,

$$a_{k}+Aa_{k-1}+Ba_{k-2}=0, \text{ where } k=2,3,4,\ldots$$

(a) Show that for $|x|<R$, the radius of convergence,

$$\left(1+Ax+Bx^{2}\right)\sum_{k=0}^{\infty}a_{k}x^{k}=a_{0}+\left(a_{1}+Aa_{0}\right)x$$

(b) Hence establish that,

$$\sum_{k=0}^{n}x^{k}=\frac{1}{1-x} \quad \text{for } |x|<1$$ *[8 marks]*

11. Use the Ratio Test to determine whether or not

$$\sum_{k=1}^{\infty}\frac{k^{2}+3k+1}{3^{k}+2} \text{ is convergent.}$$ *[9 marks]*

12. (a) Find an expression for the nth partial sum of

$$\sum_{k=1}^{\infty}\ln\left(1+\frac{1}{n}\right)$$

(b) Hence determine whether or not the series converges.   *[8 marks]*

13. Find the interval of convergence of the series

$$\sum_{k=1}^{\infty}\sin\left(\frac{\pi}{k}\right)(x-1)^{k}$$ *[12 marks]*

14. (a) Show that the function $\dfrac{1}{x\ln x\left(\ln(\ln x)\right)^{2/3}}$ is decreasing for all $x>3$

(b) By making the substitution $u=\ln x$, evaluate $\displaystyle\int_{3}^{\infty}\frac{1}{x\ln x\left(\ln(\ln x)\right)^{2/3}}\,dx$

(c) Hence determine whether $\displaystyle\sum_{k=3}^{\infty}\frac{1}{k\ln k\left(\ln(\ln k)\right)^{2/3}}$ converges.   *[15 marks]*

4 Maclaurin and Taylor series

In this chapter you will learn:

At the end of the previous chapter we looked at power series and noted that these were different from other infinite series as they were actually functions of a variable $x \in \mathbb{R}$:

$$\sum_{k=0}^{\infty} a_k x^k = a_0 + a_1 x + a_2 x^2 + a_3 x^3 + \cdots$$

If a power series is convergent, we can input a value of x within its interval of convergence and get a finite value for the sum; that is a value for the function at that point.

But what function would we be evaluating? Could it be a function with which we are already familiar, such as e^x, $\ln x$ or $\sin x$? Can we relate power series to functions such as these?

We can already make a start at answering this; we know from the main course that, for example, the function

$$f(x) = (1+3x)^{-1}$$

has a power series expansion since it is the sum to infinity of a geometric series of first term 1 and common ratio $-3x$; that is:

$$(1+3x)^{-1} = 1 - 3x + 9x^2 - 27x^3 + 81x^4 - 243x^5 + \cdots \quad |x| < \frac{1}{3}$$

If it is possible to express the function $f(x) = (1+3x)^{-1}$ as a power series, it should be possible to express other functions as power series.

In this chapter we look at methods for finding power series representations for functions and see how we can use them to make approximations for these functions and to evaluate limits.

4A Maclaurin series

As we are able to manipulate, differentiate and integrate power series (within their radius of convergence), it seems a good idea to express other types of function as series so that we can analyse them in the same way.

To this end, consider a power series with radius of convergence $R > 0$ and suppose we define a function:

$$f(x) = a_0 + a_1x + a_2x^2 + a_3x^3 + \cdots \qquad |x| < R$$

Letting $x = 0$ we immediately have:

$$f(0) = a_0$$

Since we can differentiate the power series for $|x| < R$, we have:

$$f'(x) = a_1 + 2a_2x + 3a_3x^2 + 4a_4x^3 + \cdots$$
$$\therefore f'(0) = a_1$$

Differentiating again:

$$f''(x) = 2a_2 + (3 \times 2)a_3x + (4 \times 3)a_4x^2 + \cdots$$
$$\therefore f''(0) = 2!a_2$$

$$\Rightarrow a_2 = \frac{f''(0)}{2!}$$

And again:

$$f'''(x) = (3 \times 2)a_3 + (4 \times 3 \times 2)a_4x + \cdots$$
$$\therefore f'''(0) = 3!a_3$$

$$\Rightarrow a_3 = \frac{f'''(0)}{3!}$$

Continuing in this way we will get:

$$f(x) = \frac{f(0)}{0!} + \frac{f'(0)}{1!}x + \frac{f''(0)}{2!}x^2 + \frac{f'''(0)}{3!}x^3 + \cdots = \sum_{k=0}^{\infty} \frac{f^{(k)}(0)}{k!}x^k$$

KEY POINT 4.1

The power series

$$f(x) = f(0) + f'(0)x + \frac{f''(0)}{2!}x^2 + \frac{f'''(0)}{3!}x^3 + \cdots$$

is known as the **Maclaurin series** of the function $f(x)$.

It exists provided that $f^{(k)}(0)$ exists for all $k \in \mathbb{N}$.

In Section 4D we will see that it is useful to 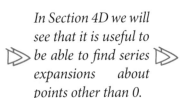 *be able to find series expansions about points other than 0.*

As we are evaluating all of the derivatives at $x = 0$, we say that the Maclaurin series of a function is centred at 0, or talk of the series expansion around 0.

We cannot find a Maclaurin series for every function we have met so far (for example $f(x) = \ln x$ does not satisfy the above condition of $f^{(k)}(0)$ existing for all $k \in \mathbb{N}$; indeed it does not exist for any $k \in \mathbb{N}$) but we can find Maclaurin series for many familiar functions.

Worked example 4.1

Find the Maclaurin series for:

(a) $f(x) = e^x$ (b) $g(x) = \sin x$

Give your answers in the form $\sum_{k=0}^{\infty} a_k x^k$

> We need to establish the first few derivatives of f(x) and evaluate them at x = 0. We see that clearly $f^{(k)}(0) = 1$ for all $k \in \{0,1,2,...\}$

(a) $f(x) = e^x \Rightarrow f(0) = 1$
$f'(x) = e^x \Rightarrow f'(0) = 1$
$f''(x) = e^x \Rightarrow f''(0) = 1$
$f'''(x) = e^x \Rightarrow f'''(0) = 1$
$\vdots$

> Use the Maclaurin series formula

So,

$$f(x) = \frac{f(0)}{0!} + \frac{f'(0)}{1!}x + \frac{f''(0)}{2!}x^2 + \frac{f'''(0)}{3!}x^3 + \cdots$$

$$= \frac{1}{0!} + \frac{1}{1!}x + \frac{1}{2!}x^2 + \frac{1}{3!}x^3 + \frac{1}{4!}x^4 \cdots$$

$$= 1 + x + \frac{x^2}{2!} + \frac{x^3}{3!} + \frac{x^4}{4!} + \cdots + \frac{x^n}{n!} + \cdots$$

$$= \sum_{k=0}^{\infty} \frac{x^k}{k!}$$

> We need to establish the first few derivatives of f(x) and evaluate them at x = 0. We see that as $f^{(4)}(x) = f(x)$ there is a cycle of 4 values that repeats continually such that $f^{(k+4)}(0) = f^{(k)}(0)$

(b) $f(x) = \sin x \Rightarrow f(0) = 0$
$f'(x) = \cos x \Rightarrow f'(0) = 1$
$f''(x) = -\sin x \Rightarrow f''(0) = 0$
$f'''(x) = -\cos x \Rightarrow f'''(0) = -1$
$f^{(4)}(x) = \sin x \Rightarrow f^{(4)}(0) = 0$
$f^{(5)}(x) = \cos x \Rightarrow f^{(5)}(0) = 1$
$\vdots$

> Use the Maclaurin series formula

So,

$$f(x) = \frac{f(0)}{0!} + \frac{f'(0)}{1!}x + \frac{f''(0)}{2!}x^2 + \frac{f'''(0)}{3!}x^3 + \cdots$$

$$= \frac{0}{0!} + \frac{1}{1!}x + \frac{0}{2!}x^2 + \frac{-1}{3!}x^3 + \frac{0}{4!}x^4 + \frac{1}{5!}x^5 \cdots$$

$$= x - \frac{x^3}{3!} + \frac{x^5}{5!} - \frac{x^7}{7!} + \cdots$$

$$= \sum_{k=0}^{\infty} (-1)^k \frac{x^{2k+1}}{(2k+1)!}$$

> To form the general term, we note that this is an alternating series and so need $(-1)^k$, and as we only have odd powers and factorials, $2k + 1$ will generate them

We found in Exercise 3C, questions 1(b) (i) and 2(b) that both these power series converge for all $x \in \mathbb{R}$ (although we did not relate the series to e^x and $\sin x$).

As mentioned above, we cannot find the Maclaurin series for $y = \ln x$. However, we can for $y = \ln(1+x)$ as this avoids the problem of $f(0)$ (and all the derivatives at $x = 0$) not existing.

Worked example 4.2

Find the Maclaurin series for $f(x) = \ln(1+x)$, giving your answer in the form $\sum a_k x^k$.

We need to establish the first few derivatives of $f(x)$ and evaluate them at $x = 0$.

We can see a pattern of alternating signs of factorials

$$f(x) = \ln(1+x) \implies f(0) = 0$$
$$f'(x) = (1+x)^{-1} \implies f'(0) = 1$$
$$f''(x) = -(1+x)^{-2} \implies f''(0) = -1$$
$$f'''(x) = 2!(1+x)^{-3} \implies f'''(0) = 2!$$
$$f^{(4)}(x) = -3!(1+x)^{-4} \implies f^{(4)}(0) = -3!$$
$$f^{(5)}(x) = 4!(1+x)^{-5} \implies f^{(5)}(0) = 4!$$
$$\vdots$$

Use the Maclaurin series formula

So,

$$f(x) = \frac{f(0)}{0!} + \frac{f'(0)}{1!}x + \frac{f''(0)}{2!}x^2 + \frac{f'''(0)}{3!}x^3 + \cdots$$

$$= \frac{0}{0!} + \frac{1}{1!}x - \frac{1}{2!}x^2 + \frac{2!}{3!}x^3 - \frac{3!}{4!}x^4 + \frac{4!}{5!}x^5 \cdots$$

$$= x - \frac{x^2}{2} + \frac{x^3}{3} - \frac{x^4}{4} + \frac{x^5}{5} \cdots$$

Again this is an alternating series but with the sum starting at $k = 1$, we need $(-1)^{k+1}$ to make the first term positive

$$= \sum_{k=1}^{\infty} \frac{(-1)^{k+1} x^k}{k}$$

EXAM HINT

Look for patterns in the first few derivatives at $x = 0$ to be confident of how the series will behave.

We found in Exercise 3C, question 2(a) that this power series converges for $-1 < x \leq 1$.

Clearly, to have any hope of the series converging to the value of the function at x, we can only take a value of x inside the interval of convergence of the Maclaurin series of a function. However, if we know that a Maclaurin series converges for particular values of x, this does not mean that it converges to the function it was derived from! We will see in the next section how we can determine when the Maclaurin series of a function does indeed converge to that function.

Exercise 4A

1. Find the first four non-zero terms of the Maclaurin series for the following functions.

(a) (i) $\cos x$ (ii) $\sin 3x$

(b) (i) $e^{\frac{x}{2}}$ (ii) e^{-3x}

(c) (i) $\sqrt{1+x}$ (ii) $\dfrac{1}{(2-3x)^2}$

(d) (i) $\tan x$ (ii) $\sec x$

2. Find the first three non-zero terms of the Maclaurin series for
$f(x) = x\sin 2x$.

[5 marks]

3. Show that the Maclaurin series up to the term in x^4 for
$\ln(1+\sin x)$ is

$$x - \frac{x^2}{2} + \frac{x^3}{6} - \frac{x^4}{12}$$

[6 marks]

4. (a) Find the term up to x^4 in the Maclaurin expansion of
$f(x) = \ln(\cos x)$.

(b) Use this series to find an approximation in terms
of π for $\ln 2$.

[7 marks]

5. (a) Show that the Maclaurin series for $f(x) = \dfrac{1}{\sqrt{4-x}}$ is

$$f(x) = \frac{1}{2}\left(1 + \frac{1}{8}x + \frac{1\times 3}{2!8^2}x^2 + \frac{1\times 3\times 5}{3!8^3}x^3 + \cdots + \frac{1\times 3\times 5\times \cdots \times (2n-1)}{n!8^n}x^n + \cdots\right)$$

(b) Find the radius of convergence of this series.   [8 marks]

6. (a) Find the Maclaurin expansion of $f(x) = x\ln(1+x)$, giving
your answer in the form $\sum a_k x^k$.

(b) Find the interval of convergence of this power series.

[9 marks]

7. (a) Find the Maclaurin expansion of $\sqrt[3]{1+x}$ up to the term in x^3.

(b) Prove that this power series converges for $|x| < 1$.   [9 marks]

8.

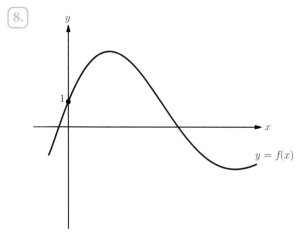

Explain why neither of the following can be Maclaurin series of
the function f(x):

(a) $\dfrac{1}{2} + \dfrac{x}{2} + \dfrac{x^2}{8} + \cdots$

(b) $1 - 3x - \dfrac{x^2}{4} + \cdots$

4B Approximations to the Maclaurin series

Have you ever wondered how a calculator or computer finds a value for, say, sin 0.5 or e^3?

Look back at the expression for the truncation error of an alternating series in Section 3B (Key point 3.8).

One possible way is to program the calculator with the Maclaurin series so that when values of x are inputted, it can simply evaluate this power series. It cannot of course use infinitely many terms of such series, so how many terms is enough to give a sufficiently accurate answer? This is similar to the issue for alternating series in chapter 3 of this option, where we found an expression for the truncation error at n terms of the series; but here, by truncating the Maclaurin series, we are actually determining an nth degree polynomial, which approximates the function.

KEY POINT 4.2

> The truncated Maclaurin series:
>
> $$\sum_{k=0}^{n} \frac{f^{(k)}(0)}{k!} x^k = \frac{f(0)}{0!} + \frac{f'(0)}{1!} x + \frac{f''(0)}{2!} x^2 + \cdots + \frac{f^{(n)}(0)}{n!} x^n$$
>
> is referred to as the ***n*th degree Maclaurin polynomial**, $p_n(x)$ of the function $f(x)$.

Using the Maclaurin series for sin x (Worked example 4.1(b)) to approximate the function near to $x = 0$ (here we use $x = 0.5$), we can see how accurate the first few Maclaurin polynomials for sin x are.

- So, for the first degree Maclaurin polynomial we have sin $x \approx x$:

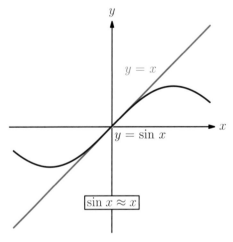

This would give us sin $0.5 \approx 0.5$, which is an error of just over 4%.

- For the third degree Maclaurin polynomial we have $\sin x \approx x - \dfrac{x^3}{3!}$.

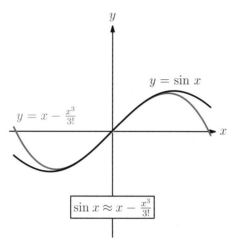

$$\sin x \approx x - \frac{x^3}{3!}$$

This would give us $\sin 0.5 \approx 0.479\,1\dot{6}$, which is only a 0.05% error.

- For the fifth degree Maclaurin polynomial we have $\sin x \approx x - \dfrac{x^3}{3!} + \dfrac{x^5}{5!}$:

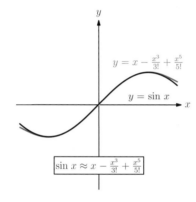

$$\sin x \approx x - \frac{x^3}{3!} + \frac{x^5}{5!}$$

This would give us $\sin 0.5 \approx 0.479\,427\,083\,4$, which is now accurate to 5DP.

Clearly, our approximation becomes more and more accurate the higher the degree of the polynomial; with the following result, we can quantify the truncation error for any Maclaurin series.

KEY POINT 4.3

For a function $f(x)$ for which all derivatives evaluated at $x = 0$ exist:

$$f(x) = \sum_{k=0}^{n} \frac{f^{(k)}(0)}{k!} x^k + R_n(x)$$

where the error term $R_n(x)$ is given by:

$$R_n(x) = \frac{f^{(n+1)}(c)}{(n+1)!} x^{n+1} \quad \text{for some } c \in \,]0, x[$$

This is sometimes referred to as the **Lagrange form of the error term**.

EXAM HINT

Although the expression for the Lagrange error term for Maclaurin series does not appear in the Formula booklet, the more general case for Taylor series, examined in Section 4D, is given in the Formula booklet.

The proof of this result is beyond the scope of the syllabus but it is possible to understand the Lagrange error term by thinking about the particular case of a 0th order (i.e. constant) Maclaurin polynomial where the error term is given by the first derivative.

The Mean Value Theorem states that there must exist some $c \in]0, x[$ such that,

$$\frac{f(x) - f(0)}{x - 0} = f'(c)$$

$$\Rightarrow f(x) = f(0) + f'(c)x$$

which is exactly the result in Key point 4.3, with $n = 0$.

This idea then generalises to higher order derivatives.

In estimating the error in taking an nth degree polynomial to approximate a function, we will not know the particular value of c, so instead we will find the largest possible error (an upper bound for the error) by taking c to be the worst case possible.

Worked example 4.3

(a) Find an expression for the error term in approximating e^x by its 2nd degree Maclaurin polynomial.

(b) Give an upper bound to 4DP on the error when using this approximation to find $e^{0.75}$.

First state the 2nd degree Maclaurin polynomial using the series found above	(a) The 2nd degree Maclaurin polynomial gives the approximation $$e^x \approx 1 + x + \frac{x^2}{2}$$
Find the error, noting that all derivatives of e^x are e^x	with error term $$R_2(x) = \frac{f^{(3)}(c)x^3}{3!} \qquad c \in]0, x[$$ $$= \frac{e^c x^3}{3!}$$
Evaluate at $x = 0.75$	(b) Taking $x = 0.75$ we have $$R_2(0.75) = \frac{e^c \, 0.75^3}{3!} \qquad c \in]0, 0.75[$$
As e^c is an increasing function, the largest possible value of c will give the largest possible value (the upper bound) on the error	$$\therefore R_2(0.75) < \frac{e^{0.75} \, 0.75^3}{3!} = 0.1489$$

EXAM HINT

For alternating series (that satisfy the appropriate conditions), it is easier to bound the error at a particular value of x using the result for the truncation error in Key point 3.8 rather than the Lagrange error term.

We can use Key point 4.3 to bound errors resulting from the truncation of Maclaurin series, but we can also determine for which values of x a Maclaurin series actually converges to the function from which it was derived. (Remember, we said at the end of the last section that a Maclaurin series does not necessarily converge to the function from which it was derived for all x in the interval of convergence.) Since

$$f(x) = \sum_{k=0}^{n} \frac{f^{(k)}(0)}{k!} x^k + R_n(x)$$

if we let $n \to \infty$, it makes sense that

$$f(x) = \sum_{k=0}^{\infty} \frac{f^{(k)}(0)}{k!} x^k$$

only if the error term tends to 0.

KEY POINT 4.4

The (infinite) Maclaurin series for $f(x)$ is precisely the same as the function $f(x)$ for all x where

$$\lim_{n \to \infty} |R_n(x)| = 0$$

Worked example 4.4

Prove that the Maclaurin series for e^x is valid for all $x \in \mathbb{R}$.

We need to show that
$$\lim_{n \to \infty} |R_n(x)| = 0$$

From Worked example 4.1
$$f^{(n)}(x) = e^x$$
$$f^{(n+1)}(x) = e^x \text{ for all } n \in \mathbb{Z}^+$$
Therefore,
$$|R_n(x)| = \left| \frac{f^{(n+1)}(c) x^{n+1}}{(n+1)!} \right| \qquad c \in]0, x[$$

$$= \left| \frac{e^c x^{n+1}}{(n+1)!} \right|$$

Simplify the modulus sign, noting that $e^c > 0$, $(n+1)! > 0$

and $|x^{n+1}| = |x|^{n+1}$

$$\therefore \lim_{n \to \infty} |R_n(x)| = \lim_{n \to \infty} \left| \frac{e^c x^{n+1}}{(n+1)!} \right|$$

$$= \lim_{n \to \infty} \frac{e^c |x|^{n+1}}{(n+1)!}$$

Noting that $e^c \le M$ for some constant $M \in \mathbb{R}$, we can apply the algebra of limits

$$\le M \lim_{n \to \infty} \frac{|x|^{n+1}}{(n+1)!} \quad \text{for some} M \in \mathbb{R}$$

From chapter 1 Mixed examination practice, question 6, we know that

$$\lim_{n \to \infty} \frac{|x|^n}{n!} = 0$$

Since $\lim_{n \to \infty} \frac{|x|^{n+1}}{(n+1)!} = 0$,

$$\lim_{n \to \infty} |R_n(x)| \le 0$$

continued . . .

EXAM HINT

$\lim\limits_{n\to\infty}\dfrac{|x|^n}{n!} = 0$ is a useful limit to know. It can be quoted in this case but you should also know how to prove it.

And since, clearly, $|R_n(x)| \geq 0$

by the Squeeze Theorem,
$$\lim_{n\to\infty}|R_n(x)| = 0$$

Hence, $e^x = \sum\limits_{k=1}^{\infty}\dfrac{x^k}{k!}$ for all $x \in \mathbb{R}$

A similar argument works for $\sin x$ or $\cos x$.

Worked example 4.5

Show that the Maclaurin series for $\cos x$: $\sum\limits_{k=0}^{\infty}(-1)^k\dfrac{x^{2k}}{(2k)!}$ converges to $\cos x$ for all $x \in \mathbb{R}$.

We need to find $f^{(n+1)}(t)$, for $f(t) = \cos t$, so we find the first few derivatives and look for a pattern. There is a cycle of 4 values that repeats continually such that $f^{(k+4)}(t) = f^{(k)}(t)$

$$f(t) = \cos t$$
$$f'(t) = -\sin t$$
$$f''(t) = -\cos t$$
$$f'''(t) = \sin t$$
$$f^{(4)}(t) = \cos t$$
$$f^{(5)}(t) = -\sin t$$
$$\vdots$$

Since all derivatives will be either $\pm\sin t$ or $\pm\cos t$, we know that $f^{(n+1)}(t)$ will be one of these

$$\therefore f^{(n+1)}(t) = \begin{cases} \pm\sin t \\ \pm\cos t \end{cases}$$

We need $|R_n(x)|$

$$|R_n(x)| = \left|\dfrac{f^{(n+1)}(c)x^{n+1}}{(n+1)!}\right|$$
$$= \dfrac{|f^{(n+1)}(c)||x^{n+1}|}{(n+1)!}$$

Since $f^{(n+1)}(t) = \begin{cases} \pm\sin t \\ \pm\cos t \end{cases}$

we know that $|f^{(n+1)}(c)| \leq 1$

$$\leq \dfrac{|x^{n+1}|}{(n+1)!}$$
$$= \dfrac{|x|^{n+1}}{(n+1)!}$$

Again $\lim\limits_{n\to\infty}\dfrac{|x|^n}{n!} = 0$

Since $\lim\limits_{n\to\infty}\dfrac{|x|^{n+1}}{(n+1)!} = 0$,
$$\lim_{n\to\infty}|R_n(x)| \leq 0$$

And since, clearly, $|R_n(x)| \geq 0$

by the Squeeze Theorem,
$$\lim_{n\to\infty}|R_n(x)| = 0$$

Hence, $\cos x = \sum\limits_{k=0}^{\infty}(-1)^k\dfrac{x^{2k}}{(2k)!}$ for all $x \in \mathbb{R}$

We see from Worked examples 4.4 and 4.5 that the values of x for which the Maclaurin series of the functions e^x and $\cos x$ are equal to the functions themselves coincide exactly with the intervals of convergence of the respective power series. This will always be the case for the functions we meet, but we still need to be able to show this for each particular function.

An example of a function that is not equal to its Maclaurin series is

$$f(x) = \begin{cases} e^{-\frac{1}{x^2}} & x \neq 0 \\ 0 & x = 0 \end{cases}$$

Investigate the Maclaurin series and graph of this function.

Exercise 4B

1. Find an upper bound on the error when using the Maclaurin polynomials of given degree to approximate the following functions for $x = 0.5$:

   (a) (i) $\cos x, p_4(x)$ (ii) $\tan x, p_3(x)$

   (b) (i) $e^{x^2}, p_2(x)$ (ii) $e^{-3x}, p_2(x)$

   (c) (i) $\sqrt{1+x}, p_3(x)$ (ii) $\dfrac{1}{(4-x)^2}, p_3(x)$

2. (a) Find the second degree Maclaurin polynomial for e^{-x}.

   (b) For what values of $x > 0$ will this polynomial approximate e^{-x} to within 0.001? Give your answer to 4DP.   *[6 marks]*

3. Using the Lagrange error term, find an upper bound on the error when using:

   (a) $x - \dfrac{x^3}{3!} + \dfrac{x^5}{5!}$ to estimate $\sin x$ for $x \in \left[-\dfrac{\pi}{6}, \dfrac{\pi}{6} \right]$

   (b) $x + \dfrac{x^3}{3}$ to estimate $\tan x$ for $x \in \left[-\dfrac{\pi}{4}, \dfrac{\pi}{4} \right]$ *[8 marks]*

4. For $|x| \leq 1$, show that

   $$\left| e^x - 1 - \dfrac{x^2}{2!} - \dfrac{x^3}{3!} \right| < \dfrac{1}{8}$$ *[6 marks]*

5. Let $f(x) = \dfrac{e^x + e^{-x}}{2}$

   (a) Find the fourth degree Maclaurin polynomial for $f(x)$.

   (b) Hence find an approximation to $f\left(\dfrac{1}{2} \right)$, giving your answer in the form $\dfrac{a}{b}$, where $a, b \in \mathbb{Z}$

   (c) Using the Lagrange error term, place an upper bound on the error in this approximation.   *[10 marks]*

6. (a) Find the first three non-zero terms of the Maclaurin series for $\arctan x$.

   (b) Show that the series

   $$\sum_{k=0}^{\infty} (-1)^k \dfrac{x^{2k+1}}{2k+1}$$

   converges for $|x| < 1$ and that it converges to $\arctan x$.   *[11 marks]*

7. What degree Maclaurin polynomial of e^x must be taken to guarantee an estimate of e to within 1×10^{-6}? *[6 marks]*

8. Show that the Maclaurin series for $\sin 2x$ converges to the function for all $x \in \mathbb{R}$. *[8 marks]*

9. (a) Use the Lagrange form of the error term to bound the error involved in approximating $-\ln(1-x)$ at $x = 0.5$ by
$$x + \frac{x^2}{2} + \frac{x^3}{3}.$$

(b) By noting that $R_3(0.5) = \frac{(0.5)^4}{4} + \frac{(0.5)^5}{5} + \cdots$ give an improved bound on the error. *[9 marks]*

10. (a) Find the first three terms of the Maclaurin Series for $(1+x)^n$.

(b) How many terms of the expansion of $(1+x)^{82}$ are needed to guarantee finding a value of 1.1^{82} accurate to within 10^{-6}? *[10 marks]*

11. Show that the Maclaurin series for $(1+x)^{-\frac{3}{2}}$ converges to the function for $|x| < 1$. *[10 marks]*

4C Maclaurin series of composite functions

The following standard Maclaurin series (which we have already met), appear in the Formula booklet:

KEY POINT 4.5

$$e^x = 1 + x + \frac{x^2}{2!} + \cdots$$

$$\ln(1+x) = x - \frac{x^2}{2} + \frac{x^3}{3} - \cdots$$

$$\sin x = x - \frac{x^3}{3!} + \frac{x^5}{5!} - \cdots$$

$$\cos x = 1 - \frac{x^2}{2!} + \frac{x^4}{4!} - \cdots$$

$$\arctan x = x - \frac{x^3}{3} + \frac{x^5}{5} - \cdots$$

These can be used to find Maclaurin series of more complicated functions. Sometimes this is straightforward.

Worked example 4.6

Using the Maclaurin series for $\cos x$, find the series expansion of $\cos(2x^3)$.

We just need to substitute $2x^3$ into the known series for $\cos x$

$$\cos(2x^3) = 1 - \frac{(2x^3)^2}{2!} + \frac{(2x^3)^4}{4!} - \frac{(2x^3)^6}{6!} + \cdots$$

$$= 1 - 2x^6 + \frac{2}{3}x^{12} - \frac{4}{45}x^{18} + \cdots$$

Often this will involve finding two separate Maclaurin series and then combining them.

Worked example 4.7

Using the Maclaurin series for $\sin x$ and e^x, find the series expansion of $e^{\sin x}$ as far as the term in x^4.

We start by substituting the series for $\sin x$, only going as far as the x^4 term

$$e^{\sin x} = e^{x - \frac{x^3}{3!} + \cdots}$$

$$\approx e^x e^{-\frac{x^3}{3!}}$$

We now use the series for e^x only going as far as x^4 and then expand

$$\approx \left(1 + x + \frac{x^2}{2!} + \frac{x^3}{3!} + \frac{x^4}{4!} + \cdots\right)\left(1 + \left(-\frac{x^3}{3!}\right) + \cdots\right)$$

$$\approx 1 + x + \frac{x^2}{2} + \frac{x^3}{6} + \frac{x^4}{24} - \frac{x^3}{6} - \frac{x^4}{6} + \cdots$$

$$\approx 1 + x + \frac{x^2}{2} - \frac{x^4}{8}$$

EXAM HINT

It is much quicker to form Maclaurin series in this way so where possible in the exam combine known series.

We can also use results on intervals where the expansion converges to the function (as we know these will be the intervals of convergence of the functions we will meet) to find the values for which the expansion of composite functions are valid.

Worked example 4.8

Find the Maclaurin series up to the term in x^3 for $\ln\left(\dfrac{\sqrt{1+2x}}{2-3x}\right)$ and state the interval in which the expansion is valid.

We know the series expansion for $\ln(1+x)$ so rearrange the original function into separate functions in this form

$$\ln\left(\frac{\sqrt{1+2x}}{2-3x}\right) = \ln\left(\sqrt{1+2x}\right) - \ln(2-3x)$$

$$= \frac{1}{2}\ln(1+2x) - \ln(2-3x)$$

$$= \frac{1}{2}\ln(1+2x) - \ln\left[2\left(1+\left(\frac{-3x}{2}\right)\right)\right]$$

$$= \frac{1}{2}\ln(1+2x) - \left\{\ln 2 + \ln\left(1+\left(\frac{-3x}{2}\right)\right)\right\}$$

Now find the series expansion for each separately

$$\frac{1}{2}\ln(1+2x) = \frac{1}{2}\left((2x) - \frac{(2x)^2}{2} + \frac{(2x)^3}{3} + \cdots\right)$$

$$= \frac{1}{2}\left(2x - 2x^2 + \frac{8x^3}{3} + \cdots\right)$$

continued . . .

$$= x - x^2 + \frac{4x^3}{3} + \cdots$$

$$\ln\left(1 + \left(\frac{-3x}{2}\right)\right) = \left(\frac{-3x}{2}\right) - \frac{\left(\frac{-3x}{2}\right)^2}{2} + \frac{\left(\frac{-3x}{2}\right)^3}{3} + \cdots$$

$$= \frac{-3x}{2} - \frac{9x^2}{8} - \frac{9x^3}{8} + \cdots$$

And
finally put
everything
together

$$\ln\left(\frac{\sqrt{1+2x}}{2-3x}\right) = \left(x - x^2 + \frac{4x^3}{3} + \cdots\right) - \ln 2 - \left(\frac{-3x}{2} - \frac{9x^2}{8} - \frac{9x^3}{8} + \cdots\right)$$

$$= x - x^2 + \frac{4x^3}{3} + \cdots - \ln 2 + \frac{3x}{2} + \frac{9x^2}{8} + \frac{9x^3}{8} + \cdots$$

$$= \ln\left(\frac{1}{2}\right) + \frac{5x}{2} + \frac{x^2}{8} + \frac{59x^3}{24} + \cdots$$

We consider the
interval of validity
separately for each
function and then
note that for both to
be valid we need the
smaller interval

Since $\ln(1+x)$ is valid when $-1 < x \le 1$,

$\ln(1+2x)$ is valid when $-1 < 2x \le 1$

i.e. when $-\dfrac{1}{2} < x \le \dfrac{1}{2}$

$\ln\left(1 + \left(\dfrac{-3x}{2}\right)\right)$ is valid when $-1 < \dfrac{-3x}{2} \le 1$

i.e. when $-\dfrac{2}{3} \le x < \dfrac{2}{3}$

Therefore, $\ln\left(\dfrac{\sqrt{1+2x}}{2-3x}\right)$ is valid when $-\dfrac{1}{2} \le x < \dfrac{1}{2}$

Exercise 4C

In this exercise you can assume all the standard Maclaurin series results given in the Formula booklet.

1. Find the first four non-zero terms of the Maclaurin series for:

   (a) (i) $\sin(3x^4)$ (ii) $\cos\left(2\sqrt{x}\right)$

   (b) (i) $\ln(2+3x)$ (ii) $\ln(1-2x)$

   (c) (i) $e^{-\frac{x^2}{2}}$ (ii) e^{x^3}

2. By combining Maclaurin series of different functions find the series expansion as far as the term in x^4 for:

   (a) (i) $\ln(1+x)\sin 2x$ (ii) $\ln(1-x)\cos 3x$

   (b) (i) $\dfrac{e^x}{1+x}$ (ii) $\dfrac{\sin x}{1-2x}$

   (c) (i) $\ln(1+\sin x)$ (ii) $\ln(1-\sin x)$

3. Find the Maclaurin series as far as the term in x^4 for $e^{3x}\sin 2x$.

   [4 marks]

4. Show that $\sqrt{1+x^2}\,e^{-x} \approx 1 - x + x^2 - \dfrac{2}{3}x^3 + \dfrac{1}{6}x^4$.

   [5 marks]

5. (a) Find the Maclaurin series for $\ln(1+4x^2+4x)$, giving your answer in the form $\sum a_k x^k$

(b) State the interval of convergence of the power series.
[6 marks]

6. (a) Find the first two non-zero terms of the Maclaurin series for $\tan x$.

(b) Hence find the Maclaurin series of $e^{\tan x}$ up to and including the term in x^4. *[6 marks]*

7. (a) By using the Maclaurin series for $\cos x$, find the series expansion for $\ln(\cos x)$ up to the term in x^4.

(b) Hence find the first two non-zero terms of the expansion of $\ln(\sec x)$ stating where the expansion is valid.

(c) Use your result from (b) to find the first two non-zero terms of the series for $\tan x$. *[8 marks]*

8. (a) Find the first 4 terms of the Maclaurin series for

$$f(x) = \ln[(2+x)^3 (1-3x)]$$

(b) Find the equation of the tangent to $f(x)$ at $x = 0$.
[10 marks]

9. (a) Find the Maclaurin series for $\ln\sqrt{\dfrac{1+x}{1-x}}$ stating the interval of convergence of the power series.

(b) Use the first three terms of this series to estimate the value of $\ln 2$, stating the value of x used.

(c) Provide an upper bound on the error in your approximation using the Lagrange error term.

(d) Refine the upper bound on the error by considering the error as a geometric series.

10. Using the standard result for e^x, form a series for $e^{\sqrt{x}}$. Why is this not a valid expansion? Does $e^{\sqrt{x}}$ have a Maclaurin series?
[13 marks]

4D Taylor series

We have seen that a Maclaurin series is valid in an interval centred on $x = 0$ and that close to this point, often just a few terms of the series are needed to give a very good approximation of the function. However, further away from $x = 0$, even within the interval where the expansion is valid, you can need many more terms of the series to get a reasonable degree of accuracy.

For example, we found above that the 5th degree Maclaurin polynomial for $\sin x$ approximated $\sin 0.5$ correct to 5DP but if we try to use the same polynomial to approximate a value further away from 0, say at $x = 2$, we would get

$$\sin 2 \approx 0.909\,297\,4$$

which is correct to only 1DP. The further away from 0 we go the worse this gets.

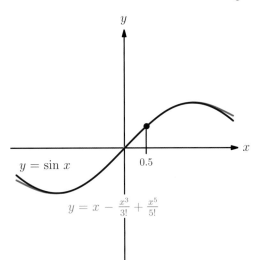

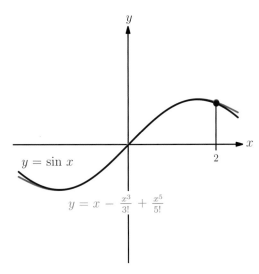

For functions such as $\sin x$ that have a Maclaurin series valid for all $x \in \mathbb{R}$, we can overcome this difficulty by simply taking higher and higher order Maclaurin polynomials to get the desired degree of accuracy. For other functions, such as $\ln(1+x)$ whose series is only convergent for $-1 < x \leq 1$, we cannot make any reasonable approximation at all outside this interval, no matter how many terms of the polynomial we take.

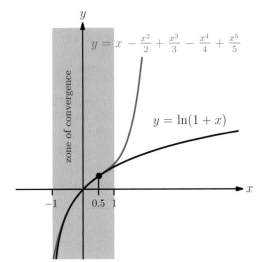

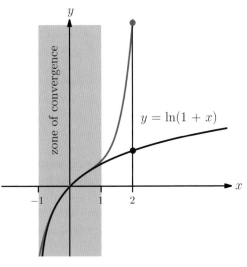

To overcome these problems we will try to convert the Maclaurin series expansion to a power series centred on a general point $x = a$ rather than $x = 0$. In this way we will be able to make a reasonable polynomial approximation of a function near to any given point.

So, starting with the Maclaurin series:

$$g(x) = g(0) + \frac{g'(0)}{1!}x + \frac{g''(0)}{2!}x^2 + \frac{g'''(0)}{3!}x^3 + \cdots$$

and letting $g(x) = f(x+a)$ so that $g^{(k)}(x) = f^{(k)}(x+a)$ we have

$$f(x+a) = f(a) + \frac{f'(a)}{1!}x + \frac{f''(a)}{2!}x^2 + \frac{f'''(a)}{3!}x^3 + \cdots$$

And finally replacing $x+a$ with x:

$$f(x) = f(a) + \frac{f'(a)}{1!}(x-a) + \frac{f''(a)}{2!}(x-a)^2 + \frac{f'''(a)}{3!}(x-a)^3 + \cdots$$

This is known as the Taylor series. All of the results we have used for Maclaurin series generalise in this way.

KEY POINT 4.6

> **Taylor approximations**
>
> For a function $f(x)$ for which all derivatives evaluated at a exist:
>
> $$f(x) = f(a) + (x-a)f'(a) + \cdots + \frac{(x-a)^n}{n!}f^{(n)}(a) + R_n(x)$$
>
> where the Lagrange error term $R_n(x)$ is given by
>
> $$R_n(x) = \frac{f^{(n+1)}(c)}{(n+1)!}(x-a)^{n+1} \quad \text{for some } c \in \,]a, x[$$

This is the form in which this error term is given in the Formula booklet; of course to reduce this to the error term of a Maclaurin series we need only let $a = 0$.

Worked example 4.9

(a) Find the Taylor series expansion for $f(x) = \ln x$ around the point $x = 1$.

(b) Using the 4th degree Taylor polynomial as an approximation for this function, find the maximum error for $x \in \left[\dfrac{1}{2}, \dfrac{3}{2}\right]$.

Start by finding the first few derivatives and look for a pattern. Here we clearly have $f^{(n)}(1) = (-1)^{n-1}(n-1)!$ for $n \geq 1$	(a) $\quad\quad\quad f(x) = \ln x \;\Rightarrow\; f(1) = 0$ $\quad\quad\quad f'(x) = x^{-1} \;\Rightarrow\; f'(1) = 1$ $\quad\quad\quad f''(x) = -x^{-2} \;\Rightarrow\; f''(1) = -1$ $\quad\quad\quad f'''(x) = 2!x^{-3} \;\Rightarrow\; f'''(1) = 2!$ $\quad\quad\quad f^{(4)}(x) = -3!x^{-4} \;\Rightarrow\; f^{(4)}(1) = -3!$ $\quad\quad\quad f^{(5)}(x) = 4!x^{-5} \;\Rightarrow\; f^{(5)}(1) = 4!$ $\quad\quad\quad\quad\quad\quad\vdots$
Apply the Taylor series formula with $a = 1$	$f(x) = \dfrac{f(1)}{0!} + \dfrac{f'(1)}{1!}(x-1) + \dfrac{f''(1)}{2!}(x-1)^2 + \dfrac{f'''(1)}{3!}(x-1)^3 + \cdots$ $= \dfrac{0}{0!} + \dfrac{1}{1!}(x-1) - \dfrac{1}{2!}(x-1)^2 + \dfrac{2!}{3!}(x-1)^3 - \dfrac{3!}{4!}(x-1)^4 \cdots$ $= (x-1) - \dfrac{(x-1)^2}{2} + \dfrac{(x-1)^3}{3} - \dfrac{(x-1)^4}{4} + \cdots + \dfrac{(-1)^{n-1}(x-1)^n}{n} + \cdots$

continued . . .

Find the error term for this truncation and look to place an upper bound on this

(b) We have:

$$f(x) = (x-1) - \frac{(x-1)^2}{2} + \frac{(x-1)^3}{3} - \frac{(x-1)^4}{4} + R_4(x)$$

Where,

$$R_4(x) = \frac{f^{(5)}(c)(x-1)^5}{5!}, \quad c \in \left]\frac{1}{2}, \frac{3}{2}\right[$$

$$= \frac{4! c^{-5}(x-1)^5}{5!}$$

$$= \frac{(x-1)^5}{5c^5}$$

Use the lower bound for c to produce the upper bound on $\dfrac{(x-1)^5}{5c^5}$

$$< \frac{(x-1)^5}{5\left(\frac{1}{2}\right)^5}$$

$$\leq \frac{\left(\frac{3}{2}-1\right)^5}{5\left(\frac{1}{2}\right)^5} = \frac{1}{5}$$

Exercise 4D

1. Find the first three non-zero terms of the Taylor series for each of the following:

    (a) (i) $\tan x$ about $x = \dfrac{\pi}{4}$

    (ii) $\sin x$ about $x = \dfrac{\pi}{2}$

    (b) (i) $\sqrt{x}$ about $x = 1$

    (ii) e^{x^2} about $x = 4$

    (c) (i) $\operatorname{cosec} x$ about $x = \dfrac{\pi}{3}$

    (ii) $\cot x$ about $x = \dfrac{\pi}{6}$

2. Use Taylor's expansion to express $\ln(3 + x)$ as a series in x, as far as the term in x^3.   [3 marks]

3. Find the Taylor expansion of e^x in powers of $(x - 3)$ up to and including the term in $(x-3)^3$.   [3 marks]

4. (a) Find a series expansion for $\sin\left(\dfrac{\pi}{6} + x\right)$ up to degree three.

    (b) Hence estimate the value of $\sin 35°$ giving your answer to 3 significant figures.

    (c) Provide an upper bound for the error in your estimate.
                                                                          [6 marks]

5. Find an upper bound for the error in using

$$1 - 2(x-1) + 3(x-1)^2 - 4(x-1)^3 \text{ to estimate } \frac{1}{x^2} \text{ for } x \in \left[\frac{3}{4}, \frac{5}{4}\right].$$

[5 marks]

6. (a) Find the second degree Taylor polynomial at $a = 8$ of
$f(x) = \sqrt[3]{x}$

(b) Show that for $7 \le x \le 9$

$$|R_2(x)| < 0.0004$$
[6 marks]

7. Show that $f(x) = \sqrt{x}$ has no Maclaurin expansion but has a
Taylor expansion about any point $x_0 \neq 0$. *[5 marks]*

8. Let $f(x) = x^{\frac{1}{x}}$, for $x \in \mathbb{R}^+$.

(a) Show that

$$f'(x) = \left(\frac{1 - \ln x}{x^{2 - \frac{1}{x}}}\right).$$

(b) Find the Taylor expansion of $f(x)$ about $x = e$ up to the
term in x^2.

(c) Find the maximum value of this polynomial and confirm
that this is the same as the maximum of $f(x)$. *[10 marks]*

9. Prove that the Taylor expansion of $\cos x$ about any value
converges to $\cos x$ for all values of x. *[8 marks]*

10. Use Taylor's theorem to show that when h is small the
error in approximating the derivative of $f(x)$ at a using

$$f'(x) = \frac{f(x+h) - f(x-h)}{2h} \text{ is approximately } \frac{1}{6}h^2 f'''(a).$$

[6 marks]

4E Applications

Representations of functions using Taylor series can be useful in
a number of contexts.

We look here at two:

- integrating a function that is otherwise very difficult to
integrate (if not impossible to integrate as a standard
function) and

- finding limits of the form '$\frac{0}{0}$' or '$\frac{\infty}{\infty}$'.

For the second we already have L'Hôpital's Rule but sometimes
it is easier to do with Taylor series, especially if the first part of
the question has already asked for a Taylor series!

We will look first at finding an expression for the integral
of a function that cannot be integrated to give a standard
function; the power series method is just about the best way of
representing the integral in this case.

*At the end of the
next chapter we
will look at a third
application of Taylor
Series: finding
approximations to
the solutions of dif-
ferential equations.*

Worked example 4.10

Find $\int \sin(x^2)\, dx$ as a power series, giving your answer in the form $\sum a_k x^k$

Using the standard result of the Maclaurin series for $\sin x$ we can find the series expansion for $\sin(x^2)$

$$\sin x = \sum_{k=0}^{\infty} \frac{(-1)^k\, x^{2k+1}}{(2k+1)!} \quad \text{for all } x \in \mathbb{R}$$

$$\therefore\ \sin(x^2) = \sum_{k=0}^{\infty} \frac{(-1)^k\, (x^2)^{2k+1}}{(2k+1)!}$$

$$= \sum_{k=0}^{\infty} \frac{(-1)^k\, x^{4k+2}}{(2k+1)!} \quad \text{for all } x \in \mathbb{R}$$

As this expansion is valid for all $x \in \mathbb{R}$ we can integrate term by term

So,

$$\int \sin(x^2)\, dx = \int \sum_{k=0}^{\infty} \frac{(-1)^k\, x^{4k+2}}{(2k+1)!}\, dx$$

$$= \sum_{k=0}^{\infty} \int \frac{(-1)^k\, x^{4k+2}}{(2k+1)!}\, dx$$

$$= \sum_{k=0}^{\infty} \frac{(-1)^k\, x^{4k+3}}{(4k+3)(2k+1)!}$$

In the next worked example we look at an alternative to L'Hôpital's Rule for a limit of the form $\dfrac{`0`}{0}$.

Worked example 4.11

Using the Maclaurin series for $\cos x$, evaluate $\displaystyle\lim_{x \to 0} \frac{\cos x - 1 + \dfrac{x^2}{2}}{x^4}$.

We hope to be able to cancel the x^4 in the denominator before taking the limit to avoid the $\dfrac{`0`}{0}$ situation
So, substitute in the Maclaurin series for $\cos x$ and simplify the fraction before taking the limit

$$\cos x = 1 - \frac{x^2}{2!} + \frac{x^4}{4!} - \frac{x^6}{6!} + \cdots$$

$$\therefore\ \frac{\cos x - 1 + \dfrac{x^2}{2}}{x^4} = \frac{\left(1 - \dfrac{x^2}{2!} + \dfrac{x^4}{4!} - \dfrac{x^6}{6!} + \cdots\right) - 1 + \dfrac{x^2}{2}}{x^4}$$

$$= \frac{\dfrac{x^4}{4!} - \dfrac{x^6}{6!} + \dfrac{x^8}{8!} \cdots}{x^4}$$

$$= \frac{1}{4!} - \frac{x^2}{6!} + \frac{x^4}{8!} \cdots$$

Now that the x^4 in the denominator has cancelled, we are free to let $x \to 0$

So:

$$\lim_{x \to 0} \frac{\cos x - 1 + \dfrac{x^2}{2}}{x^4} = \lim_{x \to 0} \left(\frac{1}{4!} - \frac{x^2}{6!} + \frac{x^4}{8!} \cdots\right)$$

$$= \frac{1}{4!} = \frac{1}{24}$$

Exercise 4E

1. Evaluate using Maclaurin series:

   (a) (i) $\lim\limits_{x\to0}\dfrac{\sin x - x}{x^3}$
   (ii) $\lim\limits_{x\to0}\dfrac{1-\cos x}{x^2}$

   (b) (i) $\lim\limits_{x\to0}\dfrac{e^x - e^{-x}}{x}$
   (ii) $\lim\limits_{x\to0}\dfrac{e^x - e^{-x}}{\sin x}$

   (c) (i) $\lim\limits_{x\to0}\dfrac{x\cos x - \sin x}{x^3}$
   (ii) $\lim\limits_{x\to0}\dfrac{3\sin x - 4x\cos x + x}{x^3}$

2. Find Maclaurin series for the following in the form $\sum a_k x^k$:

   (a) $\displaystyle\int \dfrac{\cos(x^3)-1}{x^2}\,dx$

   (b) $\displaystyle\int \dfrac{\ln(x+1)}{x}\,dx$
   [8 marks]

3. (a) Find the first three non-zero terms of the Taylor series for $\sin(x-3)$ about the point $x = 3$.

   (b) Using this series, find $\lim\limits_{x\to3}\dfrac{x^2 - 9}{\sin(x-3)}$.
   [6 marks]

4. (a) Find the Maclaurin series for $\arctan x$ as far as the term in x^7.

   (b) Hence evaluate $\lim\limits_{x\to0}\dfrac{\sin x - \arctan x}{x^3}$.
   [7 marks]

5. (a) Using the Maclaurin series for $\ln(1+x)$ and $\cos x$, show that the Maclaurin polynomial of degree 4 for $\ln(\cos x)$ is

   $$-\dfrac{1}{2}x^2 - \dfrac{1}{12}x^4.$$

   (b) Find the Maclaurin polynomial of degree 6 for $\tan(x^2)$.

   (c) Hence, evaluate $\lim\limits_{x\to0}\dfrac{\tan(x^2)}{\ln(\cos x)}$.
   [9 marks]

6. (a) By using the Maclaurin series for $\ln(1+x)$ or otherwise, find a power series expansion of $\ln\left(\dfrac{1}{1-2x^3}\right)$ up to and including the term in x^{12}.

   (b) Hence find $\lim\limits_{x\to0}\dfrac{\ln\left(\dfrac{1}{1-2x^3}\right)}{x^3}$.
   [7 marks]

7. (a) By taking the 4th degree polynomial for e^{-x^2}, find an approximation to:

   $$\int_0^1 e^{-x^2}\,dx$$

   (b) Place bounds on the error in this approximation. *[8 marks]*

8. (a) Find a power series for $\displaystyle\int_0^1 \dfrac{\sin x}{x}\,dx$ in the form $\displaystyle\sum_{k=1}^{\infty} a_k x^k$.

   (b) How many terms of this series are required to ensure an error of less than 10^{-9}?
   [10 marks]

Summary

- A **Maclaurin series** is an infinite polynomial which matches all the derivatives of a function at zero.

- The Maclaurin Series for $f(x)$ is given by:

$$f(x) = f(0) + f'(0)x + \frac{f''(0)}{2!}x^2 + \cdots$$

$$= \sum_{k=0}^{\infty} \frac{f^{(k)}(0)}{k!}x^k$$

- The **nth degree Maclaurin polynomial** of the function $f(x)$ is given by:

$$= \sum_{k=0}^{n} \frac{f^{(k)}(0)}{k!}x^k = f(0) + f'(0)x + \frac{f''(0)}{2!}x^2 + \cdots + \frac{f^{(n)}(0)}{n!}x^n$$

This is the full Maclaurin series truncated at n terms.

- The error term in using an nth degree Maclaurin polynomial is given by:

$$R_n(x) = \frac{f^{(n+1)}(c)}{(n+1)!}x^{n+1} \quad \text{for some } c \in \left]0, x\right[$$

- **Taylor approximations** generalise Maclaurin series to allow expansion about any point, a:

$$f(x) = f(a) + (x-a)f'(a) + \cdots + \frac{(x-a)^n}{n!}f^{(n)}(a) + R_n(x)$$

where the Lagrange error term $R_n(x)$ is given by

$$R_n(x) = \frac{f^{(n+1)}(c)}{(n+1)!}(x-a)^{n+1} \quad \text{for some } c \in \left]a, x\right[$$

- Taylor approximations can be used to provide a representation for the integral of functions and to enable limits of the form $\frac{`0`}{0}$ and $\frac{`\infty`}{\infty}$ to be found.

Mixed examination practice 4

1. (a) Find the first four derivatives of $f(x) = \ln(1+x)$.

   (b) Hence find the first four non-zero terms of the Maclaurin series for $f(x)$.

   (c) Using this expansion, find the exact value of the alternating harmonic series:

   $$1 - \frac{1}{2} + \frac{1}{3} - \frac{1}{4} + \cdots$$

   [7 marks]

2. Find the Taylor series expansion of $\csc x$ in ascending powers

   of $\left(x - \frac{\pi}{4}\right)$ up to and including the term in $\left(x - \frac{\pi}{4}\right)^3$.

   [5 marks]

3. (a) Find the degree 5 Maclaurin polynomial of $e^{x^2} \sin x$

   (b) Use the result of part (a) to find

   $$\lim_{x \to 0} \frac{e^{x^2} \sin x - x}{x^3}$$

   [6 marks]

4. (a) Find the Maclaurin series up to the term in x^3 for

   $$f(x) = \frac{1}{2+x}$$

   (b) Use the Lagrange error term to show that the largest error that could occur when using this polynomial to approximate $f(x)$ for $0 \le x \le 1$ is $\frac{1}{32}$.

   [7 marks]

5. (a) Find the Maclaurin series for xe^x, stating the first four non-zero terms and the general term.

   (b) Hence find a Maclaurin expansion for $\int_0^x te^t \, dt$.

   (c) Hence show that $\frac{1}{2} + \frac{1}{3} + \frac{1}{4(2!)} + \frac{1}{6(4!)} + \cdots = 1$.

   [10 marks]

6. (a) Find a Maclaurin series expansion for e^{-x^2}.

   (b) Hence evaluate $\int_0^1 e^{-x^2} \, dx$ correct to within an error of 0.001.

   [8 marks]

7. Using Taylor's theorem, show that

   $$1 - \frac{x^2}{2} \le \cos x \le 1 - \frac{x^2}{2} + \frac{x^4}{24} \quad \text{for all } x \in \mathbb{R}$$

   [6 marks]

8. (a) Show that

   $$\frac{1}{\sqrt{1-x^2}} = 1 + \frac{x^2}{2} + \frac{3x^4}{8} + \frac{5x^6}{16} + \frac{35x^8}{128} + \cdots + \frac{1 \times 3 \times 5 \times \cdots (2k-1)x^{2k}}{k!2^k}$$

(b) Find the radius of convergence of this power series.

(c) Hence find a power series for $\arcsin x$ stating the values of x for which this is convergent. *[12 marks]*

9. (a) Show that $\arctan x = \int_0^x f(t)\, dt$ for some function f.

(b) By integrating an appropriate power series, find the Maclaurin series of $\arctan x$ up to and including the term in x^7.

(c) Hence evaluate $\lim\limits_{x\to 0}\dfrac{x-\arctan x}{x^3}$

(d) (i) Use your series (up to the term in x^7) for $\arctan x$ to estimate π.

   (ii) What assumption have you made?

   (iii) Find an upper bound for the error in your estimation. *[14 marks]*

10. The function f is defined by $f(x)=\ln\left(\dfrac{1}{1-x}\right)$.

(a) Write down the value of the constant term in the Maclaurin series for $f(x)$.

(b) Find the first three derivatives of $f(x)$ and hence show that the Maclaurin series for $f(x)$ up to and including the x^3 term is:

$$x+\frac{x^2}{2}+\frac{x^3}{3}$$

(c) Use this series to find an approximate value for $\ln 2$.

(d) Use the Lagrange form of the remainder to find an upper bound for the error in this approximation.

(e) How good is this upper bound as an estimate for the actual error? *[17 marks]*

(© IB Organization 2008)

11. (a) Using the series for e^x, write down the Maclaurin expansion of e^{2x} in the form $\displaystyle\sum_{k=0}^{\infty} a_k x^k$

(b) Show that the Lagrange error term, $R_n(x)$ satisfies

$$R_n(x)\le \frac{2^{n+1}e}{(n+1)!}x^{n+1} \quad \text{if } 0\le x\le \frac{1}{2}$$

(c) Hence show that using 6 terms of the expansion in (a) to approximate e^{2x}, gives an error of less than 0.0001 in the approximation of

$$\int_0^{1/2} xe^{2x}\, dx$$

(d) How many terms are required to ensure the error is less than 10^{-9}? *[12 marks]*

5 Differential equations

In this chapter you will learn:

- to write real world problems as equations involving variables and their derivatives

- to solve these differential equations to find the original functions, by separating the variables

- to solve a different type of differential equation by using a substitution

- to solve another type of differential equation by multiplying through it by a function

- to approximate solutions to differential equations using Euler's method and Taylor series

- to represent differential equations graphically.

In the core course you will have looked at problems that involved velocity (as the rate of change of displacement) and acceleration (as the rate of change of velocity). We can model many processes in science by equations involving the rate of change of some variable, such as population growth and the cooling of bodies hotter than their surroundings. Newton's well known Second Law actually states that force is equal to the *rate of change* of momentum. To find the underlying variable from these rates of change involves solving differential equations.

In this chapter we first learn to form differential equations with emphasis on real-world applications, and then cover three methods for solving different types of differential equations.

5A Setting up differential equations

When we solve a **differential equation** we work from an equation involving derivatives to one without. You have done this already for the case where the equation can be written in the form $\dfrac{dy}{dx} = f(x)$.

As an example, consider the differential equation $\dfrac{dy}{dx} = 3x^2$.

To solve this differential equation all that is needed is integration: $y = \displaystyle\int 3x^2 \, dx = x^3 + c$

Because of the constant of integration you find that there is more than one solution to the differential equation. It could be any one of a family of solutions:

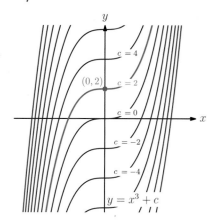

The solution $y = x^3 + c$ is called the **general solution** to the differential equation. We may also be given a **boundary condition** and told that the curve passes through a point, for example $(0, 2)$. This allows us to narrow down the general solution to the **particular solution** – in this case $y = x^3 + 2$.

Differential equations like this are used to solve problems involving rates of change and you often have to form a differential equation from the information given in a question. There are several phrases you should recognise:

KEY POINT 5.1

- 'rate of change' means the derivative (sometimes $\dfrac{dy}{dx}$, but other variables can be used)

- 'proportional to x' means a constant multiple of x, that is kx (k is a constant)

- 'inversely proportional to x' means $\dfrac{k}{x}$

- 'rate of decrease' means that the derivative is negative

Worked example 5.1

The rate of hair loss of a man is proportional to how much older than thirty he is. If he is born with $20\,000$ hairs and has $200\,000$ hairs at the age of 30, when will he be bald?

Define the variables, including units

Let H be the number of hairs

Let x be the age of the man in years

Turn the information into an equation

$$\frac{dH}{dx} = -k(x - 30)$$

The minus sign indicates that the number of hairs decreases when $x > 30$ and increases when $x < 30$

Solve the equation by integration

$$H = -\frac{kx^2}{2} + 30kx + c$$

Use the boundary conditions to find constants

When $x = 0$, $H = 20\,000$

$\therefore \quad 20\,000 = 0 + 0 + c$

$\Rightarrow \quad 20\,000 = c$

$\therefore$ When $x = 30$, $H = 200\,000$

$\therefore\ 200\,000 = -k\left(\dfrac{30^2}{2} - 30 \times 30\right) + 20\,000$

$\Rightarrow 180\,000 = 450k$

$\Rightarrow \quad\quad k = 400$

$\therefore H = -200x^2 + 12\,000x + 20\,000$

continued . . .

Interpret the requirement for baldness •

We need to find x when $H = 0$
$$0 = -200x^2 + 12000x + 20000$$

This is a quadratic equation. Solve it • by using the formula or a calculator

$$x = 61.6 \text{ or } -1.62 \ (3SF)$$

Since age must be positive
$$x = 61.6 \ (3SF)$$

Exercise 5A

1. Find the general solution of the following differential equations:

(a) (i) $\dfrac{dy}{dx} = 3\sin 2x$

(ii) $\dfrac{dy}{dx} = 4\cos\left(\dfrac{x}{3}\right)$

(b) (i) $3\dfrac{dy}{dx} - 2e^{2x} = 0$

(ii) $4e^{x/2} - \dfrac{dy}{dx} = 0$

(c) (i) $\cos^2 x \dfrac{dy}{dx} = 3$

(ii) $\cot^2 x \dfrac{dy}{dx} = 1$

2. Find the particular solution of the following differential equations:

(a) (i) $\dfrac{dy}{dx} = \dfrac{2}{x^2 + 4}$, $y = 2$ when $x = 0$

(ii) $\dfrac{dy}{dx} = \dfrac{1}{\sqrt{4 - x^2}}$, $y = \dfrac{\pi}{2}$ when $x = \sqrt{2}$

(b) (ii) $(x^2 + 1)\dfrac{dy}{dx} = 2x$, $y = 0$ when $x = 1$

(ii) $2x\dfrac{dy}{dx} = x^2 + 1$, $y = 1$ when $x = 1$

(c) (i) $\dfrac{1}{2}e^{3x}\dfrac{dy}{dx} = 3$, $y = 0$ when $x = 0$

(ii) $e^{2x-1}\dfrac{dy}{dx} = 4$, $y = 0$ when $x = \dfrac{1}{2}$

3. (a) (i) The value of an antique vase, in $, increases at a rate proportional to the time, in years, since it has been found. One year after it was found the value of the vase was $500 and it was increasing at the rate of $30 per year. Find the value of the vase 10 years after it was found.

(ii) The distance, in m, of a falling object from the top of a tower increases at a rate proportional to the time, in s, it has been falling. Initially the object is at the top of the tower. After 2 s the distance from the top of the tower is 20 m. Find the distance from the top of the tower after 3 s.

(b) (i) The rate of growth of a plant is inversely proportional to $(t+1)$, where t is the time, in weeks, since it was planted. Initially the plant was 23 cm tall and its height was increasing at the rate of 5 cm/week. Find the height of the plant after 10 weeks.

(ii) The mass of a baby increases at a rate inversely proportional to its age in months. When one month old, the baby had a mass of 4 kg, and when 2 months old it was 5 kg. Find the mass of the baby when it is 6 months old.

(c) (i) The value of a car decreases at a rate proportional to its age in years. The initial value of the car was £4500, and its value two years later was £3000. Find the equation for the value of the car which is t years old.

(ii) The price of a new games console decreases at a rate inversely proportional to the square root of time, in months, since it was released. Initially the games console cost $350, and one month later it cost $300. Find the equation for the cost of the games console after t months.

5B Separation of variables

The second type of differential equation which you need to be able to solve is one that can be written in the form:

$$\frac{dy}{dx} = f(x)g(y)$$

The method for solving such equations is called **separation of variables** and we shall refer to these differential equations as **variables separable differential equations**.

Technically this separation of $\frac{dy}{dx}$ is not mathematically valid. However, the resulting integration leads to the correct answer. Is it more important for you to get the full truth or a useful method?

KEY POINT 5.2

To solve a differential equation by separation of variables:

- get all the x values on one side and all the y values on the other side by multiplication or division
- separate $\frac{dy}{dx}$ as if it were a fraction
- integrate both sides.

Worked example 5.2

Show that the general solution to the differential equation

$$\frac{\mathrm{d}y}{\mathrm{d}x} = xy - x$$

can be written as $y = 1 + Ae^{x^2}$ if $y > 1$.

The equation can be written in the form $\frac{\mathrm{d}y}{\mathrm{d}x} = f(x)g(y)$ so use separation of variables

$$\frac{\mathrm{d}y}{\mathrm{d}x} = x(y - 1)$$

Separate variables: divide by $y - 1$ and multiply by $\mathrm{d}x$ Then integrate

$$\int \frac{1}{y-1}\,\mathrm{d}y = \int x\,\mathrm{d}x$$

$$\Rightarrow \quad \ln|y - 1| = x + c$$

Rearrange

$$\Rightarrow \quad |y - 1| = e^{x^2 + c}$$

But since $y - 1 > 0$

$$y - 1 = e^{x^2 + c}$$
$$= e^{x^2}e^c$$

Since e^c is a constant, relabel it as A

$$= Ae^{x^2}$$

$$\therefore y = 1 + Ae^{x^2}$$

Notice that when solving this type of differential equation we cannot simply add '$+c$' to the end of the solution. In the above example, we changed from $e^x e^c$ to Ae^x on the penultimate line. This is a very common trick to convert from an additive constant to a multiplicative constant.

The next example shows what to do when you are given boundary conditions.

Worked example 5.3

Solve the differential equation $\cos^2 x \dfrac{\mathrm{d}y}{\mathrm{d}x} = e^{-2y}$ for $0 \le x < \dfrac{\pi}{2}$ given that when $x = \dfrac{\pi}{4}$, $y = \dfrac{1}{2}$, giving your answer in the form $y = f(x)$.

The equation can be written in the form $\frac{\mathrm{d}y}{\mathrm{d}x} = f(x)g(y)$ so use separation of variables

$$\frac{1}{e^{-2y}}\frac{\mathrm{d}y}{\mathrm{d}x} = \frac{1}{\cos^2 x}$$

$$\Rightarrow \int e^{2y}\,\mathrm{d}y = \int \frac{1}{\cos^2 x}\,\mathrm{d}x$$

$$\Rightarrow \int e^{2y}\,\mathrm{d}y = \int \sec^2 x\,\mathrm{d}x$$

Do the integration

$$\frac{1}{2}e^{2y} = \tan x + c$$

EXAM HINT

$2c$ is just another constant. To keep the algebra simple we can rewrite it as another constant such as c' or C.

continued . . .

This is a convenient place to use boundary conditions to find c'

$$\Rightarrow e^{2y} = 2\tan x + c'$$
$$e^1 = 2\tan\frac{\pi}{4} + c'$$
$$\Rightarrow c' = e - 2$$
$$\therefore e^{2y} = 2\tan x + e - 2$$

Rearrange to get $y = f(x)$ as instructed

$$2y = \ln(2\tan x + e - 2)$$
$$\Rightarrow y = \frac{1}{2}\ln(2\tan x + e - 2)$$

EXAM HINT

Writing $\dfrac{1}{\cos^2 x}$ as $\sec^2 x$ should turn it into a more recognisable integral. This is a common trick.

Notice that the last example asked for the equation in explicit form ($y = f(x)$). If it had not done so it would have been acceptable to leave the answer in implicit form such as $e^{2y} = 2\tan x + e - 2$.

Exercise 5B

1. Find the particular solution of the following differential equations, giving your answer in the form $y = f(x)$ simplified as far as possible.

   (a) (i) $\dfrac{dy}{dx} = \dfrac{2x^2}{3y}$, $y = 0$ when $x = 0$

   (ii) $\dfrac{dy}{dx} = 4xy^2$, $y = 1$ when $x = 0$

   (b) (i) $\dfrac{dy}{dx} = \dfrac{4y}{x}$, $y = 2$ when $x = 1$

   (ii) $\dfrac{dy}{dx} = -3x^2 y$, $y = 3$ when $x = 0$

2. Find the particular solutions of the following differential equations. You do not need to give the equation for y explicitly.

   (a) (i) $\dfrac{dy}{dx} = \dfrac{\sin x}{\cos y}$, $y = 0$ when $x = \dfrac{\pi}{3}$

   (ii) $\dfrac{dy}{dx} = \dfrac{\sec^2 x}{\sec^2 y}$, $y = 0$ when $x = \dfrac{\pi}{3}$

(b) (i) $2(1+x)\dfrac{dy}{dx} = 1+y^2, y = 0$ when $x = 0$

(ii) $(1+x^2)\dfrac{dy}{dx} = 2x\sqrt{1-y^2}, y = 0$ when $x = 0$

(c) (i) $\dfrac{dy}{dx} = 2e^{x+2y}, y = 0$ when $x = 0$

(ii) $\dfrac{dy}{dx} = e^{x-y}, y = 2$ when $x = 0$

3. Find the general solution of the following differential equations, giving your answer in the form $y = f(x)$ simplified as far as possible.

(a) (i) $2y\dfrac{dy}{dx} = 3x^2$ (ii) $\dfrac{1}{y^2}\dfrac{dy}{dx} = 2x$

(b) (i) $x\dfrac{dy}{dx} = \sec y$ (ii) $\csc x\dfrac{dy}{dx} = 1+y^2$

(c) (i) $(x-1)\dfrac{dy}{dx} = x(y+3)$ (ii) $(1-x^2)\dfrac{dy}{dx} = xy+y$

4. Solve the differential equation $\dfrac{dy}{dx} = 2y(1-x)$ given that when

$x = 1, y = 1$. Give your answer in the form $y = f(x)$.   *[6 marks]*

5. Given that $\dfrac{dN}{dt} = -kN$, where k is a positive constant, show that

$N = Ae^{-kt}$.   *[6 marks]*

6. Find the general solution of the differential equation

$x\dfrac{dy}{dx} - 4 = y^2$, giving your answer in the form $y = f(x)$.   *[6 marks]*

7. Given that $\dfrac{dy}{dx} = \sqrt{\dfrac{1-y^2}{1-x^2}}$ and that $y = \dfrac{\sqrt{3}}{2}$ when $x = \dfrac{1}{2}$, show

that $2y = x\sqrt{k} + \sqrt{1-x^2}$, where k is a constant to be found. *[7 marks]*

5C Homogeneous differential equations

A homogeneous differential equation is one of the form:

$$\frac{dy}{dx} = f\left(\frac{y}{x}\right)$$

For example $\dfrac{dy}{dx} = \dfrac{y^2}{x^2}$ and $\dfrac{dy}{dx} = \dfrac{x^2+y^2}{2xy}$ are both homogeneous

because

$$\frac{dy}{dx} = \left(\frac{y}{x}\right)^2 \text{ and } \frac{dy}{dx} = \frac{1}{2}\left(\frac{x^2}{xy}+\frac{y^2}{xy}\right) = \frac{1}{2}\left(\frac{1}{\left(\frac{y}{x}\right)}+\frac{y}{x}\right) \text{ respectively.}$$

The first we can already solve by separating variables but the second requires a new approach.

KEY POINT 5.3

Any homogeneous differential equation can be converted to a variables separable differential equation (if it is not already) by making the change of variable (or substitution):

$$y = vx$$

Here v is a variable and not a constant, so in making this substitution we must be sure to differentiate the product when replacing $\dfrac{dy}{dx}$:

$$\frac{dy}{dx} = \frac{d}{dx}(vx)$$

$$= x\frac{dv}{dx} + (v \times 1)$$

$$= x\frac{dv}{dx} + v$$

We will use this method to solve the second equation given above.

Worked example 5.4

Find the general solution of $\dfrac{dy}{dx} = \dfrac{x^2 + y^2}{2xy} \ x, y > 0$ in the form $y^2 = f(x)$.

Once we realise that we can't separate the variables we consider whether it is homogeneous. It is (see above) and so we use the change of variable $y = vx$

Let $y = vx$

Change everything into v and x including $\dfrac{dy}{dx}$ and then simplify

Then, $\dfrac{dy}{dx} = \dfrac{d}{dx}(vx)$

$$= x\frac{dv}{dx} + v$$

and so,

$$x\frac{dv}{dx} + v = \frac{x^2 + (vx)^2}{2x(vx)}$$

$$\Rightarrow x\frac{dv}{dx} + v = \frac{x^2 + v^2 x^2}{2vx^2}$$

$$\Rightarrow x\frac{dv}{dx} + v = \frac{1 + v^2}{2v}$$

continued . . .

$$\Rightarrow x\frac{dv}{dx} = \frac{1+v^2}{2v} - v$$

$$\Rightarrow x\frac{dv}{dx} = \frac{1-v^2}{2v}$$

Separate the variables and solve as normal

$$\therefore \int \frac{2v}{1-v^2}\,dv = \int \frac{1}{x}\,dx$$

$$\Rightarrow \quad -\ln\left|1-v^2\right| = \ln x + C$$

$$\Rightarrow \quad \ln\left|1-v^2\right| = \ln\tfrac{1}{x} - C$$

$$\Rightarrow \quad 1-v^2 = e^{\ln\frac{1}{x}-C}$$

$$= e^{\ln\frac{1}{x}}e^{-C}$$

$$= \frac{A}{x}$$

Replace v with $\dfrac{y}{x}$

$$\therefore 1 - \frac{y^2}{x^2} = \frac{A}{x}$$

$$\Rightarrow \quad x^2 - y^2 = Ax$$

$$\Rightarrow \quad y^2 = x(x-A)$$

Exercise 5C

1. Use a substitution $y = vx$ to find the general solution to the following homogeneous differential equations. You may leave your answers in implicit form.

   (a) (i) $\dfrac{dy}{dx} = \left(\dfrac{y}{x}\right)^2 - 2$ (ii) $\dfrac{dy}{dx} = \left(\dfrac{y}{x}\right)^2 - \dfrac{4y}{x}$

   (b) (i) $\dfrac{dy}{dx} = \dfrac{x+2y}{x}$ (ii) $\dfrac{dy}{dx} = \dfrac{xy - y^2}{x^2}$

   (c) (i) $x\dfrac{dy}{dx} = 3x - 4y$ (ii) $x\dfrac{dy}{dx} = 2xy + y^2$

   (d) (i) $\dfrac{dy}{dx} = \dfrac{y}{x} + e^{-\frac{y}{x}}$ (ii) $\dfrac{dy}{dx} = \dfrac{1}{\cos\left(\dfrac{y}{x}\right)} + \dfrac{y}{x}$

2. (a) Find the general solution to the equation $\dfrac{dy}{dx} = \dfrac{x+y}{x}$.

   (b) Find the particular solution for which $y = 3$ when $x = e$. *[7 marks]*

3. (a) Using a substitution $y = vx$ find the general solution to the differential equation $\dfrac{dy}{dx} = \dfrac{x^2 + y^2 + xy}{x^2}$, giving your answer in the form $y = f(x)$.

   (b) Find the particular solution which passes through the point $(1,1)$.

   [9 marks]

4. (a) Define the term 'homogeneous differential equation'.

(b) Show that $xy\dfrac{dy}{dx} = x^2 + y^2$ is a homogeneous differential equation.

(c) Find the particular solution for which $y = 4$ when $x = 1$, giving your answer in the form $y^2 = f(x)$. *[10 marks]*

5. (a) Write the differential equation $\dfrac{dy}{dx} = \dfrac{4x + y}{x - y}$ in the form $\dfrac{dy}{dx} = f\left(\dfrac{y}{x}\right)$.

(b) Hence find the general solution of the equation $\dfrac{dy}{dx} = \dfrac{4x + y}{x - y}$

in the form $2\ln|x| = f\left(\dfrac{y}{x}\right)$. *[8 marks]*

6. (a) Show that the substitution $x = X - 1$, $y = Y + 3$ turns

$\dfrac{dy}{dx} = \dfrac{4x - y + 7}{2x + y - 1}$ into a homogeneous differential equation.

(b) Hence find the particular solution with $x = 0$, $y = 3$ giving your answer in the form $f(x, y) = c$. *[9 marks]*

7. (a) A particular solution of the differential equation

$x\dfrac{dv}{dx} = f(v)$ has $v = 2$ when $x = e$.

If k is the value of v when $x = 1$, show that $\displaystyle\int_k^2 \dfrac{1}{f(y)}\,dy = 1$.

(b) (i) The differential equation $\dfrac{dy}{dx} = \ln y - \ln x$ has a particular

solution with $x = e$, $y = 2e$. Show that $\displaystyle\int_k^2 \dfrac{1}{\ln v - v}\,dv = 1$.

(ii) Hence find the value of k to three significant figures. *[14 marks]*

8. Prove that if $\dfrac{dy}{dx} = f\left(\dfrac{y}{x}\right)$, the substitution $y = vx$ produces

a differential equation in variables separable form. *[5 marks]*

5D Linear differential equations

Although not homogeneous, we already have the necessary tools to solve a differential equation such as:

$$x^2\frac{dy}{dx} + 2xy = e^x$$

because the left hand side (LHS) is of a convenient form.

We notice that $2x$ is the derivative of x^2 and $\dfrac{dy}{dx}$ the derivative of y, which means we have an expression that has resulted from the differentiation of a product $(x^2 y)$ using the product rule. Therefore we can write the equation equivalently as:

$$\frac{d}{dx}(x^2 y) = e^x$$

Now, we can integrate both sides and rearrange to get:

$$x^2 y = \int e^x \, dx$$

$$\Rightarrow y = \frac{e^x + C}{x^2}$$

When faced with a differential equation where we cannot separate the variables, the LHS will often be more complicated. However, this method does suggest a way to deal with these cases.

Consider, in general, a first order differential equation similar to that above:

$$\frac{dy}{dx} + P(x)y = Q(x)$$

where $P(x)$ and $Q(x)$ are just functions of x. This is known as a **linear differential equation**.

Note that if there is a function in front of $\dfrac{dy}{dx}$, we can divide through the equation by that function to get it to this form.

We now wish to make the LHS the derivative of a product as above; to do this we multiply through the equation by a function $I(x)$:

$$I(x)\frac{dy}{dx} + I(x)P(x)y = I(x)Q(x)$$

Notice that if $I(x)$ is chosen such that $I'(x) = I(x)P(x)$ then we have the LHS in the form that we require. From here we can proceed exactly as above:

$$\frac{d}{dx}(I(x)y) = I(x)Q(x)$$

$$\Rightarrow y = \frac{1}{I(x)}\int I(x)Q(x) \, dx$$

The only remaining question is to decide on the function $I(x)$ to make this work.

We need:

$$I'(x) = I(x)P(x)$$

$$\Rightarrow \frac{I'(x)}{I(x)} = P(x)$$

$$\Rightarrow \int \frac{I'(x)}{I(x)} \, dx = \int P(x) \, dx$$

$$\Rightarrow \ln|I(x)| = \int P(x) \, dx$$

$$\Rightarrow I(x) = e^{\int P(x)\, dx}$$

This function $I(x)$ is known as the **integrating factor**.

KEY POINT 5.4

Given a first order linear differential equation:

$$\frac{dy}{dx} + P(x)y = Q(x)$$

multiply through by the integrating factor, $I(x) = e^{\int P(x)\,dx}$,

and solve the resulting differential equation.

Worked example 5.5

Solve the differential equation $\cos x \dfrac{dy}{dx} - 2y\sin x = 3$ for $x \in \left]-\dfrac{\pi}{2}, \dfrac{\pi}{2}\right[$

where $y = 1$ when $x = 0$.

We first check to see whether the LHS is the derivative of a product. It isn't (although if the 2 weren't there it would be). Therefore we start by dividing through by $\cos x$ to get the equation in the correct form for applying the integrating factor

$$\cos x \frac{dy}{dx} - 2y\sin x = 3$$

$$\Rightarrow \frac{dy}{dx} - 2y\frac{\sin x}{\cos x} = \frac{3}{\cos x}$$

$$\Rightarrow \frac{dy}{dx} - (2\tan x)y = 3\sec x$$

Find the integrating factor

$$I(x) = e^{\int P(x)\,dx}$$

making sure not to miss the $-$ sign on $P(x)$

$$I(x) = e^{\int -2\tan x\,dx}$$

$$= e^{-2\ln|\sec x|}$$

$$= e^{\ln(\sec x)^{-2}}$$

$$= e^{\ln\cos^2 x}$$

$$= \cos^2 x$$

We now multiply through by $\cos^2 x$ and check that the LHS is of the form

$$\frac{d}{dx}(y\cos^2 x) = \cos^2 x\frac{dy}{dx} - 2\cos x\sin x$$

So,

$$\cos^2 x\frac{dy}{dx} - (2\cos^2 x\tan x)y = 3\cos^2 x\sec x$$

$$\Rightarrow \cos^2 x\frac{dy}{dx} - (2\cos x\sin x)y = 3\cos x$$

$$\Rightarrow \qquad \frac{d}{dx}(y\cos^2 x) = 3\cos x$$

We can now integrate both sides

$$y\cos^2 x = \int 3\cos x\,dx$$

$$= 3\sin x + c$$

And finally we need to find the constant C and rearrange into the form $y = f(x)$

Since $x = 0, y = 1$

$1\cos^2 0 = 3\sin 0 + c$

$$\Rightarrow c = 1$$

$\therefore y\cos^2 x = 3\sin x + 1$

$$\Rightarrow y = \sec^2 x(3\sin x + 1)$$

Exercise 5D

1. Use an integrating factor to find the general solution to each of the following linear differential equations:

   (a) (i) $\dfrac{dy}{dx} + 2y = e^x$ (ii) $\dfrac{dy}{dx} - 4y = e^x$

   (b) (i) $\dfrac{dy}{dx} + y\cot x = 1$ (ii) $\dfrac{dy}{dx} - (\tan x)y = \sec x$

   (c) (i) $\dfrac{dy}{dx} + \dfrac{y}{x} = \dfrac{1}{x^2}$ (ii) $\dfrac{dy}{dx} + \dfrac{y}{x} = \dfrac{1}{x^3}$

2. Find the particular solution of the linear differential equation
   $$\frac{dy}{dx} + y = e^x$$
   which has $y = e$ when $x = 1$.   *[8 marks]*

3. Find the general solution to the differential equation
   $$x^2 \frac{dy}{dx} - 2xy = \frac{x^4}{x-3}$$
       [8 marks]

4. Find the general solution of the differential equation
   $$\frac{dy}{dx} + y\sin x = e^{\cos x}$$
       [8 marks]

5. Find the particular solution of the linear differential equation
   $$x^2 \frac{dy}{dx} + xy = \frac{2}{x}$$ that passes through the point $(1,1)$.   *[10 marks]*

6. Given that $\cos x \dfrac{dy}{dx} + y\sin x = \cos^2 x$ and that $y = 2$ when $x = 0$, find y in terms of x.   *[12 marks]*

7. Why do we ignore the constant of integration when finding the integrating factor?

8. Find the general solution to the differential equation
   $$x\frac{dy}{dx} + 2y = 1 + \frac{1}{x}\frac{dy}{dx}$$
       [12 marks]

9. (a) Use the substitution $z = \dfrac{1}{y}$ to transform the equation
   $$\frac{dy}{dx} + xy = xy^2$$
   into a linear differential equation in x and z.

   (b) Solve the resulting equation, writing z in terms of x.

   (c) Find the particular solution to the original equation that has $y = 1$ when $x = 1$.   *[14 marks]*

10. (a) Using the substitution $z = y^2$ or otherwise, solve the equation

$$2y\frac{dy}{dx} + \frac{y^2}{x} = x^2$$

given that when $x = 4$, $y = -5$. Give your answer in the form $y = f(x)$.

(b) Use another substitution to find the general solution to the equation

$$\cos y \frac{dy}{dx} + \tan x \sin y = \sin x \qquad \textit{[15 marks]}$$

5E Approximations to solutions

Although we can now solve a good number of first order differential equations, there will still be some that cannot be solved in terms of an exact algebraic expression. In these cases it is possible to find an often very good numerical approximation to the solution.

We will consider two such methods here:

- a method based on using the gradient of points around the solution curve to move closer and closer to the solution at a particular value of x

- forming a Taylor polynomial to approximate the solution curve.

Before developing the first of these methods, we will look at representing solutions to such differential equations graphically.

Given a differential equation:

$$\frac{dy}{dx} = f(x, y)$$

we can find the gradient at any given point (a,b) by simply putting these values of $x = a$ and $y = b$ into the equation. Although we could pick any coordinates for this, it is easiest to choose integer-valued points.

For example, given the differential equation:

$$\frac{dy}{dx} = x - y^2 + 2$$

we can find the gradient at the point $(2,3)$:

$$\frac{dy}{dx} = 2 - 3^2 + 2 = -5$$

Continuing this process for a range of coordinates, we can build up a table showing the gradient at various points:

		x			
	-2	**-1**	**0**	**1**	**2**
-2	-4	-3	-2	-1	0
-1	-1	0	1	2	3
y **0**	0	1	2	3	4
1	-1	0	1	2	3
2	-4	-3	-2	-1	0

And from here we can represent the gradient at each point graphically by drawing the tangent at that point:

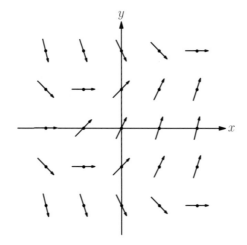

KEY POINT 5.5

> A plot of the tangents at all points (x, y) is called the **slope field** of a differential equation.

From the slope field, we can then construct approximate solution curves that correspond to different initial conditions. To do so we just observe two rules.

Solution curves:

1. follow the direction of the tangents at each point

2. do not cross.

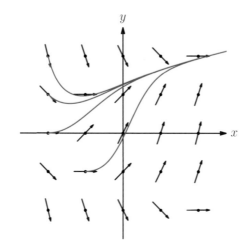

The slight drawback here is that, without finding enough tangents to form the slope field in some detail, it can be difficult to get a good impression of what the solution curves should look like, and of course, it is very time consuming to generate the tangents at a large number of points.

However, the process of generating the slope field can be made easier by finding the relationship between all points with the same gradient.

KEY POINT 5.6

A curve on which all points have the same gradient is known as an **isocline**.

To find isoclines set $\dfrac{dy}{dx} = c$ for some constant c.

In the example above, with $\dfrac{dy}{dx} = x - y^2 + 2$ the isoclines will be given by:

$$c = x - y^2 + 2 \implies y^2 = x + 2 - c.$$

Therefore, on the isocline corresponding to:

- $c = 0$ ($y^2 = x + 2$), the tangents at every point will have gradient 0

- $c = 1$ ($y^2 = x + 1$), the tangents at every point will have gradient 1 and so on.

This allows us to sketch a dense slope field quickly (and without having to fill in the sort of table we used above).

To do this, we first sketch a few isoclines, and then go along each isocline and draw arrows corresponding to the appropriate gradient.

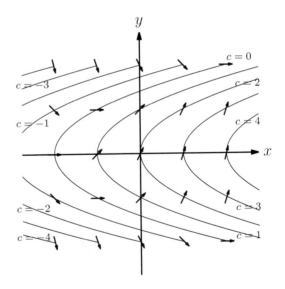

We can then construct the family of solution curves:

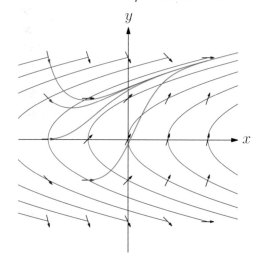

Using this idea of the slope field and solution curves, we can reconstruct the curve relating to a particular initial condition by starting at the point (x_0, y_0) of the initial condition and then moving step-by-step in the direction of the slope field to other points that lie approximately on the solution curve:

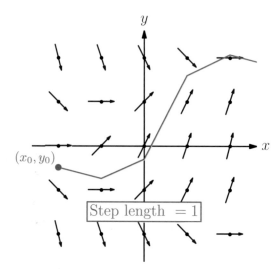

Obviously, this only gives an approximation to the solution curve, but the accuracy can be improved by taking smaller step lengths and more of them:

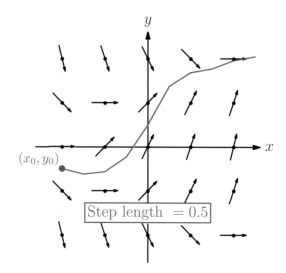

This process is known as **Euler's method** and can be summarised as follows.

KEY POINT 5.7

Given the differential equation:

$$\frac{dy}{dx} = f(x, y) \text{ with } y = y_0 \text{ when } x = x_0$$

- Start at the point (x_0, y_0) and find the gradient $m_0 = f(x_0, y_0)$.

- Move a fixed step h in the x-direction and calculate the corresponding distance k in the y-direction from the gradient of the slope field: $k = m_0 h$

- Using the new point $(x_0 + h, y_0 + k)$ repeat the above.

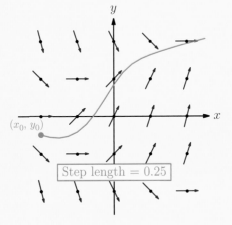

Continuing the above generates a sequence of points that approximate the solution curve.

Worked example 5.6

Using Euler's method with a step length of 0.25, approximate the solution, y, of the differential equation

$$\frac{dy}{dx} = x - y^2 + 2$$

when $x = 1$, given that $y = 1$ when $x = 0$. Give your answer to 3SF.

Find the gradient at the point (0, 1) by substituting into the differential equation

$$x_0 = 0, \ y_0 = 1$$
$$\therefore m_0 = 0 - 1^2 + 2 = 1$$

The x step length is 0.25 so this gives x_1 immediately.
Using $y = mx$ find the corresponding y-distance and add to y_0

$$x_1 = 0 + 0.25 = 0.25$$
$$y_1 = 1 + (1 \times 0.25) = 1.25$$

continued . . .

Find the gradient at the point (0.25, 1.25) by substituting into the differential equation

$$\therefore m_1 = 0.25 - 1.25^2 + 2 = 0.6875$$

The x step length is 0.25 so find x_2 by adding this step length to x_1
Using $y = mx$ find the corresponding y-distance and add to y_1

$$x_2 = 0.25 + 0.25 = 0.5$$
$$y_2 = 1.25 + (0.6875 \times 0.25)$$
$$= 1.421875$$

Now continue with the above process until $x = 1$ is reached. It may be helpful to record the information in a table to keep track of the calculations, but for lengthy decimals record only the first few decimal places and use the ANS button on your calculator in subsequent calculations

x	y	m
0	1	1
0.25	1.25	0.6875
0.5	1.421 875	$0.5 - 1.421875^2 + 2$ $= 0.47827$
0.75	$1.421875 + (0.47827 \times 0.25)$ $= 1.54144$	$0.75 - 1.54144^2 + 2$ $= 0.37395$
1	$1.54144 + (0.37395 \times 0.25)$ $= 1.63493$	

Round to 3SF

$$y(1) \approx 1.63$$

EXAM HINT

In the exam you can start filling in a table such as this immediately; it is a good idea to record your working at each stage.

We will now look at the second method of approximating solutions to differential equations, this time using our knowledge of Taylor series from chapter 4 of this option.

Given a differential equation

$$\frac{dy}{dx} = f(x, y) \qquad \text{with} \quad x = x_0, y = y_0$$

we can form a Taylor series for the solution, y, about the point $x = x_0$ given in the boundary condition:

Taylor series were looked at in Section 4D.

$$y = y(x_0) + y'(x_0)(x - x_0) + \frac{y''(x_0)}{2!}(x - x_0)^2 + \frac{y'''(x_0)}{3!}(x - x_0)^3 + \dots$$

where $y(x_0)$ means y evaluated at the point $x = x_0$.

Truncating this series to a polynomial of some desired degree (usually 3 or 4) will produce an approximation to the solution as required.

The only difficulty here is in finding the derivatives, $y', y'', y''', \dots$ This can be done by successively differentiating the original differential equation with respect to x:

$$y'' = \frac{d}{dx}\left(\frac{dy}{dx}\right) = \frac{d}{dx}\big(f(x,y)\big)$$

$$y''' = \frac{d}{dx}\left(\frac{d}{dx}\big(f(x,y)\big)\right)$$

and so on as required, before evaluating each derivative at $x = x_0$, $y = y_0$.

NB. To differentiate $f(x,y)$ here we will need to use the technique of implicit differentiation.

KEY POINT 5.8

The solution of a differential equation:

$$\frac{dy}{dx} = f(x,y) \qquad x = x_0, y = y_0$$

can be approximated by forming a Taylor polynomial for y about the point x_0:

$$y = y(x_0) + y'(x_0)(x - x_0)$$
$$+ \frac{y''(x_0)}{2!}(x - x_0)^2 + \frac{y'''(x_0)}{3!}(x - x_0)^3 + \dots$$

where y'', y''', etc. can be found by successively differentiating the original differential equation with respect to x.

Worked example 5.7

Find a Taylor polynomial of degree 3 to approximate the solution of the differential equation

$$\frac{dy}{dx} = x^2 + y^2,\ x = 1, y = 0$$

and use this polynomial to find an approximation of $y(1.1)$ to 4DP.

Form a Taylor polynomial about the point $x = 1$, the given initial point. To do this we will need $y(1), y'(1), y''(1)$ and $y'''(1)$. We are given $y(1)$ and we can immediately evaluate $y'(1)$ by substituting $x = 1, y = 0$ into the differential equation

$y(1) = 0$
$y'(1) = 1^2 + 0^2 = 1$

We then need to find $y''(1)$ and $y'''(1)$ by first differentiating the differential equation

$$y'' = \frac{d}{dx}(y')$$
$$= \frac{d}{dx}(x^2 + y^2)$$

Use the chain rule for $\frac{d}{dx}(y^2)$

$$= 2x + 2yy'$$

continued . . .

Evaluate at $x = 1, y = 0, y' = 1$

$$\therefore y''(1) = (2\times 1) + (2\times 0 \times 1)$$
$$= 2$$

Follow the same procedure for $y'''(1)$

Similarly,

$$y''' = \frac{d}{dx}(y'')$$
$$= \frac{d}{dx}(2x + 2yy')$$

Apply the product rule and the chain rule to yy'

$$= 2 + 2(y' \, y' + yy'')$$
$$= 2\left(1 + (y')^2 + yy''\right)$$
$$\therefore y'''(1) = 2\left(1 + 1^2 + (0\times 2)\right)$$
$$= 4$$

Now form the Taylor polynomial

Therefore the Taylor polynomial of degree 3 is

$$y \approx y(1) + y'(1)(x-1) + \frac{y''(1)}{2!}(x-1)^2 + \frac{y'''(1)}{3!}(x-1)^3$$
$$\approx 0 + 1(x-1) + \frac{2}{2!}(x-1)^2 + \frac{4}{3!}(x-1)^3$$
$$\approx (x-1) + (x-1)^2 + \frac{2}{3}(x-1)^3$$

So

$$y(1.1) \approx 1.1 - 1 + (1.1-1)^2 + \frac{2}{3}(1.1-1)^3$$
$$\approx 0.1107$$

Exercise 5E

1. Use Euler's method with step length $h = 0.1$ to find an approximate value of y when $x = 0.4$ for the following differential equations:

(a) (i) $\dfrac{dy}{dx} = x^2 - y^2$, $y = 1$ at $x = 0$

(ii) $\dfrac{dy}{dx} = \ln(x + y)$, $y = 2$ at $x = 0$

(b) (i) $\dfrac{dy}{dx} - y^2 = \sin(x^2)$, $y = 1$ at $x = 0$

(ii) $\dfrac{dy}{dx} - y = 2e^x$, $y = 0$ at $x = 0$

(c) (i) $(x + y)\dfrac{dy}{dx} = 3x^2 + y^2$, $y = 2$ at $x = 0$

(ii) $(x + y)\dfrac{dy}{dx} = e^{x+0.2y}$, $y = 1$ at $x = 0$

2. For the following differential equations, find the equation of the isoclines and hence by sketching these construct the slope field and solution curves.

(a) (i) $\dfrac{dy}{dx} = 2x - y$ (ii) $\dfrac{dy}{dx} = \dfrac{x}{y}$

(b) (i) $\dfrac{dy}{dx} = xy$ (ii) $\dfrac{dy}{dx} = xy + 2x$

(c) (i) $\dfrac{dy}{dx} = 2x - y^2$ (ii) $\dfrac{dy}{dx} = x^2 + y - 3$

3. Find a Taylor polynomial of degree 3 about the point x_0 that approximates the solution of the following differential equations:

(a) (i) $\dfrac{dy}{dx} = y^2 - x, \ y_0 = 1$ at $x_0 = 0$

(ii) $(1 + 2x)\dfrac{dy}{dx} = x + 4y^2, \ y_0 = \dfrac{1}{2}$ at $x_0 = 0$

(b) (i) $\dfrac{dy}{dx} = \cos x - \sin y + x^2, \ y_0 = \dfrac{\pi}{2}$ at $x_0 = -\pi$

(ii) $\sin x \dfrac{dy}{dx} + y \cos x = y^2, \ y_0 = \sqrt{2}$ at $x_0 = \dfrac{\pi}{4}$

4. For the differential equation
$$\frac{dy}{dx} = (y + 1)(x - 3)$$

(a) Give the equations of the isoclines.

(b) Construct the slope field.

(c) Sketch the solution curves.

(d) What can you say about the solution curve corresponding to the initial condition $x = 0, y = -1$? *[9 marks]*

5. For the differential equation
$$\frac{dy}{dx} = \frac{(x + y)}{xy + 2}$$

with $y = 1$ when $x = 0$, use Euler's method with step length $h = 0.2$ to find an approximate value of y when $x = 1$. Give your answer correct to three decimal places. *[9 marks]*

6. Consider the differential equation
$$\frac{dy}{dx} = xe^y$$

with the boundary condition $x = 1, y = 0.3$.

(a) Use Euler's method with $h = 0.1$ to find an approximate value of y when $x = 1.3$.

(b) Solve the differential equation.

(c) (i) Find the percentage error in your approximation from part (a).

(ii) How can this error be decreased? *[14 marks]*

7. The function $y = f(x)$ satisfies the differential equation
$f'(x) = x^2 y$ with $f(0) = 0.5$.

(a) (i) Use Euler's method with step length $h = 0.25$ to find an approximate value of $f(1)$.

    (ii) How can your approximation be made more accurate?

(b) Solve the differential equation and hence find the actual value of $f(1)$.

(c) Sketch the graph of your solution and use it to explain why your approximation from part (a) is smaller than the actual value of $f(1)$.   *[17 marks]*

8. For the differential equation $(1 + x) y' = y^2 + e^x$

(a) (i) Show that:

$$y'' = \frac{y'(2y - 1) + e^x}{1 + x}$$

$$y''' = \frac{2y''(y - 1) + 2(y')^2 + e^x}{1 + x}$$

    (ii) Given also that $y = 1$ at $x = 0$, find a 3rd degree Taylor polynomial about $x = 0$ to approximate the solution.

(b) Hence find an approximation to the solution at $x = 0.1$.   *[12 marks]*

9. Consider the differential equation

$$\frac{d^2 y}{dx^2} = 6xe^{-x^2}$$

with boundary conditions $y = 3$ and $\dfrac{dy}{dx} = 1$ when $x = 0$.

(a) Find an expression for $\dfrac{dy}{dx}$ in terms of x.

(b) Use the Euler method with step length 0.2 to find the approximate value of y when $x = 1$.   *[12 marks]*

Summary

- 'Rate of change' means the derivative (sometimes $\frac{dy}{dx}$, but other variables can be used).

  'Proportional to x' means a constant multiple of x, that is kx (k is a constant).

  'Inversely proportional to x' means $\frac{k}{x}$.

  'Rate of decrease' means that the derivative is negative.

- A **differential equation** of the form $\frac{dy}{dx} = f(x)g(y)$ can be solved by **separation of variables**:

  $\int \frac{1}{g(y)} dy = \int f(x) dx$.

- A differential equation which can be written in the form $\frac{dy}{dx} = f\left(\frac{y}{x}\right)$ is called a homogeneous differential equation.

- A substitution $y = vx$ turns homogeneous differential equations into **variables separable differential equations**.

- A **linear differential equation** can be written as $\frac{dy}{dx} + P(x)y = Q(x)$.

- Linear differential equations can be solved by multiplying through by the **integrating factor**:

  $$I(x) = e^{\int P(x)dx}$$

  This turns the equation into $\frac{dy}{dx}(I(x)\,y) = I(x)Q(x)$.

- A plot of the tangents at all points (x, y) is called the **slope field** of a differential equation.

  Drawing a slope field enables us to construct approximate solution curves to a differential equation. These different solution curves are determined by the initial conditions.

- An **isocline** is a curve on which all tangents have the same gradient.

- **Euler's method** for approximating solutions to differential equations at a given point states that given the differential equation:

  $$\frac{dy}{dx} = f(x, y) \text{ with } y = y_0 \text{ when } x = x_0$$

  - Start at the point (x_0, y_0) and find the gradient $m_0 = f(x_0, y_0)$.
  - Move a fixed step h in the x-direction and calculate the corresponding distance k in the y-direction from the gradient of the slope field: $k = m_0 h$.
  - Using the new point $(x_0 + h, y_0 + k)$ repeat the above.

- The solution of a differential equation

  $$\frac{dy}{dx} = f(x, y) \text{ with } x = x_0, y = y_0$$

  can be approximated by forming a Taylor polynomial for y about the point x_0:

  $$y = y(x_0) + y'(x_0)(x - x_0) + \frac{y''(x_0)}{2!}(x - x_0)^2 + \frac{y'''(x_0)}{3!}(x - x_0)^3 + \cdots$$

  where y'', y''', etc. can be found by successively differentiating the original differential equation w.r.t. x.

Mixed examination practice 5

1. (a) Sketch on graph paper the slope field for the differential equation

$$\frac{dy}{dx} = x - y$$

at the points (x, y) where $x \in \{0,1,2,3,4\}$ and $y \in \{0,1,2,3,4\}$.

(b) On the slope field sketch the curve that passes through the point $(0,3)$.

(c) Solve the differential equation to find the equation of this curve. Give your answer in the form $y = f(x)$. *[14 marks]*

(© IB Organization 2007)

2. (a) For the differential equation

$$\cos x \frac{dy}{dx} + y\sin x + 2y^3 = 0$$

and the boundary condition $y = 1$ at $x = 0$, find a 3rd degree Taylor polynomial to approximate the solution close to $x = 0$.

(b) Use this polynomial to approximate the solution at $x = 0.2$. Give your answer to 3 significant figures. *[9 marks]*

3. Solve the differential equation

$$x^2 \frac{dy}{dx} = 3xy + 2y^2$$

given that $y = 4$ at $x = 2$. Give your answer in the form $y = f(x)$. *[9 marks]*

4. A curve that passes through the point (1, 2) is defined by the differential equation

$$\frac{dy}{dx} = 2x(1 + x^2 - y)$$

(a) (i) Use Euler's method to get an approximate value of y when $x = 1.3$, taking steps of 0.1. Show intermediate steps to four decimal places in a table.

(ii) How can a more accurate answer be obtained using Euler's method?

(b) Solve the differential equation, giving your answer in the form $y = f(x)$. *[14 marks]*

5. Consider the differential equation

$$\frac{dy}{dx} - 4xy = e^{2x^2}$$

with $y = 4$ when $x = 0$.

(a) Use the Euler method with step length $h = 0.05$ to find an approximation to the value of y when $x = 0.2$.

(b) Use the integrating factor method to solve the differential equation and hence find the exact value of y when $x = 1$.

(c) How can the difference between the values found in (a) and (b) be decreased? *[17 marks]*

6. Given the differential equation

$$x^2 \frac{dy}{dx} = y + xy$$

with boundary condition $y = 1$ at $x = 1$:

(a) (i) Show that $y'' = \dfrac{y'(1-x) + y}{x^2}$.

    (ii) Find a degree 2 Taylor polynomial close to $x = 1$ to approximate the solution.

    (iii) Hence find an approximation to the solution at $x = 1.1$.

(b) (i) Solve the differential equation exactly, giving your answer in the form $y = f(x)$.

    (ii) Hence find the true solution at $x = 1.1$, giving your answer to 5 decimal places.

(c) Find the percentage error in your approximation, to 2 significant figures. *[17 marks]*

7. Given that $\dfrac{1}{2}\dfrac{dy}{dx} = \dfrac{y^2 + 1}{x^2 + 1}$ and that $y = 0$ when $x = 0$, express y

in terms of x. *[9 marks]*

8. Solve the differential equation

$$(1 + x)\frac{dy}{dx} - xy = xe^{-x}$$

given that $y = 1$ at $x = 0$. Give your answer in the form $y = f(x)$. *[9 marks]*

9. (a) Show that

$$x \frac{dy}{dx} = y + \frac{x}{\ln y - \ln x}$$

is a homogeneous differential equation.

(b) If $x > 0, y > 0$, find the general solution to the differential equation, giving your answer in the form $ye^{y/x} = f(x)$. *[11 marks]*

6 Summary and mixed examination practice

Introductory problem revisited

Consider a wedding cake with four layers:

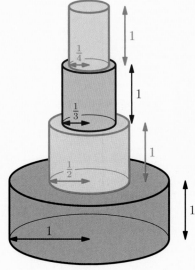

Each layer has a thickness of 1. The first layer has a radius of 1, the second a radius of $\frac{1}{2}$, the third a radius of $\frac{1}{3}$ and the fourth a radius of $\frac{1}{4}$.

Find the volume of the cake and the surface area (excluding the bottom of the first layer) that needs covering with icing.

Now imagine there are infinitely many layers to the cake. What can you say about the volume of the cake and the surface area that needs icing now?

We note that each layer of the cake is a cylinder so the volumes will be given by:

$$V_1 = \pi \times 1^2 \times 1 = \pi$$

$$V_2 = \pi \times \left(\frac{1}{2}\right)^2 \times 1 = \frac{\pi}{2^2}$$

$$V_3 = \pi \times \left(\frac{1}{3}\right)^2 \times 1 = \frac{\pi}{3^2}$$

$$V_4 = \pi \times \left(\frac{1}{4}\right)^2 \times 1 = \frac{\pi}{4^2}$$

$$\therefore V = V_1 + V_2 + V_3 + V_4$$

$$= \pi + \frac{\pi}{2^2} + \frac{\pi}{3^2} + \frac{\pi}{4^2}$$

$$= \pi\left(1 + \frac{1}{2^2} + \frac{1}{3^2} + \frac{1}{4^2}\right)$$

Continuing this series for the cake with infinitely many layers we get $V = \pi\sum_{k=1}^{\infty}\frac{1}{k^2}$,

which we now know to be a convergent p-series and so we can conclude that the volume of this infinitely layered cake is finite!

If we did not know this p-series result (or if we did and wanted an upper bound on the volume) we could say:

$$V = \pi\left\{1 + \frac{1}{2^2} + \frac{1}{3^2} + \frac{1}{4^2} + \frac{1}{5^2} + \frac{1}{6^2} + \frac{1}{7^2} + \frac{1}{8^2} + \ldots\right\}$$

$$\leq \pi\left\{1 + \left(\frac{1}{2^2} + \frac{1}{2^2}\right) + \left(\frac{1}{4^2} + \frac{1}{4^2} + \frac{1}{4^2} + \frac{1}{4^2}\right) + \left(\frac{1}{8^2} + \ldots\right) + \ldots\right\}$$

$$= \pi\left\{1 + \frac{1}{2}\left(\frac{1}{2} + \frac{1}{2}\right) + \frac{1}{4}\left(\frac{1}{4} + \frac{1}{4} + \frac{1}{4} + \frac{1}{4}\right) + \frac{1}{8}\left(\frac{1}{8} + \ldots\right) + \ldots\right\}$$

$$= \pi\left\{1 + \frac{1}{2}(1) + \frac{1}{4}(1) + \frac{1}{8}(1) + \ldots\right\}$$

$$= \pi\left(\frac{1}{1 - \frac{1}{2}}\right) \quad \text{(sum of a geometric sequence)}$$

$$= 2\pi$$

Either way the volume is finite (and $\leq 2\pi$). In fact it can be shown that $\sum_{k=1}^{\infty}\frac{1}{k^2} = \frac{\pi^2}{6}$ so $V = \frac{\pi^3}{6}$.

Now for the surface area of each cylinder which is made up of the top and the sides.

If we first deal with the tops of each layer, looking down from above we see that when taken together we get the full circle of radius 1; that is a total surface area of $\pi \times 1^2 = \pi$. This will be the same no matter how many layers we have.

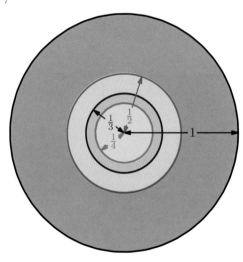

We can also establish this in a more formal way by noting that the top of each layer is made up of the circular area of the top of the cylinder minus the circular area of the layer above.

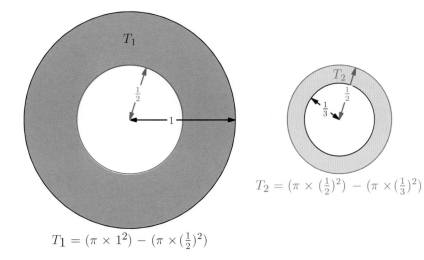

$$T_1 = (\pi \times 1^2) - (\pi \times (\tfrac{1}{2})^2)$$

$$T_2 = (\pi \times (\tfrac{1}{2})^2) - (\pi \times (\tfrac{1}{3})^2)$$

So,

$$T_1 = (\pi \times 1^2) - \left(\pi \times \left(\frac{1}{2}\right)^2\right)$$

$$T_2 = \left(\pi \times \left(\frac{1}{2}\right)^2\right) - \left(\pi \times \left(\frac{1}{3}\right)^2\right)$$

$$T_3 = \left(\pi \times \left(\frac{1}{3}\right)^2\right) - \left(\pi \times \left(\frac{1}{4}\right)^2\right)$$

$$T_4 = \left(\pi \times \left(\frac{1}{4}\right)^2\right) - \left(\pi \times \left(\frac{1}{5}\right)^2\right)$$

$$\therefore T = (\pi \times 1^2) - \left(\pi \times \left(\frac{1}{5}\right)^2\right) \quad \text{(all other terms between cancel out)}$$

$$= \pi\left(1 - \left(\frac{1}{5}\right)^2\right)$$

The same pattern of cancellation will occur for the cake with n layers, leaving us with just:

$$T_n = \pi\left(1 - \left(\frac{1}{n+1}\right)^2\right)$$

Then letting $n \to \infty$ so we have infinitely many layers for the cake,

$$T = \lim_{n \to \infty} T_n$$

$$= \pi \lim_{n \to \infty}\left(1 - \left(\frac{1}{n+1}\right)^2\right)$$

$$= \pi\left(1 - (0)^2\right) \quad \text{(algebra of limits)}$$

$$= \pi$$

To finish we need to add to this the surface area of the sides of the cylinders (curved surface area of cylinder is given by $2\pi rh$).

$$S_1 = 2\pi \times 1 \times 1 = 2\pi$$

$$S_2 = 2\pi \times \frac{1}{2} \times 1 = \frac{2\pi}{2}$$

$$S_3 = 2\pi \times \frac{1}{3} \times 1 = \frac{2\pi}{3}$$

$$S_4 = 2\pi \times \frac{1}{4} \times 1 = \frac{2\pi}{4}$$

$$\therefore S = S_1 + S_2 + S_3 + S_4$$

$$= 2\pi + \frac{2\pi}{2} + \frac{2\pi}{3} + \frac{2\pi}{4}$$

$$= 2\pi \left(1 + \frac{1}{2} + \frac{1}{3} + \frac{1}{4} \right)$$

Continuing this series for the cake with infinitely many layers we get,

$$S = 2\pi \sum_{k=1}^{\infty} \frac{1}{k}$$

which we now know to be a divergent *p*-series and so we conclude that even though the surface area of the top of each layer is finite (total π) the total surface area when including the area of the sides is infinite.

Therefore we have a cake with finite volume but infinite surface area; that is, a cake that we could eat but could not find enough icing to cover...

Summary

- Limits behave as expected algebraically; that is, if the sequence $\{a_n\}$ **converges** to a limit a and the sequence $\{b_n\}$ to a limit b, then:

$$\lim_{n\to\infty}\left(pa_n + qb_n\right) = p\lim_{n\to\infty}a_n + q\lim_{n\to\infty}b_n = pa + qb \text{ for } p,q \in \mathbb{R}$$

$$\lim_{n\to\infty}\left(a_n b_n\right) = \left(\lim_{n\to\infty}a_n\right)\left(\lim_{n\to\infty}b_n\right) = ab$$

$$\lim_{n\to\infty}\left(\frac{a_n}{b_n}\right) = \frac{\lim_{n\to\infty}a_n}{\lim_{n\to\infty}b_n} = \frac{a}{b} \text{ when } b \neq 0$$

- If the sequence $\{a_n\}$ **diverges**, then for some constant $c \in \mathbb{R}$:

$$\lim_{n\to\infty}\left(\frac{c}{a_n}\right) = 0 \text{ and } \lim_{n\to\infty}\left(\frac{a_n}{c}\right) = \infty$$

- It is usually necessary to manipulate a_n into a form where the numerator and denominator both have finite limits so that the algebra of limits can be applied. This can often be achieved by dividing through by the highest power of n.

- If a sequence is sandwiched between two other sequences, both of which converge to the same limit, then that sequence is squeezed and must converge to the limit too.

    The **Squeeze Theorem**: if we have sequences $\{a_n\}, \{b_n\}$ and $\{c_n\}$ such that

$$a_n \leq b_n \leq c_n \text{ for all } n \in \mathbb{Z}^+ \text{ and } \lim_{n\to\infty}a_n = \lim_{n\to\infty}c_n = L < \infty$$

    then $\lim_{n\to\infty}b_n = L$

- If for any sequence $\{x_n\}$ such that $x_n \to x_0$ we have that $f(x_n) \to L$, then $L \in \mathbb{R}$ is said to be the limit of the function.

- To show that the limit of a function does not exist at a point x_0, find two sequences $x_n \to x_0$ and $y_n \to x_0$, but for which $f(x_n)$ and $f(y_n)$ do not tend to the same limit.

- If we find the limit of a function at point x_0 by having a sequence that approaches from below, we write $\lim_{x \to x_0^-} f(x)$.

  If we do so by having a sequence that approaches from above we write $\lim_{x \to x_0^+} f(x)$.

  We need both the limit from above and the limit from below to exist and coincide for the limit to exist at that point. If they do then:

  $$\lim_{x \to x_0} f(x) = \lim_{x \to x_0^+} f(x) = \lim_{x \to x_0^-} f(x)$$

- The Squeeze Theorem and the algebra of limits hold for functions as well.

- We can use **L'Hôpital's Rule** to find limits of functions of the form $\dfrac{`0`}{0}$ and $\dfrac{`\infty`}{\infty}$:

  Given functions $f(x)$ and $g(x)$ that are differentiable in the neighbourhood of a point a and $g(x) \neq 0$, if either:

  $$\lim_{x \to a} f(x) = \lim_{x \to a} g(x) = 0 \quad \text{or} \quad \lim_{x \to a} f(x) = \lim_{x \to a} g(x) = \infty$$

  then $\lim_{x \to a} \dfrac{f(x)}{g(x)} = \lim_{x \to a} \dfrac{f'(x)}{g'(x)}$ provided that the latter exists.

- It may be necessary to manipulate functions that have limits of the form '$0 \times \infty$' or '$\infty - \infty$' into quotients so that l'Hôpital's Rule can then be applied.

- A function $f(x)$ is continuous at the point x_0 if $\lim_{x \to x_0} f(x) = f(x_0)$

  Both the limit and the value $f(x_0)$ must exist for $f(x)$ to be continuous there.

- To show that a function is not continous at a point x_0, find a sequence $x_n \to x_0$ but for which $f(x_n) \nrightarrow f(x_0)$.

  The function is said to be continuous if it is continuous at all points of its domain.

- The derivative of a function $f(x)$ at the point x_0 is given by $f'(x_0) = \lim_{h \to 0} \dfrac{f(x_0 + h) - f(x_0)}{h}$

  Or equivalently by $f'(x_0) = \lim_{x \to x_0} \dfrac{f(x) - f(x_0)}{x - x_0}$ if the limit exists.

  If not, then the function is not differentiable at that point.

- For a function $f(x)$ to be differentiable at a point x_0:

  - $f(x)$ must be continuous at x_0 (and hence $\lim_{x \to x_0} f(x)$ must already exist)

  - $f(x)$ must not have a 'sharp point' at x_0

  - the tangent to $f(x)$ at x_0 must not be vertical.

- A function that is differentiable at a point, is continuous at that point.

- **Rolle's Theorem** for differentiable functions states that:

  For a function $f(x)$, that is continuous on an interval $[a,b]$ and differentiable on $]a,b[$,

  if $f(a) = f(b)$ then there must exist a point $c \in]a,b[$ such that $f'(c) = 0$.

- The **Mean Value Theorem** is a generalisation of Rolle's Theorem that states that:

  For a function $f(x)$, that is continuous on an interval $[a,b]$ and differentiable on $]a,b[$, there must exist a point $c \in]a,b[$ such that $f'(c) = \dfrac{f(b) - f(a)}{b - a}$.

- The **Fundamental Theorem of Calculus** links the concepts of differentiation and integration (to find the area under a curve). For a continuous function $f(x)$ on the interval $[a,b]$,

$$\frac{d}{dx} \int_a^x f(t)\, dt = f(x)$$

  and for any function $g(x)$ such that $g'(x) = f(x)$

$$\int_a^b f(x)\, dx = g(b) - g(a).$$

- The **improper integral**

$$\int_a^\infty f(x)\, dx = \lim_{b \to \infty} \int_a^b f(x)\, dx$$

  is convergent (exists) if the limit is finite. Otherwise the integral is divergent (does not exist).

- Convergence or divergence of improper integrals can be established by comparison with other known convergent or divergent integrals; that is, if $0 \le f(x) \le g(x)$ for all $x \ge a$ then:

  - $\int_a^\infty f(x)\, dx$ is convergent if $\int_a^\infty g(x)\, dx$ is convergent.

  - $\int_a^\infty g(x)\, dx$ is divergent if $\int_a^\infty f(x)\, dx$ is divergent.

- $\int_a^\infty \dfrac{1}{x^p}\, dx$ converges only for $p > 1$.

- If $\int_a^\infty |f(x)|\, dx$ converges, then so does $\int_a^\infty f(x)\, dx$.

- Improper integrals of increasing functions or decreasing functions can be approximated by the sum of infinitely many rectangles of width 1.

  - For a *decreasing function* $f(x)$ for all $x > a$, we have an *upper and lower sum* such that:

$$\sum_{k=a+1}^\infty f(k) < \int_a^\infty f(x)\, dx < \sum_{k=a}^\infty f(k)$$

  - For an *increasing function* $g(x)$ for all $x > a$, we have an *upper and lower sum* such that:

$$\sum_{k=a}^\infty g(k) < \int_a^\infty g(x)\, dx < \sum_{k=a+1}^\infty g(k)$$

- The nth partial sum, S_n, of a series is the sum of the first n terms:

$$S_n = u_1 + u_2 + \cdots + u_n$$

  An infinite series converges to S if the sequence of its partial sums $S_1, S_2, S_3, S_4, \ldots$ converges to S.

$$S = \lim_{n \to \infty} S_n = \sum_{k=1}^\infty u_k$$

- **Divergence Test**

  If $\lim_{k \to \infty} u_k \neq 0$ or if the limit does not exist, the series $\displaystyle\sum_{k=1}^{\infty} u_k$ is divergent.

- **Comparison Test**

  Given two series of positive terms $\displaystyle\sum_{k=1}^{\infty} a_k$ and $\displaystyle\sum_{k=1}^{\infty} b_k$ such that $a_k \leq b_k$ for all k, then if:

  - $\displaystyle\sum_{k=1}^{\infty} b_k$ is convergent to a limit S, $\displaystyle\sum_{k=1}^{\infty} a_k$ is also convergent to a limit T where $T \leq S$

  - $\displaystyle\sum_{k=1}^{\infty} a_k$ is divergent, so is $\displaystyle\sum_{k=1}^{\infty} b_k$.

- **Limit Comparison Test**

  Given two series of positive terms $\displaystyle\sum_{k=1}^{\infty} a_k$ and $\displaystyle\sum_{k=1}^{\infty} b_k$, where $\lim_{n \to \infty} \dfrac{a_n}{b_n} = l > 0$, then if one series converges so does the other and if one series diverges so does the other.

- **Integral Test**

  Given a positive decreasing function $f(x)$, $x > 1$, if $\displaystyle\int_1^{\infty} f(x)\,dx$ is

  - convergent then $\displaystyle\sum_{k=1}^{\infty} f(k)$ is convergent

  - divergent then $\displaystyle\sum_{k=1}^{\infty} f(k)$ is divergent

- An **alternating series** is one with alternately positive and negative terms.

- **Alternating Series Test**

  If for an alternating series $\displaystyle\sum_{k=1}^{\infty} u_k$:

  - $|u_{k+1}| < |u_k|$ for all $k \in \mathbb{Z}^+$ and $\lim_{k \to \infty} |u_k| = 0$

  then the series is convergent.

- If $S = \displaystyle\sum_{k=1}^{\infty} u_k$ is the sum of an alternating series that satisfies:

  $$|u_{k+1}| < |u_k| \text{ for all } k \in \mathbb{Z}^+ \text{ and } \lim_{k \to \infty} |u_k| = 0$$

  then the error in taking the first n terms as an approximation to S (the **truncation error**) is less than the absolute value of the $(n + 1)$th term:

  $$|S - S_n| < |a_{n+1}|$$

- A series $\displaystyle\sum_{k=1}^{\infty} u_k$ is **absolutely convergent** if the series $\displaystyle\sum_{k=1}^{\infty} |u_k|$ is convergent.

  If a series $\displaystyle\sum_{k=1}^{\infty} u_k$ is convergent but $\displaystyle\sum_{k=1}^{\infty} |u_k|$ is divergent, then the series is **conditionally convergent**.

An absolutely convergent series is convergent.

- **Ratio Test**

  Given a series $\sum\limits_{k=1}^{\infty} u_k$:

  - If $\lim\limits_{k \to \infty} \left| \dfrac{u_{k+1}}{u_k} \right| < 1$, then the series is absolutely convergent (and hence convergent).

  - If $\lim\limits_{k \to \infty} \left| \dfrac{u_{k+1}}{u_k} \right| > 1$, then the series is divergent.

  - If $\lim\limits_{k \to \infty} \left| \dfrac{u_{k+1}}{u_k} \right| = 1$, then the Ratio Test is inconclusive.

- A **power series** is an infinite series of the form:

$$\sum_{k=0}^{\infty} a_k (x-b)^k = a_0 + a_1(x-b) + a_2(x-b)^2 + a_3(x-b)^3 + \cdots$$

  It may converge:

  - for all $x \in \mathbb{R}$

  - only for a single value $b \in \mathbb{R}$

  - for all $x \in \mathbb{R}$ such that $|x-b| < R$, where $R \in \mathbb{R}^+$.

- The largest number $R \in \mathbb{R}^+$ such that a power series converges for $|x-b| < R$ and diverges for $|x-b| > R$ is called the **radius of convergence** of the power series. It may be determined by the Ratio Test. If:

  - $R = \infty$ then the series converges for all $x \in \mathbb{R}$

  - $R = 0$ then the series converges only when $x = b$.

- The **interval of convergence** of a power series is the set of all points for which the series converges. It always includes all points such that $|x-b| < R$ but may also include end point(s) of this interval.

  A power series can be differentiated or integrated term by term over any interval contained within its interval of convergence.

- A **Maclaurin series** is an infinite polynomial which matches all the derivatives of a function at zero.

- The Maclaurin series for $f(x)$ is given by:

$$f(x) = f(0) + f'(0)x + \frac{f''(0)}{2!}x^2 + \cdots$$

$$= \sum_{k=0}^{\infty} \frac{f^{(k)}(0)}{k!} x^k$$

- The *n*th degree **Maclaurin polynomial** of the function $f(x)$ is given by:

$$= \sum_{k=0}^{n} \frac{f^{(k)}(0)}{k!} x^k = f(0) + f'(0)x + \frac{f''(0)}{2!}x^2 + \cdots + \frac{f^{(n)}(0)}{n!}x^n$$

  This is the full Maclaurin series truncated at n terms.

- The error term in using an *n*th degree Maclaurin polynomial is given by:

$$R_n(x) = \frac{f^{(n+1)}(c)}{(n+1)!} x^{n+1} \quad \text{for some } c \in \,]0, x[$$

- **Taylor approximations** generalise Maclaurin series to allow expansion about any point, a:

$$f(x) = f(a) + (x-a)f'(a) + \cdots + \frac{(x-a)^n}{n!} f^{(n)}(a) + R_n(x)$$

where the Lagrange error term $R_n(x)$ is given by

$$R_n(x) = \frac{f^{(n+1)}(c)}{(n+1)!}(x-a)^{n+1} \quad \text{for some } c \in \left]a, x\right[$$

- Taylor approximations can be used to provide a representation for the integral of functions and to enable limits of the form $\frac{\text{'0'}}{0}$ and $\frac{\text{'}\infty\text{'}}{\infty}$ to be found.

- 'Rate of change' means the derivative (sometimes $\frac{dy}{dx}$, but other variables can be used).

  'Proportional to x' means a constant multiple of x, that is kx (k is a constant).

  'Inversely proportional to x' means $\frac{k}{x}$.

  'Rate of decrease' means that the derivative is negative.

- A **differential equation** of the form $\frac{dy}{dx} = f(x)g(y)$ can be solved by **separation of variables**:

  $\int \frac{1}{g(y)} dy = \int f(x) dx$.

- A differential equation which can be written in the form $\frac{dy}{dx} = f\left(\frac{y}{x}\right)$ is called a *homogeneous differential equation*.

- A substitution $y = vx$ turns homogeneous differential equations into **variables separable differential equations**.

- A **linear differential equation** can be written as $\frac{dy}{dx} + P(x)y = Q(x)$.

- Linear differential equations can be solved by multiplying through by the **integrating factor**:

  $$I(x) = e^{\int P(x)dx}$$

  This turns the equation into $\frac{dy}{dx}\left(I(x)\, y\right) = I(x)Q(x)$.

- A plot of the tangents at all points (x, y) is called the **slope field** of a differential equation.

  Drawing a slope field enables us to construct approximate solution curves to a differential equation. These different solution curves are determined by the initial conditions.

- An **isocline** is a curve on which all tangents have the same gradient.

- **Euler's method** for approximating solutions to differential equations at a given point states that given the differential equation:

  $$\frac{dy}{dx} = f(x, y) \text{ with } y = y_0 \text{ when } x = x_0$$

  - Start at the point (x_0, y_0) and find the gradient $m_0 = f(x_0, y_0)$.

  - Move a fixed step h in the x-direction and calculate the corresponding distance k in the y-direction from the gradient of the slope field: $k = m_0 h$.

  - Using the new point $(x_0 + h, y_0 + k)$ repeat the above.

- The solution of a differential equation

  $$\frac{dy}{dx} = f(x, y) \text{ with } x = x_0, y = y_0$$

  can be approximated by forming a Taylor polynomial for y about the point x_0:

  $$y = y(x_0) + y'(x_0)(x - x_0) + \frac{y''(x_0)}{2!}(x - x_0)^2 + \frac{y'''(x_0)}{3!}(x - x_0)^3 + \cdots$$

  where y'', y''', etc. can be found by successively differentiating the original differential equation w.r.t. x.

1. Solve the differential equation

$$e^{-3x}\frac{dy}{dx} + ye^{-3x}\tan x = \cos x \quad \text{for } x \in \left[0, \frac{\pi}{2}\right[$$

given that $y = 1$ when $x = 0$. Give your answer in the form $y = f(x)$. *[13 marks]*

2. Let $f(x) = e^{-x^2} + \cos 2x$.

(a) Assuming the Maclaurin series for e^x and $\cos x$, show that

$$f(x) = 2 - 3x^2 + \frac{7}{6}x^4 - \frac{23}{90}x^6 + \cdots$$

(b) Hence find $\lim\limits_{x \to 0} \dfrac{e^{-x^2} + \cos 2x - 2}{x^2}$. *[8 marks]*

3. Find:

(a) $\lim\limits_{x \to a} \dfrac{x^p - a^p}{x^q - a^q}$.

(b) $\lim\limits_{x \to 0} \dfrac{e^x - 1 - x - \dfrac{x^2}{2}}{x^3}$. *[6 marks]*

4. (a) (i) By considering the gradients of $\ln x$ and x, show that
   $\ln n < n$ for $n \geq 1$.

   (ii) Hence show that $\displaystyle\sum_{k=2}^{\infty} \frac{1}{\ln k}$ diverges.

   (b) Use the Comparison Test to determine whether $\displaystyle\sum_{k=3}^{\infty} \frac{\ln k}{k}$ converges or diverges. *[7 marks]*

5. Consider the differential equation $\dfrac{dy}{dx} = ye^{-x^2}$ with the boundary condition $y = 2$ when $x = 0$.

   (a) Use Euler's method with step length $h = 0.1$ to find an approximate value of y when $x = 0.3$. Give your answer to three decimal places.

   (b) (i) Use differentiation to find the values of $\dfrac{d^2y}{dx^2}$ and $\dfrac{d^3y}{dx^3}$ when $x = 0$.

   (ii) Find the Maclaurin series expansion for y, up to and including the term in x^3.

   (iii) Hence find another approximation for the value of y when $x = 0.3$.

   (c) Explain how you can improve the accuracy of each of your approximations above. *[20 marks]*

6. (a) Find a and b such that the function

$$f(x) = \begin{cases} \cos x + a & x \le 0 \\ x \sin\left(\dfrac{1}{x}\right) + 1 & 0 < x \le \dfrac{1}{\pi} \\ \dfrac{\pi^2}{2}x^2 + b & x > \dfrac{1}{\pi} \end{cases}$$

is continuous everywhere.

(b) Show that $f(x)$ is differentiable at $x = \dfrac{1}{\pi}$ but not at $x = 0$.   *[9 marks]*

7. Consider the differential equation $\dfrac{dy}{dx} = \dfrac{(9x+y)(4x+y)}{x^2}$ for $x > 0$.

(a) Show that this can be written in the form $\dfrac{dy}{dx} = f\left(\dfrac{y}{x}\right)$.

(b) Hence solve the equation, giving your answer in the form $y = f(x)$.   *[13 marks]*

8. (a) Evaluate the improper integral $\displaystyle\int_1^\infty \dfrac{1}{x^2}\,dx$.

(b) Hence show that the improper integral $\displaystyle\int_1^\infty \dfrac{\cos x}{x}\,dx$ exists

(is convergent).   *[10 marks]*

9. (a) Find the Maclaurin series for $\sin x$ up to the term in x^5.

(b) Show that, for $|x| \le 2$:

$$\left| \sin x - x + \dfrac{x^3}{3!} \right| \le \dfrac{4}{15}$$ *[9 marks]*

10. (a) Find $\displaystyle\int_2^\infty \dfrac{1}{x \ln x}\,dx$

(b) Hence determine whether $\displaystyle\sum_{k=2}^\infty \dfrac{1}{k \ln k - 1}$ converges or diverges.   *[8 marks]*

11. Consider the differential equation

$$\dfrac{dy}{dx} + \dfrac{xy}{4 - x^2} = 1$$

where $|x| < 2$ and $y = 1$ when $x = 0$.

(a) Use Euler's methods with $h = 0.25$ to find an approximate value of y when $x = 1$, giving your answer to two decimal places.

(b) (i) By first finding an integrating factor, solve this differential equation. Give your answer in the form $y = f(x)$.

(ii) Calculate, correct to 2 decimal places, the value of y when $x = 1$.

(c) Sketch the graph of $y = f(x)$ for $0 \le x \le 1$. Use your sketch to explain why your approximate value of y is greater than the true value of y. [24 marks]

(© IB Organization 2005)

12. (a) Show that the series $\displaystyle\sum_{k=1}^{\infty} \frac{(-1)^{k+1} k}{k^2 + 1}$ converges.

(b) Find the minimum number of terms it is necessary to take to ensure that an approximation of this sum is correct to 1 decimal place. [1 mark]

13. Consider the improper integral $I = \displaystyle\int_{10}^{\infty} \frac{1}{x^2 + 3x + 2} \, dx$.

(a) Show that $\dfrac{1}{x^2 + 3x + 2} = \dfrac{A}{x+1} + \dfrac{B}{x+2}$

where A and B are constants to be found.

(b) Hence find the exact value of I.

(c) (i) Find the upper and lower sums for I.

   (ii) By using the result in part (a) and writing out the first few partial sums, deduce that:

$$\sum_{k=1}^{n} \frac{1}{k^2 + 3k + 2} = \frac{1}{2} - \frac{1}{n+2}$$

   (iii) Hence evaluate the upper and lower sums.

(d) Hence show that $\dfrac{1}{12} < \ln\left(\dfrac{12}{11}\right) < \dfrac{1}{11}$. [15 marks]

14. (a) Find $\displaystyle\lim_{x \to \infty} x \sin\left(\frac{1}{x}\right)$

(b) Determine whether $\displaystyle\sum_{k=1}^{\infty} k \sin\left(\frac{1}{k}\right)$ converges or diverges. [6 marks]

15. (a) Use Taylor's theorem to prove that $\ln(1+x) \le x$.

(b) By making an appropriate choice of x, hence prove that:

$$\sqrt[n]{a_1 a_2 \ldots a_n} \le \frac{a_1 + a_2 + \cdots + a_n}{n}$$ [9 marks]

16. (a) Find the radius of convergence of the infinite series:

$$\frac{1}{2}x + \frac{1 \times 3}{2 \times 5}x^2 + \frac{1 \times 3 \times 5}{2 \times 5 \times 8}x^3 + \frac{1 \times 3 \times 5 \times 7}{2 \times 5 \times 8 \times 11}x^4 + \cdots$$

(b) Determine whether the series $\displaystyle\sum_{k=1}^{\infty} \sin\left(\frac{1}{k} + k\pi\right)$ is convergent or divergent. [15 marks]

17. (a) Determine the radius of convergence of the power series:

$$\sum_{k=1}^{\infty} \frac{(x-4)^k}{\sqrt[3]{k}}$$

(b) Find the set of all x points for which the series converges (the interval of convergence). *[10 marks]*

18. (a) Using the Mean Value Theorem, show that for all positive integers n:

$$n\ln\left(1+\frac{1}{n}\right) \le 1$$

(b) Show that for all real numbers s, such that $0 < s < 4$:

$$\frac{1}{s} + \frac{1}{4-s} \ge 1$$

(c) By integrating the inequality of part (b) over the interval $[t, 2]$ or otherwise, show that for all real numbers t, such that $0 < t \le 2$:

$$\ln\left(\frac{4-t}{t}\right) \ge 2-t$$

(d) Hence or otherwise, show that for all positive integers n:

$$n\ln\left(1+\frac{1}{n}\right) \ge \frac{2n}{2n+1}$$

(e) Using parts (a) and (d) or otherwise, show that:

$$\lim_{n\to\infty}\left(1+\frac{1}{n}\right)^n = e$$

[19 marks]

(©IB Organization 2002)

19. (a) Find the degree 5 Maclaurin polynomial for the function
$$f(x) = e^{x^2}$$

(b) (i) Show that
$$f^{(6)}(x) = \left(64^6 x^6 + 480x^4 + 720x^2 + 120\right)e^{x^2}$$

(ii) Show that $f^{(6)}(x)$ is increasing for all $x > 0$.

(c) (i) Using the answer to part (a), find an estimate for
$$\int_0^{\frac{1}{2}} e^{x^2}\, dx$$

Give your answer to 5DP.

(ii) Using part (b) and the Lagrange error term, place an upper bound on this estimate. *[18 marks]*

Answers

Chapter 1

Exercise 1A

1. (a) (i) $\dfrac{3}{2}$ (ii) -2

   (b) (i) $\dfrac{1}{3}$ (ii) 4

   (c) (i) 0 (ii) 0

   (d) (i) $\dfrac{9}{16}$ (ii) $\dfrac{3}{2}$

2. (b) $\dfrac{27}{125}$

3. (b) 2

4. 0

5. 1

Exercise 1B

1. (a) 0 (b) 4
   (c) 0 (d) 0

3. (c) 1

4. (a) 1 (b) 1

5. (b) 0

6. (a) $a = e$ (b) $\ln x < x$
   (c) 3

7. (d) (i) e (ii) That limit of function is function of limit.

Exercise 1C

1. (a) (i) $\lim\limits_{x \to x_0^+} f(x) = 5$

   $\lim\limits_{x \to x_0^-} f(x) = 5$

   $\lim\limits_{x \to x_0} f(x) = 5$

   (ii) $\lim\limits_{x \to x_0^+} f(x) = \dfrac{1}{3}$

   $\lim\limits_{x \to x_0^-} f(x) = \dfrac{1}{3}$

   $\lim\limits_{x \to x_0} f(x) = \dfrac{1}{3}$

   (b) (i) $\lim\limits_{x \to x_0^+} f(x) = \infty$

   $\lim\limits_{x \to x_0^-} f(x) = -\infty$

   $\lim\limits_{x \to x_0} f(x)$ does not exist

   (ii) $\lim\limits_{x \to x_0^+} f(x) = -\infty$

   $\lim\limits_{x \to x_0^-} f(x) = \infty$

   $\lim\limits_{x \to x_0} f(x) =$ does not exist

   (c) (i) $\lim\limits_{x \to x_0^+} f(x) = -\infty$

   $\lim\limits_{x \to x_0^-} f(x)$ does not exist

   $\lim\limits_{x \to x_0} f(x)$ does not exist

   (ii) $\lim\limits_{x \to x_0^+} f(x) = 0$

   $\lim\limits_{x \to x_0^-} f(x)$ does not exist

   $\lim\limits_{x \to x_0} f(x)$ does not exist

   (d) (i) $\lim\limits_{x \to x_0^+} f(x) = 2$

   $\lim\limits_{x \to x_0^-} f(x) = 2$

   $\lim\limits_{x \to x_0} f(x) = 2$

   (ii) $\lim\limits_{x \to x_0^+} f(x) = -7$

   $\lim\limits_{x \to x_0^-} f(x) = -8$

   $\lim\limits_{x \to x_0} f(x)$ does not exist

   (e) (i) $\lim\limits_{x \to x_0^+} f(x) = 3$

   $\lim\limits_{x \to x_0^-} f(x) = 3$

   $\lim\limits_{x \to x_0} f(x) = 3$

   (ii) $\lim\limits_{x \to x_0^+} f(x) = 2$

   $\lim\limits_{x \to x_0^-} f(x) = 2$

   $\lim\limits_{x \to x_0} f(x) = 2$

2. (a)

   (b) $\lim\limits_{x \to -5^-} f(x) = 6$, $\lim\limits_{x \to -5^+} f(x) = -1$
   (c) $\lim\limits_{x \to -3} f(x) = -5$
   (d) Yes
   (e) $x = -5, 1$

3. (a) 2 (b) $\dfrac{2}{3}$

4. $a = -3$
   $b = 4$
   $c = 1$

5. (b) No; $\lim_{x \to 0} f(x)$

6. (b) 4

7. (a) 1   (b) −1

    (c) Does not exist

8. (b) $\dfrac{9}{2}$

9. 0

10. Does not exist

Exercise 1D

1. (a) (i) 2   (ii) 1

    (b) (i) 4π (ii) 6

    (c) (i) 1   (ii) $\dfrac{3}{4}$

2. (a) −2   (b) $\dfrac{1}{4}$

    (c) $\dfrac{1}{6}$ (d) 2

    (e) ∞ (f) $\dfrac{9}{4}$

3. (a) 0   (b) 0   (c) $\dfrac{1}{2}$

4. (a) −1   (b) ∞ (c) ∞

5. (a) Second set of differentiation not necessary

    (b) −4

6. $\dfrac{1}{4}$

7. 9

8. 0

9. −1

Exercise 1E

1. (a) (i) Yes   (ii) Yes

    (b) (i) Yes   (ii) Yes

    (c) (i) No   (ii) Yes

    (d) (i) No   (ii) No

    (e) (i) Yes   (ii) No

    (f) (i) Yes   (ii) No

2. (a) (i) 1   (ii) 0

    (iii) Does not exist

    (iv) 2   (v) 2

    (vi) 2

    (b) All $x \in \mathbb{R}$ except $x = 0, 1$

3. $k = -1$

4. (a) $a = -1, b = -2$

    (b) All $x \in \mathbb{R}$ except $x = -4$

6.

> Consider a sequence
> such as $x_k = x_0 + \dfrac{\sqrt{2}}{k}$

Exercise 1F

1. (a)

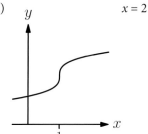

$x = 2$

    (b)

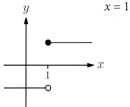

$x = 1$

    (c)

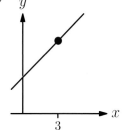

    (d)

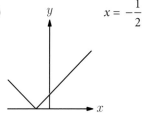

$x = -\dfrac{1}{2}$

    (e)

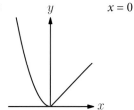

$x = 0$

    (f)

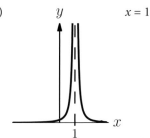

$x = 1$

    (g)

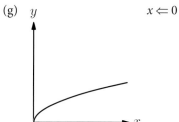

$x \Leftarrow 0$

2. (a)

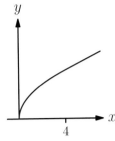

(b) All $x \in \mathbb{R}$

(c) All $x \in \mathbb{R}$ except $x = 0$

3. (a)

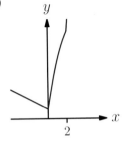

(b) All $x \in \mathbb{R}$

(c) All $x \in \mathbb{R}$ except $x = 0, 2$

4. All $x \in \mathbb{R}$, except $x = -3, 1, 3$

5. $b = 16$, $c = -20$

6. (b) $\sin\left(\dfrac{1}{x}\right) - \dfrac{1}{x}\cos\left(\dfrac{1}{x}\right)$

9. (a) $a = 3$, $b = -2$

(b) All $x \in \mathbb{R}$, except $x = \dfrac{2}{3}$

10. (b) $f'(0) = 0$

(c) $2x\sin\left(\dfrac{1}{x}\right) - \cos\left(\dfrac{1}{x}\right)$

11.

> Let $f(x) = g(x) + kx$, where $g(x)$ is function in previous question.

Exercise 1G

1. (a) (i) $x = \dfrac{5}{2}$ (ii) $x = -1$

(b) (i) $x = \dfrac{\pi}{2}$ (ii) $x = 2\pi, 6\pi$

(c) (i) $x = \pm\dfrac{1}{\sqrt{3}}$ (ii) $x = 1$

2. (a) (i) $x = 2$ (ii) $x = 0$

(b) (i) $x = 0.881$ (ii) $x = 0.680$

(c) (i) $x = \dfrac{2}{\sqrt{3}}$ (ii) $x = 16$

3. 30

5. (b) $f(1) \neq f(4)$

12. (c) 0.732

13.

> Use Rolle's Theorem and induction.

15. 1 root. Use Rolle's Theorem

Mixed examination practice 1

1. (a) $a = 2$, $b = 1$

(b) All $x \in \mathbb{R}$, except $x = -1$

2. 1

4. (a) $\dfrac{1}{2}$ (b) 1501

5. (a) $e^{\ln\left(x^x\right)}$ (b) 1

(c) That limit of function is function of limit

7. (a) $\dfrac{-5}{8}$ (b) $-\dfrac{1}{2}$

9. (c) 0

10. (c) 5

11. (a) 1   (b) e

(c) That limit of function is function of limit

Chapter 2

Exercise 2A

1. (a) (i) e^{x^2} (ii) $2\cos^5 x$

(b) (i) $-2\sin(2x^3)$ (ii) $-5\sqrt{t^2 + 3}$

(c) (i) $\dfrac{t^3 + 3}{t^2 + 2t + 5}$ (ii) $\dfrac{e^t}{t^2 + 7}$

(d) (i) e^{-b^3} (ii) $-3\cos^2(2a^2)$

2. (a) (i) $f(x)$ (ii) $g(y)$

(b) (i) $f(b)$ (ii) $-g(a)$

(c) (i) 0   (ii) 0

(d) (i) $f(b) - f(a)$ (ii) 0

(e) (i) $(f(x))^2$ (ii) $-(f(t))^{\frac{1}{3}}$

3. (a) $\dfrac{1}{x}$ (b) $f'(x)$

4. (a) (i) $3x^2 \ln\left(\dfrac{b}{a}\right)$ (ii) $3x^2 \ln\left(\dfrac{b}{a}\right)$

(b) No

5. (a) $2x\sin(x^4) - \sin(x^2)$

(b) $\dfrac{1}{2} y^{-\frac{1}{2}} e^{-y^2} - \dfrac{1}{4} y^{-\frac{3}{4}} e^{-y}$

Exercise 2B

1. (a) 1   (b) 4   (c) Diverges
   (d) $\dfrac{1}{2}$

2. (a) Diverges   (b) Converges
   (c) Converges   (d) Converges
   (e) Diverges   (f) Converges

3. (a) $p < 0$ (b) $p > 1$

4. 1

5. $\dfrac{\pi}{2}$

7. (b) 4

8. (b) $\ln \dfrac{5}{2}$

9. 2

12. Yes

> Integrate by parts

Exercise 2C

1. (a) $\displaystyle\sum_{k=2}^{\infty} e^{-k^2} < \int_1^{\infty} e^{-x^2}\,dx < \sum_{k=1}^{\infty} e^{-k^2}$

   (b) $\displaystyle\sum_{k=6}^{\infty} \frac{1}{\sqrt{k+2}} < \int_5^{\infty} \frac{1}{\sqrt{x+2}}\,dx$
   $\displaystyle < \sum_{k=5}^{\infty} \frac{1}{\sqrt{k+2}}$

   (c) $\displaystyle\sum_{k=3}^{\infty} \frac{\ln k}{k^2} < \int_2^{\infty} \frac{\ln x}{x^2}\,dx < \sum_{k=2}^{\infty} \frac{\ln k}{k^2}$

2. (a) $\displaystyle\sum_{k=10}^{\infty} -\frac{1}{k^2} < \int_{10}^{\infty} -\frac{1}{x^2}\,dx < \sum_{k=11}^{\infty} -\frac{1}{k^2}$

   (b) $\displaystyle\sum_{k=1}^{\infty} \ln\left(\frac{k^2}{k^2+1}\right) < \int_1^{\infty} \ln\left(\frac{x^2}{x^2+1}\right)dx$
   $\displaystyle < \sum_{k=2}^{\infty} \ln\left(\frac{k^2}{k^2+1}\right)$

   (c) $\displaystyle\sum_{k=2}^{\infty} \frac{1}{e^{-k}-e^{k}} < \int_2^{\infty} \frac{1}{e^{-x}-e^{x}}\,dx$
   $\displaystyle < \sum_{k=3}^{\infty} \frac{1}{e^{-k}-e^{k}}$

3. (a) $\displaystyle\sum_{k=0}^{\infty} -\frac{1}{(k+2)^3} < \int_0^{\infty} -\frac{1}{(x+2)^3}\,dx$
   $\displaystyle < \sum_{k=1}^{\infty} -\frac{1}{(k+2)^3}$

   (b) $\displaystyle\sum_{k=1}^{\infty} \frac{1}{k^2+8k+17} < \int_0^{\infty} \frac{1}{x^2+8x+17}\,dx$
   $\displaystyle < \sum_{k=0}^{\infty} \frac{1}{k^2+8k+17}$

4. (c) $\displaystyle\sum_{k=4}^{\infty} \frac{1}{e^{k}+e^{-k}} < \int_3^{\infty} \frac{1}{e^{x}+e^{-x}}\,dx$
   $\displaystyle < \sum_{k=3}^{\infty} \frac{1}{e^{k}+e^{-k}}$

5. (a) $\displaystyle\sum_{k=11}^{\infty} 2^{-k} < \int_{10}^{\infty} 2^{-x}\,dx < \sum_{k=10}^{\infty} 2^{-k}$

   (b) $\dfrac{1}{1024} < \displaystyle\int_{10}^{\infty} 2^{-x}\,dx < \dfrac{1}{512}$

Mixed examination practice 2

1. (a) $\dfrac{1}{2}$ (b) $\dfrac{1}{5}$

2. (a) $\ln\left(\cos^2 3b + 1\right)$
   (b) $\ln\left(\cos^2 3x + 1\right)$

3. (a) $a = 1, b = n, f(x) = \dfrac{1}{x}$
   (c) 0

4. (b) $\dfrac{1}{2}$

6. (b) $\displaystyle\sum_{k=1}^{\infty} e^{-k^2} < \int_0^{\infty} e^{-x^2}\,dx < \sum_{k=0}^{\infty} e^{-k^2}$

7. (b) ∞ (c) Diverges

8. (a) $k = 21$ (b) 3

9. (b) Converges

⬤ Chapter 3

Exercise 3A

1. (a) $1.00, 1.25, 1.36, 1.42$
   (b) $0.866, 1.73, 1.73, 0.866$
   (c) $0.167, 0.310, 0.435, 0.546$
   (d) $0.368, 0.503, 0.553, 0.571$

2. (a) $\dfrac{n}{2}(3n+5)$, divergent
   (b) $\dfrac{n(19-n)}{10}$, divergent
   (c) $\dfrac{1}{2}\left(1-\left(\dfrac{1}{3}\right)^n\right)$, convergent

(d) $6(1.2^n - 1)$, divergent

(e) $\dfrac{1}{15}\left(1 - \left(\dfrac{1}{16}\right)^n\right)$, convergent

3. (a) $3(2k-1)$ (b) $2 \times 3^{k-1}$

(c) $-3 \times \dfrac{5}{4^k}$ (d) $\ln\left(\dfrac{k}{k-1}\right)$

(e) $\dfrac{1}{3 \times 2^k}$

Exercise 3B

1. (a) (i) Compare to $\displaystyle\sum \dfrac{1}{k^2}$

(ii) Compare to $\displaystyle\sum \dfrac{1}{k^2}$

(b) (i) Compare to $\displaystyle\sum \dfrac{1}{k^{3/2}}$

(ii) Compare to $\displaystyle\sum \dfrac{1}{k^3}$

(c) (i) Compare to $\displaystyle\sum \dfrac{1}{k^2}$

(ii) Compare to $\displaystyle\sum \dfrac{1}{k^{3/2}}$

(d) (i) Compare to $\displaystyle\sum \left(\dfrac{1}{2}\right)^{k-1}$

(ii) Compare to $\displaystyle\sum \left(\dfrac{1}{2}\right)^{k-1}$

(e) (i) Compare to $\displaystyle\sum \left(\dfrac{3}{4}\right)^{k}$

(ii) Compare to $\displaystyle\sum \left(\dfrac{1}{2}\right)^{k}$

(f) (i) Compare to $\displaystyle\sum \dfrac{1}{k^2}$

(ii) Compare to $\displaystyle\sum \dfrac{1}{k^2}$

2. (a) (i) Compare to $\displaystyle\sum \dfrac{1}{k}$

(ii) Compare to $\displaystyle\sum \dfrac{1}{\sqrt{k}}$

(b) (i) Divergence Test $\left(\lim = \dfrac{1}{2}\right)$

(ii) Divergence Test $\left(\lim = \dfrac{3}{2}\right)$

(c) (i) Compare to $\displaystyle\sum \dfrac{1}{k}$

(ii) Compare to $\displaystyle\sum \dfrac{1}{k}$

(d) (i) Compare to $\displaystyle\sum \left(\dfrac{4}{3}\right)^{k}$

(ii) Compare to $\displaystyle\sum \left(\dfrac{\pi}{3}\right)^{k}$

(e) (i) Divergence Test (lim = 1)
(ii) Divergence Test (lim = ∞)

(f) (i) Divergence Test (lim = e)
(ii) Divergence Test (lim = e^{-1})

3. (a) (i) Converges $\left(\dfrac{1}{k^3}\right)$

(ii) Diverges $\left(\dfrac{1}{k}\right)$

(b) (i) Converges $\left(\dfrac{1}{5}\right)^{k}$

(ii) Converges $\left(\dfrac{2}{3}\right)^{k}$

(c) (i) Diverges $\left(\dfrac{1}{k}\right)$

(ii) Converges $\left(\dfrac{1}{k^2}\right)$

(d) (i) Converges $\left(\dfrac{1}{k^2}\right)$

(ii) Converges $\left(\dfrac{1}{k^3}\right)$

(e) (i) Diverges $\left(\dfrac{1}{\sqrt{k}}\right)$

(ii) Converges $\left(\dfrac{1}{k^{4/3}}\right)$

4. (a) (i) Diverges (ii) Diverges
(b) (i) Converges (ii) Diverges
(c) (i) Converges (ii) Converges
(d) (i) Converges (ii) Converges
(e) (i) Diverges (ii) Converges

5. (a) (i) Converges, 0.202
(ii) Converges, 0.302
(b) (i) Diverges
(ii) Diverges
(c) (i) Converges, 7.71×10^{-3}
(ii) Diverges
(d) (i) Converges, 0.402
(ii) Converges, 2.76×10^{-7}
(e) (i) Diverges
(ii) Converges, 1.35×10^{-22}

6. (a) (i) Absolutely convergent
    (ii) Absolutely convergent
    (b) (i) Divergent
    (ii) Divergent
    (c) (i) Conditionally convergent
    (ii) Absolutely convergent
    (d) (i) Conditionally convergent
    (ii) Conditionally convergent
    (e) (i) Absolutely convergent
    (ii) Absolutely convergent

7. (a) (i) Converges   (ii) Diverges
    (b) (i) Diverges   (ii) Converges
    (c) (i) Converges   (ii) Converges
    (d) (i) Diverges   (ii) Converges
    (e) (i) Converges   (ii) Diverges

8. (a) Diverges (Limit Comparison Test: $\sum \dfrac{1}{k}$)

    (b) Converges (Comparison Test: $\sum \dfrac{1}{k^{3/2}}$)

    (c) Converges (Alternating Series Test)

9. (a) $x \geq e^2$

    (b) Converges (Comparison with $\sum \dfrac{1}{k^2}$)

10. Converges absolutely

11. (b) 4

12. (a) Converges (Comparison Test: $\sum \dfrac{1}{k^{3/2}}$)

    (b) Diverges (Ratio Test)

13. (b) 1

14. (a) $n = 2$

    (c) Conditional

15. $c > 27$

17. (a) $\displaystyle\sum_{k=n+1}^{\infty} f(k) < \int_n^{\infty} f(x)\,dx < \sum_{k=n}^{\infty} f(k)$

    (b) $\displaystyle\sum_{k=1}^{\infty} f(k) - \sum_{k=1}^{n} f(k) < \int_n^{\infty} f(x)\,dx$

    (c) 4×10^{-4} (d) 23

18. (b) Diverges

> Express as the sum of two fractions

19. (a) Converges for $a > 1$
    Diverges for $a \leq 1$
    (b) (i) Converges conditionally
    (ii) Converges absolutely

Exercise 3C

1. (a) (i) $R = 0$; only converges at $x = 0$

    (ii) $R = 0$; only converges at $x = -3$

(b) (i) $R = \infty$; converges for all $x \in \mathbb{R}$

    (ii) $R = \infty$; converges absolutely for all $x \in \mathbb{R}$

(c) (i) $R = 5$; converges absolutely for all $x \in \,]{-5}, 5[$

    (ii) $R = 1$; converges for all $x \in \,]{-1}, 1[$

(d) (i) $R = 2$; converges for all $x \in [3, 7[$

    (ii) $R = 1$; converges for all $x \in [0, 2]$

2. (a) Converges absolutely for $x \in \,]{-1}, 1[$
    Diverges at $x = -1$
    Converges conditionally at $x = 1$
    (b) Converges absolutely for all $x \in \mathbb{R}$
    (c) Converges absolutely for all $x \in \mathbb{R}$

3. Converges absolutely for all $x \in \mathbb{R}$

4. $]{-5}, {-3}[$ Diverges at $x = -5, -3$

5. (a) All $x \in \mathbb{R}$

    (b) $f'(x) = 1 + x + \dfrac{x^2}{2!} + \dfrac{x^3}{3!} + \dfrac{x^4}{4!} + \dots$

    Holds for all $x \in \mathbb{R}$

6. (a) $R = 3$ (b) $x \in [-7, 1[$

7. (a) Converges absolutely for $x \in \,]{-4}, 4[$
    Diverges at $x = -4, 4$

    (b) Converges absolutely for $x \in \left[-\dfrac{1}{2}, \dfrac{1}{2}\right]$

    (c) Converges absolutely for $x \in \,]{-1}, 1[$
    Diverges at $x = -1$
    Converges conditionally at $x = 1$

Mixed examination practice 3

1. (a) Diverges (Comparison Test: $\sum \dfrac{1}{k}$)

    (b) Converges (Limit Comparison Test: $\sum \dfrac{1}{k^2}$)

2. (a) ∞

    (b) 2

3. (b) Converges

4. (b) $\dfrac{85}{72} < \displaystyle\sum_{n=1}^{\infty} \dfrac{1}{n^3} < \dfrac{263}{216}$

6. (c) $\dfrac{\pi^2}{12}$

7. Diverges (Test for Divergence)

8. (b) $A = B = 2$

(d) $\dfrac{2}{3}$

9. (a) Divergent (Comparison Test: $3^{-2} \sum \left(\dfrac{3}{e}\right)^n$)

(b) Conditionally convergent (Alternating Series Test)

(c) Absolutely convergent (Integral Test)

11. Convergent

12. (a) $\ln(n+1)$　　(b) Diverges

13. $0 \le x < 2$

14. (b) ∞　　　　(c) Diverges

Chapter 4

Exercise 4A

1. (a) (i) $1 - \dfrac{x^2}{2} + \dfrac{x^4}{24} - \dfrac{x^6}{720} + \ldots$

(ii) $3x - \dfrac{9}{2}x^3 + \dfrac{81}{40}x^5 - \dfrac{243}{560}x^7 + \ldots$

(b) (i) $1 + \dfrac{x}{2} + \dfrac{x^2}{8} + \dfrac{x^3}{48} + \ldots$

(ii) $1 - 3x + \dfrac{9}{2}x^2 - \dfrac{9}{2}x^3 + \ldots$

(c) (i) $1 + \dfrac{x}{2} - \dfrac{x^2}{8} + \dfrac{x^3}{16} + \ldots$

(ii) $\dfrac{1}{4} + \dfrac{3}{4}x + \dfrac{27}{16}x^2 + \dfrac{27}{8}x^3 + \ldots$

(d) (i) $x + \dfrac{1}{3}x^3 + \dfrac{2}{15}x^5 + \dfrac{17}{315}x^7$

(ii) $1 + \dfrac{1}{2}x^2 + \dfrac{5}{24}x^4 + \dfrac{61}{720}x^6 + \ldots$

2. $2x^2 - \dfrac{4}{3}x^4 + \dfrac{4}{15}x^6 + \ldots$

4. (a) $-\dfrac{x^2}{2} - \dfrac{x^4}{12} + \ldots$　　(b) $\dfrac{\pi^2}{18} + \dfrac{\pi^4}{972}$

5. (b) $R = 4$

6. (a) $\displaystyle\sum_{k=2}^{\infty}(-1)^k \dfrac{x^k}{k-1}$　　(b) $-1 < x \le 1$

7. (a) $1 + \dfrac{1}{3}x - \dfrac{1}{9}x^2 + \dfrac{5}{81}x^3 + \ldots$

8. (a) Not equal to $f(0)$.

(b) $f(x)$ an increasing function at $x = 0$ but first derivative of series is negative at $x = 0$

Exercise 4B

1. (a) (i) 1.25×10^{-4}　　(ii) 4.28×10^{-2}

(b) (i) 0.187　　　　(ii) 0.5625

(c) (i) 2.44×10^{-3}　　(ii) 1.70×10^{-4}

2. (a) $1 - x + \dfrac{x^2}{2}$　　(b) $0 < x < 0.1817$

3. (a) 1.43×10^{-5}　　(b) 1.27

5. (a) $1 + \dfrac{x^2}{2!} + \dfrac{x^4}{4!}$　　(b) $\dfrac{433}{384}$

(c) 1.36×10^{-4}

6. (a) $x - \dfrac{x^3}{3} + \dfrac{x^5}{5} + \ldots$

7. 17

9. (a) $\dfrac{1}{4}$　　　　(b) $\dfrac{1}{32}$

> Factorise $\dfrac{(0.5)^4}{4}$ from the expression for $R_3(0.5)$.

10. (a) $1 + nx + \dfrac{n(n-1)}{2}x^2$

(b) 30

Exercise 4C

1. (a) (i) $3x^4 - \dfrac{9}{2}x^{12} + \dfrac{81}{40}x^{20} - \dfrac{243}{560}x^{28} + \ldots$

(ii) $1 - 2x + \dfrac{2}{3}x^2 - \dfrac{4}{45}x^3 + \ldots$

(b) (i) $\ln 2 + \dfrac{3}{2}x - \dfrac{9}{8}x^2 + \dfrac{9}{8}x^3 + \ldots$

(ii) $-2x - 2x^2 - \dfrac{8}{3}x^3 - 4x^4 + \ldots$

(c) (i) $1 - \dfrac{x^2}{2} + \dfrac{x^4}{8} - \dfrac{x^6}{48} + \ldots$

(ii) $1 + x^3 + \dfrac{x^6}{2} + \dfrac{x^9}{6} + \ldots$

2. (a) (i) $2x^2 - x^3 - \dfrac{2}{3}x^4 + \ldots$

(ii) $-x - \dfrac{1}{2}x^2 + \dfrac{25}{6}x^3 + 2x^4 + \ldots$

(b) (i) $1 + \dfrac{1}{2}x^2 - \dfrac{1}{3}x^3 + \dfrac{3}{8}x^4 + \ldots$

(ii) $x + 2x^2 + \dfrac{23}{6}x^3 + \dfrac{23}{3}x^4 + \ldots$

(c) (i) $x - \dfrac{x^2}{2} + \dfrac{x^3}{6} - \dfrac{x^4}{12} + \cdots$

(ii) $-x - \dfrac{x^2}{2} - \dfrac{x^3}{6} - \dfrac{x^4}{12} + \cdots$

3. $2x + 6x^2 + \dfrac{23}{3}x^3 + 5x^4 + \cdots$

5. (a) $\displaystyle\sum_{k=1}^{\infty} \dfrac{(-2)^{k+1}}{k} x^k$

(b) $-\dfrac{1}{2} < x \le \dfrac{1}{2}$

6. (a) $x + \dfrac{x^3}{3} + \cdots$

(b) $1 + x + \dfrac{x^2}{2} + \dfrac{x^3}{2} + \dfrac{3}{8}x^4 + \cdots$

7. (a) $-\dfrac{x^2}{2} - \dfrac{x^4}{12} + \cdots$

(b) $\dfrac{x^2}{2} + \dfrac{x^4}{12} + \cdots$

(c) $x + \dfrac{x^3}{3} + \cdots$

8. (a) $\ln 8 - \dfrac{3}{2}x - \dfrac{39}{8}x^2 - \dfrac{71}{8}x^3 + \cdots$

(b) $y = -\dfrac{3}{2}x + \ln 8$

9. (a) $\displaystyle\sum_{k=1}^{\infty} \dfrac{x^{2k-1}}{2k-1}; -1 < x < 1$

(b) $\ln 2 \approx 0.687552; x = \dfrac{3}{5}$
(c) 0.949
(d) 0.00625

10. No Maclaurin series as derivatives at $x = 0$ do not exist.

Exercise 4D

1. (a) (i) $1 + 2\left(x - \dfrac{\pi}{4}\right) + 2\left(x - \dfrac{\pi}{4}\right)^2 + \cdots$

(ii) $1 - \dfrac{1}{2}\left(x - \dfrac{\pi}{2}\right)^2 + \dfrac{1}{24}\left(x - \dfrac{\pi}{2}\right)^4 + \cdots$

(b) (i) $1 + \dfrac{1}{2}(x-1) - \dfrac{1}{8}(x-1)^2 + \cdots$

(ii) $e^{16} + 8e^{16}(x-4) + 33e^{16}(x-4)^2 + \cdots$

(c) (i) $\dfrac{2}{3}\sqrt{3} - \dfrac{2}{3}\left(x - \dfrac{\pi}{3}\right) + \dfrac{5}{9}\sqrt{3}\left(x - \dfrac{\pi}{3}\right)^2 + \cdots$

(ii) $\sqrt{3} - 4\left(x - \dfrac{\pi}{6}\right) + 4\sqrt{3}\left(x - \dfrac{\pi}{6}\right)^2 + \cdots$

2. $\ln 3 + \dfrac{1}{3}x - \dfrac{1}{18}x^2 + \dfrac{1}{81}x^3 + \cdots$

3. $e^3 + e^3(x-3) + \dfrac{1}{2}e^3(x-3)^2 + \dfrac{1}{6}e^3(x-3)^3 \cdots$

4. (a) $\dfrac{1}{2} + \dfrac{1}{2}\sqrt{3}x - \dfrac{1}{4}x^2 - \dfrac{1}{12}\sqrt{3}x^3 + \cdots$

(b) 0.574
(c) 1.39×10^{-6}

5. $\dfrac{80}{729}$

6. (a) $2 + \dfrac{1}{12}(x-8) - \dfrac{1}{288}(x-8)^2 + \cdots$

8. (b) $e^{\frac{1}{e}} - \dfrac{e^{\frac{1}{e}-3}}{2}(x-e)^2 + \cdots$

(c) $e^{\frac{1}{e}}$

Exercise 4E

1. (a) (i) $-\dfrac{1}{6}$ (ii) $\dfrac{1}{2}$

(b) (i) 2 (ii) 2

(c) (i) $-\dfrac{1}{3}$ (ii) $\dfrac{3}{2}$

2. (a) $\displaystyle\sum_{k=1}^{\infty}(-1)^k \dfrac{x^{6k-2}}{(2k)!}$ (b) $\displaystyle\sum_{k=1}^{\infty}(-1)^{k+1}\dfrac{x^k}{k^2}$

3. (a) $(x-3) - \dfrac{1}{6}(x-3)^3 + \dfrac{1}{120}(x-3)^5 + \cdots$

(b) 6

4. (a) $x - \dfrac{x^3}{3} + \dfrac{x^5}{5} - \dfrac{x^7}{7} + \cdots$ (b) $\dfrac{1}{6}$

5. (b) $x^2 + \dfrac{x^6}{3}$ (c) -2

6. (a) $2x^3 + 2x^6 + \dfrac{8x^9}{3} + 4x^{12} + \cdots$ (b) 2

7. (a) $\dfrac{23}{30}$ (b) error $< 2.38 \times 10$

8. (a) $\displaystyle\sum_{k=1}^{\infty} \dfrac{(-1)^{k-1}}{(2k-1)(2k-1)!}x^{2k-1}$ (b) 6

Mixed examination practice 4

1. (a) $f'(x) = (1+x)^{-1}; f''(x) = -(1+x)^{-2};$

     $f'''(x) = 2(1+x)^{-3}; f^4(x) = -6(1+x)^{-4}$

(b) $x - \dfrac{x^2}{2} + \dfrac{x^3}{3} - \dfrac{x^4}{4} + \cdots$

(c) $\ln 2$

2. $\sqrt{2}-\sqrt{2}\left(x-\dfrac{\pi}{4}\right)+\dfrac{3\sqrt{2}}{2}\left(x-\dfrac{\pi}{4}\right)^2-$

$\dfrac{11\sqrt{2}}{6}\left(x-\dfrac{\pi}{4}\right)^3+\dots$

3. (a) $x+\dfrac{5x^3}{6}+\dfrac{41\,x^5}{120}+\dots$

(b) $\dfrac{5}{6}$

4. (a) $\dfrac{1}{2}-\dfrac{x}{4}+\dfrac{x^2}{8}-\dfrac{x^3}{16}+\dots$

5. (a) $x+\dfrac{x^2}{1!}+\dfrac{x^3}{2!}+\dfrac{x^4}{4!}+\dots+\dfrac{x^n}{(n-1)!}+\dots$

(b) $\dfrac{x^2}{2}+\dfrac{x^3}{3(1!)}+\dfrac{x^4}{4(2!)}+\dots+\dfrac{x^n}{n(n-2)!}+\dots;$

$-1<x<1$

6. (a) $\displaystyle\sum_{k=0}^{\infty}(-1)^k\dfrac{x^{2k}}{k!}$

(b) $\dfrac{5651}{7560}$

8. (b) $R=1$

(c) $x+\dfrac{x^3}{6}+\dfrac{3x^5}{40}+\dfrac{5x^7}{112}+$

$\dfrac{1\times3\times5\times\dots\times(2k-1)x^{2k+1}}{k!\,2^k(2k+1)}+\dots;-1<x<1$

9. (a) $f(t)=\dfrac{1}{1+t^2}$

(b) $x-\dfrac{x^3}{3}+\dfrac{x^5}{5}-\dfrac{x^7}{7}+\dots$

(c) $\dfrac{1}{3}$

(d) (i) $\dfrac{304}{105}$ (iii) $\dfrac{4}{9}$

10. (a) 0

(b) $f'(x)=\dfrac{1}{1-x};$

$f''(x)\dfrac{1}{(1-x)^2};$

$f'''(x)=\dfrac{2}{(1-x)^3}$

(c) $\dfrac{2}{3}$

(d) $\dfrac{1}{4}$

(e) Approximately 10 times too large.

11. (a) $\displaystyle\sum_{k=0}^{\infty}\dfrac{2^k}{k!}x^k$ (d) 11

Chapter 5

Exercise 5A

1. (a) (i) $y=-\dfrac{3}{2}\cos2x+c$ (ii) $y=12\sin\left(\dfrac{x}{3}\right)+c$

(b) (i) $y=\dfrac{1}{3}e^{2x}+c$ (ii) $y=8e^{\frac{x}{2}}+c$

(c) (i) $y=3\tan x+c$ (ii) $y=\tan x-x+c$

2. (a) (i) $y=\arctan\left(\dfrac{x}{2}\right)+2$

(ii) $y=\arcsin\left(\dfrac{x}{2}\right)+\dfrac{\pi}{4}$

(b) (i) $y=\ln(x^2+1)-\ln2$

(ii) $y=\dfrac{1}{4}x^2+\dfrac{1}{2}\ln|x|+\dfrac{3}{4}$

(c) (i) $y=-2e^{-3x}+2$ (ii) $y=-2e^{1-2x}+2$

3. (a) (i) \$1985   (ii) 45 m

(b) (i) 35.0 cm   (ii) 6.58 kg

(c) (i) $4500-375t^2$ (ii) $350-50\sqrt{t}$

Exercise 5B

1. (a) (i) $y=\dfrac{2}{3}x^{3/2}$ (ii) $y=\dfrac{1}{1-2x^2}$

(b) (i) $y=2x^4$ (ii) $y=3e^{-x^3}$

2. (a) (i) $\sin y=\dfrac{1}{2}-\cos x$

(ii) $\tan y=\tan x-\sqrt{3}$

(b) (i) $2\arctan y=\ln|1+x|$

(ii) $\arcsin y=\ln(1+x^2)$

(c) (i) $e^{-2y}=-4e^x+5$

(ii) $e^y=e^x+e^2-1$

3. (a) (i) $y=\pm\sqrt{x^3+c}$ (ii) $y=-\dfrac{1}{x^2+c}$

(b) (i) $y=\arcsin(\ln|x|+c)$

(ii) $y=\tan(c-\cos x)$

(c) (i) $y=Ae^x(x-1)-3$ (ii) $y=\dfrac{A}{1-x}$

4. $y=e^{-(1-x)^2}$

6. $y=2\tan(\ln x^2+c)$

7. $k=3$

Exercise 5C

1. (a) (i) $\dfrac{1}{3}\ln\left|\dfrac{y-2x}{y+x}\right|=\ln|x|+c$

(ii) $\dfrac{1}{5}\ln\left|\dfrac{y-5x}{y}\right| = \ln|x| + c$

(b) (i) $\ln\left|\dfrac{y}{x}+1\right| = \ln|x| + c$

(ii) $\dfrac{x}{y} = \ln|x| + c$

(c) (i) $-\dfrac{1}{5}\ln\left|3-\dfrac{5y}{x}\right| = \ln|x| + c$

(ii) $\ln\left|\dfrac{y}{x}\left(1-\dfrac{y}{x}\right)\right| = \ln|x| + c$

(d) (i) $e^{\frac{y}{x}} = \ln|x| + c$

(ii) $\sin\left(\dfrac{y}{x}\right) = \ln|x| + c$

2. (a) $y = x\ln|x| + cx$

(b) $y = x\ln|x| + \left(\dfrac{3-e}{e}\right)x$

3. (a) $y = x\tan(\ln|x| + c))$

(b) $y = x\tan\left(\ln|x| + \dfrac{\pi}{4}\right)$

4. (a) A homogeneous differential equation is one of the form $\dfrac{dy}{dx} = f\left(\dfrac{y}{x}\right)$

(c) $y^2 = 2x^2(\ln|x| + 8)$

5. (a) $\dfrac{dy}{dx} = \dfrac{4+\dfrac{y}{x}}{1-\dfrac{y}{x}}$

(b) $2\ln|x| = \arctan\left(\dfrac{y}{2x}\right) - \ln\left(4+\dfrac{y^2}{x^2}\right) + c$

6. (b) $(x-y+4)^3(4x+y+1)^2 = 16$

7. (b) (ii) 3.79

Exercise 5D

1. (a) (i) $y = \dfrac{1}{3}e^x + ce^{-2x}$

(ii) $y = -\dfrac{1}{3}e^x + ce^{4x}$

(b) (i) $y = -\cot x + c\csc x$

(ii) $y = \dfrac{x+c}{\cos x}$

(c) (i) $y = \dfrac{\ln|x|}{x} + \dfrac{c}{x}$

(ii) $y = -\dfrac{1}{x^2} + \dfrac{c}{x}$

2. $y = \dfrac{1}{2}e^x + \dfrac{1}{2}e^{2-x}$

3. $y = x^2\ln|x-3| + cx^2$

4. $y = e^{\cos x}(x+c)$

5. $y = -\dfrac{2}{x^2} + \dfrac{3}{x}$

6. $y = (x+2)\cos x$

8. $y = \dfrac{x^2+c}{2(x^2-1)}$

9. (a) $\dfrac{dz}{dx} - xz = -x$

(b) $z = 1 + ce^{\frac{x^2}{2}}$

(c) $y = 1$

10. (a) $y = -\sqrt{\dfrac{x^3}{4} + \dfrac{36}{x}}$

(b) $\sin y = \cos x(\ln\sec x + c)$

Exercise 5E

1. (a) (i) 0.708   (ii) 2.32
(b) (i)1.57   (ii) 1.07
(c) (i) 2.89   (ii) 1.45

2. (a) (i)

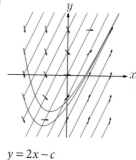

$y = 2x - c$

(ii)

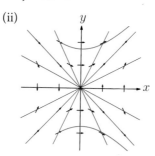

$y = \dfrac{x}{c}$ $c \neq 0$

(b) (i)

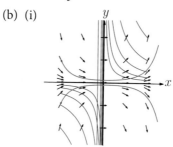

$y = \dfrac{c}{x}$ $x \neq 0$

(ii)

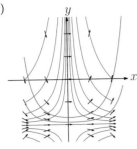

$$y = \frac{c}{x} - 2 \quad x \neq 0$$

(c) (i)

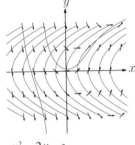

$$y^2 = 2x - c$$

(ii)

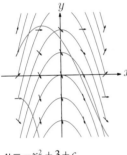

$$y = -x^2 + 3 + c$$

3. (a) (i) $1 + x + \frac{1}{2}x^2 + \frac{2}{3}x^3$

(ii) $\frac{1}{2} + x + \frac{3}{2}x^2 + \frac{4}{3}x^3$

(b) (i) $\frac{\pi}{2} + (\pi^2 - 2)(x + \pi) - \pi(x + \pi)^2 + \dfrac{(3 + 4\pi^2)(x + \pi)^3}{6}$

(ii) $\sqrt{2} + \sqrt{2}\left(x - \frac{\pi}{4}\right) + \frac{3\sqrt{2}}{2}\left(x - \frac{\pi}{4}\right)^2 + \frac{11\sqrt{2}}{6}\left(x - \frac{\pi}{4}\right)^3$

4. (a) $y = \dfrac{c}{x - 3} - 1$

(b)

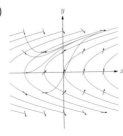

(c)

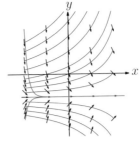

(d) Solution is constant or in equilibrium.

5. 1.629

6. (a) 0.825

(b) $y = -\ln\left(-\dfrac{x^2}{2} + \dfrac{1}{2} + e^{-0.3}\right)$

(c) (i) 11.0%
(ii) Take smaller h.

7. (a) (i) 0.615
(ii) use smaller step length

(b) $y = \dfrac{1}{2}e^{\frac{1}{3}x^3}$; $f(1) = 0.698$

(c) The tangent is always below the curve.

8. (a) (ii) $1 + 2x + \frac{3}{2}x^2 + \frac{3}{2}x^3$ (b) 1.2165

9. (a) $\dfrac{dy}{dx} = 4 - 3e^{-x^2}$ (b) 4.58

Mixed examination practice 5

1. (a)

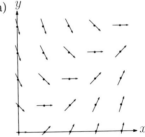

(b)

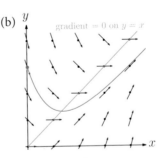

(c) $y = x - 1 + 4e^{-x}$

2. (a) $1 - 2x + \dfrac{11}{2}x^2 - \dfrac{56}{3}x^3$

(b) 0.671

3. $y = \dfrac{x^3}{6 - x^2}$

4. (a) (i) 2.141

   (ii) Take smaller steps

   (b) $y = x^2 + e^{1-x^2}$

5. (a) 4.46

   (b) $y = (x+4)e^{2x^2}$; $y = 4.55$

   (c) Take a smaller step length

6. (a) (ii) $1 + 2(x-1) + \dfrac{1}{2}(x-1)^2$

   (iii) 1.205

   (b) (i) $y = xe^{\frac{x-1}{x}}$

   (ii) 1.204 69

   (c) 0.026%

7. $y = \dfrac{2x}{\left(1-x^2\right)}$

8. $y = \dfrac{5e^x - 2xe^{-x} - e^{-x}}{4(1+x)}$

9. (b) $ye^{y/x} = Ax^2$

◼ Chapter 6

Mixed examination practice 6

1. $y = \dfrac{1}{3}(e^{3x} + 2)\cos x$

2. (b) −3

3. (a) $\dfrac{pa^{p-q}}{q}$ (b) $\dfrac{1}{6}$

4. (b) Diverges

5. (a) 2.674

   (b) (i) $\dfrac{d^2 y}{dx^2} = 2, \dfrac{d^3 y}{dx^3} = -2$

   (ii) $y \approx 2 + 2x + x^2 - \dfrac{x^3}{3}$

   (iii) 2.681

   (c) For (a) take smaller step length; for (b) take more terms.

6. (a) $a = 0, b = \dfrac{1}{2}$

7. (b) $y = -6x - \dfrac{x}{\ln x + C}$

8. (a) 1

9. (a) $x - \dfrac{x^3}{3!} + \dfrac{x^5}{5!} + \dots$

10. (a) ∞ (b) Diverges

11. (a) 1.83

   (b) (i) $y = \sqrt{4-x^2}\left\{ \arcsin\left(\dfrac{x}{2}\right) + \dfrac{1}{2} \right\}$

   (ii) $y(1) = 1.77$

   (c) Gradient is decreasing; hence the chords produced by Euler's method will track higher than the true curve.

12. (b) 19

13. (a) $A = 1, B = -1$

   (b) $\ln\left(\dfrac{12}{11}\right)$

   (c) (i) $\displaystyle\sum_{k=11}^{\infty} \dfrac{1}{k^2 + 3k + 2} < I < \sum_{k=10}^{\infty} \dfrac{1}{k^2 + 3k + 2}$

   (iii) Upper sum $= \dfrac{1}{11}$

   Lower sum $= \dfrac{1}{12}$

14. (a) 1

   (b) Diverges (Divergence Test)

15.

> Take $x_k = \dfrac{na_k}{a_1 + a_2 + \dots + a_n}$

16. (a) $\dfrac{3}{2}$

   (b) Convergent

17. (a) $R = 1$

   (b) $x \in [3,5[$

19. (a) $1 + x^2 + \dfrac{x^4}{2}$

   (c) (i) 0.54479

   (ii) 6.59×10^{-4}

Glossary

Words that appear in **bold** in the definitions of other terms are also defined in this glossary. The abstract nature of this option means that some defined terms can realistically only be explained in terms of other, more simple concepts.

Term	Definition	Example
absolutely convergent	A series with both positive and negative terms which still **converges** when all the terms are made positive.	$1 - \frac{1}{2} + \frac{1}{4} - \frac{1}{8} + \dots$ is absolutely convergent because $1 + \frac{1}{2} + \frac{1}{4} + \frac{1}{8} + \dots$ is convergent.
alternating series	A series whose terms are alternately positive and negative.	$1 - \frac{1}{2} + \frac{1}{3} - \frac{1}{4} + \dots$
Alternating Series Test	A test for convergence of series, stating that an alternating series whose terms tend to 0 is always convergent.	The series $1 - \frac{1}{2} + \frac{1}{3} - \frac{1}{4} + \dots$ is convergent.
boundary condition	The value of the unknown function at one point, which allows us to find a **particular solution** of a **differential equation**.	If we know the velocity of an object in order to find its displacement we need one boundary condition, for example its position when $t = 0$.
Comparison Test	A test for convergence of series based on comparing it to another series.	Since $\frac{1}{k^2+1} < \frac{1}{k^2}$ and $\sum \frac{1}{k^2}$ converges, the comparison test states that $\sum \frac{1}{k^2+1}$ also converges.
Comparison Test for improper integrals	A test to determine whether an **improper integral** converges by comparing it to another improper integral.	$\int\limits_{1}^{\infty} \frac{\cos x}{x^2}\,dx$ converges because $\left\| \frac{\cos x}{x^2} \right\| \leq \frac{1}{x^2}$ and we know that $\int\limits_{1}^{\infty} \frac{1}{x^2}\,dx$ converges.
conditionally convergent	A *convergent* series which **diverges** when all the terms are made positive.	$1 - \frac{1}{2} + \frac{1}{3} - \frac{1}{4} + \dots$ is conditionally convergent because it is convergent, but the series $1 + \frac{1}{2} + \frac{1}{3} + \frac{1}{4} + \dots$ is divergent.
continuous	A function which satisfies $\lim\limits_{x \to x_0} f(x) = f(x_0)$ for every point x_0.	The function shown above is not continuous because $\lim\limits_{x \to 1} f(x) = 2$, but $f(1) = 3$.

Term	Definition	Example
converges (to a limit)	When the terms of a sequence u_n get arbitrarily close to a limit as n increases.	The sequence $u_n = \dfrac{1}{n}$ converges to 0.
differential equation	An equation involving an unknown function and its derivatives.	$\dfrac{dy}{dx} - 3y = 5$ is an example of a differential equation.
Divergence Test	A test for convergence of series, stating that if the terms of the series do not tend to 0 then the series diverges.	The series $1 + 2 + 3 + \ldots$ diverges.
diverges	When a sequence does not **converge**.	The sequence $u_n = n$ diverges to infinity.
Euler's method	An approximate method for solving a differential equation where the solution curve is approximated by a sequence of straight line segments.	The shorter the line segments, the more accurate the approximation.
Fundamental Theorem of Calculus	The result relating differentiation and integration: $\dfrac{d}{dx}\displaystyle\int_a^x f(t)\,dt = f(x)$.	$\dfrac{d}{dx}\displaystyle\int_0^x \sin t\,dt = \sin x$
general solution	A most general form of a function which satisfies a **differential equation**.	The general solution of the equation $\dfrac{dy}{dx} = 2y$ is $y = Ae^{2x}$.
harmonic series	The series $\displaystyle\sum_{k=1}^{\infty} \dfrac{1}{k}$.	The harmonic series diverges, although its terms tend to 0.
improper integrals	Definite integrals where one or both limits are infinite.	$\displaystyle\int_0^{\infty} e^{-x}\,dx$ is a convergent definite integral.
Integral Test	A test for convergence of a series based on comparing it to an **improper integral**.	We can tell that the series $\displaystyle\sum \dfrac{1}{n^2}$ converges because $\displaystyle\int_1^{\infty} \dfrac{1}{x^2}\,dx$ converges.
integrating factor	A function used in solving a first order **differential equation**: $I(x) = e^{\int P(x)\,dx}$	Multiplying the equation by the integrating factor allows us to use the product rule to integrate the equation.
interval of convergence	The interval of values of x for which a **power series** converges.	The series $1 + x + x + x^2 + x^3 + \ldots$ has interval of convergence $]-1, 1[$.
isocline	A curve on which all points have the same gradient.	Isoclines are used to sketch a **slope field** of a **differential equation**.
l'Hôpital's rule	The result about limits of functions stating that, if two functions f and g both tend to either 0 or ∞ as $x \to a$, then $\displaystyle\lim_{x \to a} \dfrac{f(x)}{g(x)} = \lim_{x \to a} \dfrac{f'(x)}{g'(x)}$.	$\displaystyle\lim_{x \to 0} \dfrac{\sin x}{x} = \lim_{x \to 0} \dfrac{\cos x}{1} = \cos 0 = 1$
Lagrange form of the error term	An expression for estimating the error when a function is approximated by a **Maclaurin series** or **Taylor approximations**.	When $\sin(0.2)$ is approximated by $0.2 - \dfrac{0.2^3}{3!}$ the error is equal to $\dfrac{\sin(c)}{4!} \times 0.2^4$ for some $c \in]0, 0.2[$.

Term	Definition	Example
Limit Comparison Test	A test for convergence of series based on looking at the limit of the ratios of the terms of the two series.	As $\dfrac{1/2^k}{1/(2^k-1)} \to 1$, and $\sum \dfrac{1}{2^k}$ converges, then $\sum \dfrac{1}{2^k-1}$ also converges.
linear differential equation	A differential equation in which both $\dfrac{dy}{dx}$ and y only appear as linear terms.	$\dfrac{dy}{dx} = y^2$ is not a linear differential equation.
lower sum	The sum of rectangles drawn under the graph in order to approximate the value of an **improper integral**.	The lower sum for $\displaystyle\int_2^\infty \dfrac{1}{x^2}\,dx$ is $\displaystyle\sum_3^\infty \dfrac{1}{k^2}$.
Maclaurin series	A **power series** constructed in order to approximate a given function.	$\sin x = x - \dfrac{x^3}{3!} + \dfrac{x^5}{5!} - \ldots$
Mean Value Theorem	The result stating that for a continuous and differentiable function we can always find a tangent parallel to a given chord.	For $f(x) = x^2$, since $f(2) = 4$ and $f(3) = 9$ we can conclude that there is $x \in\,]0,2[$ for which $f'(x) = 5$.
nth degree Maclaurin polynomial	A polynomial formed by taking the terms of **Maclaurin series** up to power n.	$x - \dfrac{x^3}{3!}$ is the 3rd degree Maclaurin polynomial for $\sin x$.
nth partial sum	The sum of the first n terms of a series. A series **converges** if the sequence of its partial sums converges.	The partial sums of $\displaystyle\sum_1^\infty \dfrac{1}{k^2}$ are $S_1 = 1, S_2 = \dfrac{3}{2}, S_3 = \dfrac{11}{6}$, etc.
particular solution	One possible function which satisfies a **differential equation**.	$y = 5e^{2x}$ and $y = \dfrac{1}{2}e^{2x}$ are two examples of particular solutions of the equation $\dfrac{dy}{dx} = 2y$.
power series	A series containing only natural powers of x.	$2 + \dfrac{1}{2}x - 4x^3 + \ldots$
p-series	A series of the form $\displaystyle\sum_{k=1}^\infty \dfrac{1}{k^p}$.	The p-series converges when $p > 1$ and diverges otherwise.
radius of convergence	The largest value of $\lvert x \rvert$ for which a **power series** converges.	The series $1 + x + x + x^2 + x^3 + \ldots$ converges for $\lvert x \rvert < 1$, so the radius of convergence is 1.
Ratio Test	A test for convergence of a series based on looking at the ratios of its terms.	The Ratio Test can be used to find the **radius of convergence** of a **power series**.
Rolle's Theorem	The result stating that if a continuous function takes equal values at two points, then there must be a turning point between them. This is a special case of the **Mean Value Theorem**.	For $f(x) = x^2$, since $f(1) = f(-1)$ we can conclude that there is $x \in\,]-1,1[$ for which $f'(x) = 0$.
separation of variables	A method for solving a **differential equation** based on integrating the equation with respect to x and y separately.	$\dfrac{dy}{dx} = \dfrac{x^2}{y^3}$ can be solved by separation of variables.

Term	Definition	Example
slope field	A plot of tangents at various points in the plane in order to represent solutions of a first order **differential equation**.	Solution curves can be sketched by following the direction of the tangents.
Squeeze Theorem	The result about limit of sequences stating that, if two sequences **converge** to the same limit, and a third sequence can be 'squeezed' between them, then the third sequence converges to the same limit.	Since $-\dfrac{1}{n} \leq \dfrac{\sin n}{n} \leq \dfrac{1}{n}$, and $-\dfrac{1}{n}$ and $\dfrac{1}{n}$ both converge to 0, it follows that $\dfrac{\sin n}{n}$ converges to 0.
Taylor approximations	A result showing how to approximate a function by a power series and how to estimate the error in such approximation.	This result applies to **Maclaurin series** as a special case.
truncation error	The difference between a **partial sum** and the full sum of a series.	We know that $\displaystyle\sum_{1}^{\infty} \dfrac{1}{2^k} = 2$. If we approximate the series by $\dfrac{1}{2} + \dfrac{1}{4} + \dfrac{1}{8} = 0.875$, the truncation error is 0.125.
upper sum	The sum of rectangles drawn above the graph in order to approximate the value of an **improper integral**.	The upper sum for $\displaystyle\int_{2}^{\infty} \dfrac{1}{x^2}\,\mathrm{d}x$ is $\displaystyle\sum_{2}^{\infty} \dfrac{1}{k^2}$.
variables separable differential equations	**Differential equations** that can be solved by the method of **separation of variables**.	$\dfrac{\mathrm{d}y}{\mathrm{d}x} = \dfrac{x^2}{y^3}$ can be solved by separation of variables.

Index

Acknowledgements

The authors and publishers are grateful for the permissions granted to reproduce materials in either the original or adapted form. While every effort has been made, it has not always been possible to identify the sources of all the materials used, or to trace all copyright holders. If any omissions are brought to our notice, we will be happy to include the appropriate acknowledgements on reprinting.

IB exam questions © International Baccalaureate Organization. We gratefully acknowledge permission to reproduce International Baccalaureate Organization intellectual property.

Cover image: Thinkstock

Diagrams in the book were created by Ben Woolley.